this is the labrador retriever

by dorothy howe

ISBN 0-87666-332-3

Distributed in the U.S.A. by T.F.H. Publications, Inc., 211 West Sylvania Avenue, P.O. Box 27, Neptune City, N.J. 07753; in England by T.F.H. (Gt. Britain) Ltd., 13 Nutley Lane, Reigate, Surrey; in Canada to the book store and library trade by Clarke, Irwin & Company, Clarwin House, 791 St. Clair Avenue West, Toronto 10, Ontario; in Canada to the pet trade by Rolf C. Hagen Ltd., 3225 Sartelon Street, Montreal 382, Quebec; in Southeast Asia by Y.W. Ong, 9 Lorong 36 Geylang, Singapore 14; in Australia and the south Pacific by Pet Imports Pty. Ltd., P.O. Box 149, Brookvale 2100, N.S.W., Australia. Published by T.F.H. Publications Inc. Ltd., The British Crown Colony of Hong Kong.

ON THE FRONT COVER:
RUPERT YORKSHIRE FLAX (black bitch) by Ch. Kinley York-
shireman x Rupert Grace; and Am. BDA. CH. JO-DEAN'S DREAM-
DUST DAIQUIRI (yellow) by Eng. Am. Ch. Sandylands Midas x
Ch. Walden's Blackbird C.D.

FLAX—Semper Fidelis

CONTENTS

INTRODUCTION

Having been asked to write a book on Labradors, I have attempted to write one that might stimulate enough interest in persons who love dogs to induce some of them to become dedicated breeders of Labradors. The range of this book is intended to arouse interest among persons beyond the novice stage and develop into the search for a better understanding of how to go about the breeding of typical Labradors.

As few technical words as possible are used because looking up words in a dictionary interrupts the train of thought, as do footnotes. Practical experience is the basis for many ideas introduced in this book and it is hoped that they will be of use to other breeders.

Some understanding of genetics and its application to the production of the type of Labrador that is desired may seem beyond the understanding of the beginner. Yet we generally accept hereditary traits in human beings as well as the influence of environment without questioning how or why. Perhaps the words *gene* and *genetics* are the stumbling blocks as they are not used in ordinary conversation. Genetics is a very complicated subject and beyond the scope of a book such as this, however a few of the basic principles should be understood and applied in the breeding of Labradors even by beginners. It is only through some understanding of how genes function that we can have any control over the results of mating selected dogs and bitches. Without this knowledge, only luck determines what happens, and relying on chance is a very unsatisfactory method of progressing towards a goal.

The investigation of the pedigrees of satisfactorily productive dogs and bitches down through the history of the breed to the present day becomes a fascinating study. Certain names repeatedly appear, those of male lines in particular showing which stud dogs were used most often. The bitches these stud dogs were bred to are the important ones to notice for it is often their influence that determines the successful results. The few pedigrees given here represent the most important line which has come down to our present day Labrador in America in both show and field trial events.

Photographs have been included that will help demonstrate how certain kennels have developed their particular lines. Unfortunately, photographs taken in this country generally do not show the dogs to best advantage; therefore, I have included many more British pictures. Another reason for the predominant choice of British photographs is that pictures of our Labradors appear in American magazines from time to time and are familiar to fanciers here. Also with imported stud dogs being used to a considerable extent, it is of interest to visualize their ancestors.

Since the majority of persons buy young puppies not knowing how a typical eight or nine week old Labrador puppy should appear, I have included some photographs of puppies of that age. Every effort should be made to educate the public regarding the difference between an ordinary puppy and a good one. All puppies are appealing, but it is what they grow up to be that is important.

Each year a judge is appointed to choose what he considers the best dog and bitch. In England, Crufts is the dog show that is outstanding in this breed, and the Labrador Club Specialty show is the criterion in the United States. Therefore I have listed the winning Labradors of each sex from these shows as well as Dual and National champions to include field trial dogs.

It will be noticed that few names of the breeders and owners of Labradors have been included in this book. The reason for this is the belief that it is names of dogs and kennels that are the important ones to remember. It is not intended to pass judgment on particular Labradors or breeders; rather an effort has been made here to indicate how certain directions have been established in the past and have influenced today's outstanding and typical Labradors. As might be expected, opinions will differ on certain matters and it is up to the reader to form his own conclusions. Photographs too have been presented as representing what judges have chosen and are not necessarily the author's opinion of the best examples of the breed. Here I acknowledge indebtedness to the following persons: my friend Bertha McCormick for the many photographs and her perseverance in taking them over the years, Mr. Gerald Massey for his many letters and patience in waiting for my decisions about photographs, Major Hales Parkenham-Mahon and Lady Barlow for photographs, Mrs. Hall, Mrs. Pauling, and Frau Brulin for photographs and information about chocolate Labradors, Lars Eckberg of the Swedish Embassy for his translations, Director James Baker of the Cornell Veterinary Virus Research Laboratory for answering my questions so promptly, Codman Hislop for the picture of Flax, Elizabeth Clark for photographs of her paintings by Ward Binks, Dr. Schnelle for advising me on many kennel problems over the years and writing the article herein on hip dysplasia, Leslie Jones without whose encouragement and help this book might not have been written, and my husband who gave me the time to do it.

Dorothy Howe

1. ORIGIN OF THE LABRADOR

I quote from Leslie Sprake's *The Labrador Retriever*, printed in 1933, and from the section written by Lord George Scott:

"There is no authentic information as to the origin of the pure black water dog of Newfoundland of the type imported into England in the early part of the nineteenth century, nor is the origin of the name 'Labrador' known. It is certain that none of these dogs came from Labrador. In 1922 W. E. Cormack, a native of St. John's, made a journey on foot across Newfoundland . . . he saw small water dogs . . . it is presumed that these dogs were established in part of Newfoundland long before they were seen by Cormack.

"About and before 1830 there was a considerable trade between Poole Harbour and Newfoundland. The 2nd Earl of Malmesbury (1778–1841) is said to have imported the St. John's breed of dogs to Heron Court. The 3rd Earl (1807–1889) imported many and bred them. Also between 1865 and 1875 Lord Malmesbury, Mr. C. J. Radclyffe (of Hyde, Wareham), Mr. Montague Guest and Lord Winborne bought a lot of black water dogs imported from Newfoundland by one Hawker, the owner of a trading schooner which plied between Newfoundland and Poole.

"The above mentioned importations were the origin of the Labrador Retriever, it has not been ascertained who first gave these imported Newfoundland dogs the name of 'Labrador' . . ."

Lady Jacqueline Barlow writes from St. John's, Newfoundland: "The breed we know as the Labrador Retriever, formerly the St. John's water dog, is still to be seen unpedigreed but unmistakable, along the east and south-east coast of Newfoundland. It was used originally to retrieve fish (cod) that escaped from the hook on the surface. They were preferred by fishermen because their short, water-repellent coat did not hold the ice, unlike that of the long-haired lumbering Newfoundland dog. Labrador was part of Newfoundland but I suspect few people knew that at the time. Many Labrador owners would be surprised to see how many dogs

14

The Royal Family in England has always been interested in Labradors. This photograph shows King George VI with Windsor Bob (by Dual Ch. Staindrop Saighdear AD ex F.T.Ch. Braeroy Fudge AD). The Prime Minister at the present time has a Sandylands yellow Labrador. Photo thanks to *Our Dogs* and *The Field*.

in Newfoundland have the unmistakable characteristics of their own dogs. The dogs were mostly black, sometimes yellow, and rarely chocolate."

Through the enthusiasm of Lady Barlow in Newfoundland, a Labrador Club has been started. Her imported Ch. Knaith Beatty won Best in Show at the first Newfoundland Kennel Club all-breed show a few years ago and became the first Labrador Champion in Newfoundland. A television film, *The Labrador Retriever in Newfoundland*, was made there with Lady Barlow and her Labradors, and was shown throughout Canada in 1968.

In England, Lord George Scott wrote in 1933: "There have been several phases; what may be called big dogs with plenty of bone, have now been succeeded by a rather smaller type, maybe because the latter are considered more active, though this is by no means a certainty. One of the puzzles in judging Labradors is this difference in type, but so long as each type is right in make and shape, it must be left to the individual choice—avoiding with care on the one side the clumsy mastiff-headed bad-shouldered animal, and on the other, with even more care, the weedy snipey-looking beast, with all the appearance of a cross between a pointer and a lucher . . . the only vay to ascertain if a dog is descended from those of the early istory of the Labrador is by pedigree."

SCANDAL OF GLYNN, about 1910. Sired by F.T. Ch. Peter of Faskally
ex Shelagh of Glynn. Bred by Lord Vivian. His call to fame was being the
sire of Dual Ch. Banchory Bolo. Painting by Ward Binks.

2. DEVELOPMENT OF THE BREED

IN GENERAL

Records from private kennel stud books, the British Labrador
Club stud book published in 1949, various club year books and the
continuous printed records of our Labrador Club give the history
of the breed related to the performance of Labradors and their

progeny and, as such, are extremely valuable to breeders. Good photographs of great ones as they occur are of considerable help when matched with pedigrees. Judges as well as breeders might do well to become familiar with these.

The early history of the breed developed as a result of upper class Englishmen being such keen sportsmen and their feeling the need for a retrieving dog. They appreciated the imported water dogs called by this time Labradors, and some started breeding them and keeping records of what they did.

In Scotland the Dukes of Buccleuch have continuously bred Labradors based on the original ones from Newfoundland. It can be seen through photographs and pedigrees that their efforts to

IRISH CH. STROKESTOWN DUKE OF BLAIRCOURT 1950 AJ By Darky of Elmbank AE ex Craigluscar Dusk of Blaircourt AH. Bred by Mr. and Mrs. Grant Cairns, owned by Major H. Pakenham-Mahon. Three-time winner of the Irish Labrador Club show and many field trial wins. He sired many champions and dual champions around the world, among them Ch. Loughderg Strokestown Urch, winner of two BIS. His influence is being felt even today. Major Pakenham-Mahon is now running a yellow F.T.Ch. Strokestown Derry in field trials with great success.

CH. BANCHORY LUCKY, CH. BANCHORY DIPPER, BANCHORY
RANDO, F.T. CH. BANCHORY BOLO, CH. INGLESTON BEN (1921).
Painted by Ward Binks and owned by Mrs. Robert Clark, Jr.

keep the breed pure have been successful since at the present time
Buccleuch Labradors are obviously comparable to the early ones
and these breeders have not followed whims of fashion such as is
often the case.

The Kennel Club did not list Labradors as a separate breed until
1904, at which time there were seven entries all registered by
Munden Kennels though one of the bitches was bred at Buccleuch
Kennels. Up to this time they were all registered as just plain
retrievers, later to be separated into the various breeds as we know
them. They were not sure as to how to classify them; for instance,
one litter was registered as half Golden Retriever and half Labradors
—whether the separation was by color or coat length is not stated.
However we do know that their parents, Golden Morn and Lime-
kilm Rhoda, are considered today as Labradors. The field of genetics was not understood at that time and it was not realized that in
the first cross from pure bred Labradors the puppies come black
with short coats but that the second generation would show some
traits of the original breeds involved.

The first retrievers listed in the Stud Books of the Kennel Club
came in all colors and coat textures, with Flatcoats (called wavy-
coated in those days) having the majority of those called liver (later
changed to chocolate). According to the stud book privately printed

by Buccleuch Kennels, the chocolates in that kennel came through Field Trial Champion Peter of Faskally. This famous stud dog is behind practically all our present day imported Labradors by way of being an ancestor of Dual Champion Banchory Bolo, Champion Ilderston Ben, Dual Champion Bramshaw Bob, Dual Champion Titus of Whitmore and on through our American Labradors both show and field trial stock of today.

In 1899 Ben of Hyde was whelped. This yellow Labrador was responsible for the starting of most of the best kennels of yellow Labradors as owners of black bitches sent them to be bred to Ben. A black bitch, Velvet, was responsible for the foundation of Knaith Kennels in Scotland.

There was much duplication of names in early pedigrees listed in the stud books and the only way to identify them was stating they were Lord Grimston's Susan or the Duke of Hamilton's Sam, with the year of their whelping making it possible to tell which was which.

Of course, in the early days of breeding in Britain, with few Labradors to work with, there was much inbreeding and there must have been careful culling of inferior stock in order for the sound type to have come down to us today. The British evidently realized that inbreeding in itself never proves to be the cause of deterioration. However inbreeding does assist the continuation of qualities that already exist and prevents their disappearance from the breed. It is apparent that if such things as nervousness, stupidity, and strange temperaments are present in the make-up of a dog and bitch being bred together, the certain way to keep on reproducing these unwanted characteristics is to breed together nearly related specimens of the same degenerate strain. On the other hand, when inbreeding produces superior qualities in the progeny inbreeding becomes a powerful tool for the good if properly used. A discerning eye, a keen ability to weigh the facts presented, and a willingness to select and retain only the best is of major importance if inbreeding is to be successful.

It is remarkable that those first few dogs and bitches when bred together produced such an outstanding number of genes for desirable qualities that they were able to bring forth progeny which became typical for the breed of Labrador as we know it. It is obvious that in the formation of our Labrador as a separate breed those

CH. SANDYLANDS TWEED OF BLAIRCOURT AS 1958 By Ruler of Blaircourt AQ ex Ch. Tessa of Blaircourt AR. Bred by Mr. and Mrs. Grant Cairns, owned by Mrs. G. Broadley. (Pedigree 20.)

CH. RULER OF BLAIRCOURT AQ 1956 By Forbes of Blaircourt AL ex Olivia of Blaircourt AP. Bred and owned by Mr. and Mrs. Grant Cairns. Reserve BIS Crufts.

persons responsible for its continuation after leaving Newfoundland had what was needed to work with in the way of high quality breeding stock and also had the intelligence and powers of observation and above all the needed courage to drastically cull out inferior stock.

The great Labradors of the past after the first inbreeding, as seen through pedigrees in the stud books, have been developed through line breeding. It should be understood that the more generations that are investigated in a pedigree the more knowledge one is able to obtain, and at least five generations must be studied in order to prove much of anything. As previously mentioned progress is very slow without great bitches to breed to important stud dogs. In many instances, valuable brood bitches and stud dogs are not discovered until several years of life have been wasted on inferior mates and we will never know how many were never given an opportunity to prove their worth. It is often possible through the study of pedigrees to discover such valuable Labradors while they are still young and to make certain that their progeny get into the hands of breeders who appreciate their worth.

A successful line of bitches came through:

CRAIGLUSCAR BLACK GEM dam of
    Craigluscar Emperor sire of
        Ch. Imp of Blaircourt dam of
        Tessa of Blaircourt dam of
            Ch. Sandylands Tweed of Blaircourt
    Craigluscar Crocus dam of
        Hawk of Luscander—sire of
        Ch. Sam of Blaircourt
    Craigluscar Dusk of Blaircourt—dam of
        Ch. Strokestown Duke of Blaircourt see progeny pedigree #17
        Forbes of Blaircourt—sire of
        Ch. Ruler of Blaircourt
        Fiona of Blaircourt—dam of
            Lawrie of Blaircourt—sire of
            Olivia of Blaircourt
    Olivia of Blaircourt—dam of
        Ch. Ruler of Blaircourt
        Ch. Sam of Blaircourt

CH. DRINK-
STONE PONS
OF WINGAN
1931 By Ch.
Banchory Danilo
ex Drinkstone
Peg. Bred by Dr.
M. Home owned
in USA by Jay F.
Carlisle and
David Elliot.
Grandsire of Lena
and F. T. Ch.
Timber Town
Clansman.

Tracing pedigrees is relatively easy in this country because the American Kennel Club has always followed the policy of listing the registration numbers of parents of individual dogs as well as the dogs themselves. This has not been done until relatively recently in the British publications. Their system has been to list only certain dogs in their annual stud books, with their color, but with some of the ancestors without numbers. All registered dogs however are listed in their monthly Kennel Club magazine but have been very difficult to trace because there had been no coding system until recently. They now have a system which indicates

CH. RUPERT SAM HOWE 1960 By Eng. Can. Am. Ch. Sam of Blaircourt ex Ch. Rupert Aurora Borealis. Bred by Dorothy Howe, owned and handled by Mary Swan.

the month and year of gazettes in which names can be found. This makes it very easy to trace back a certain number of generations.

In the United States, imported dogs are listed in the AKC stud books with a star annotated to indicate that the AKC has the records, but we cannot trace the pedigrees. The American system has also changed in that full pedigrees up to three generations were at first given in the stud books but entries have now been reduced to just sire and dam. With the huge volume of dogs being registered, only those dogs and bitches that have produced progeny are currently listed in the stud book. The present system is in a way unfortunate because we can no longer see whole litters listed together, which is still possible in England.

Certain interesting information can be found through the listing of whole litters. Proportions of various colors and distribution of males and females can be seen, as well as circumstances wherein breeders have repeated certain matings. The continued use of a particular stud dog in some kennels and various studs in others might indicate something important but, on the other hand, might just have been a convenient way to do things.

AMERICAN CH. RUPERT AURORA BOREALIS 1958 Bitch By Ch. Kinley Comet ex Rupert Colchester Reef. Bred, owned and handled by Dorothy Howe.

In 1916 the need was felt for a Labrador Club in England and it was founded with Lord Knutsford (then Hon. A. Holland Hibbert) of Munden Kennels as chairman and Lorna, Countess Howe (then Mrs. Quintin Dick) of Banchory Kennels as secretary. At this time the standard for the breed was written which has been rather closely followed on both sides of the ocean ever since.

At this time too the breed was gaining increased popularity among persons of all classes. Lady Howe had great enthusiasm for the breed and was rather unique in that she bred very few dogs but owned a great many important ones. She had the faculty of recognizing a good one when she saw it, and as breeders soon realized that any dog would be given every chance to prove himself in both show and field trial under her ownership, she had not much trouble in acquiring any dog she desired. She seemed to know every Labrador in the country and of any litter about to be whelped, and many breeders refused to let a puppy go until Lady Howe had been to look the litter over. In this way she built up her kennel by choice of the country's best dogs and she dominated both field trials and show for many years without actually breeding many Labradors herself. A list of her Labradors reads like "Who's Who," with many Crufts and field trial winners as well as dual champions in her Banchory Kennels. Many of the outstanding stud dogs of that era belonged to Lady Howe and she encouraged beginners and game keepers to take an interest in the breed. She judged at both trials and shows and held important positions in The Kennel Club and the Labrador Club throughout her life.

It was through a gift of a Labrador from Lady Howe after the first World War that interest in the breed developed in America. Long Island, being in the eastern flyway for migrating waterfowl, was the logical place for the foundation of the breed in this country. The need for a retrieving water dog was great and it did not take long for sportsmen in this country to import Labradors. The professionals who understood the art of breeding and training them were often brought over with these dogs in the early days. We were fortunate in having David Elliot arrive so early in the history of the breed in this country. His philosophy and patience in teaching dogs and their owners has had a lasting influence on those of us who came in contact with him.

With the importing of Peggy of Shipton by the Arden Kennels

CH. KNAITH BEATTY 1965 By Coultercraigs Simon ex Knaith Bandlass. Bred by Mrs. Wormald owned in Newfoundland by Lady Barlow. The first Newfoundland champion made up in four shows with one Best In Show win.

The Hon. W. Averill Harriman and his brother the breed became important. Peggy when bred to the English dog Hiwood Risk, produced the greatest of all American-bred bitches F.T.Ch. Tar of Arden and her sister Pitch of Arden. (There was also a yellow brother, Fitz of Arden, in this litter). Another great bitch arrived when Peggy was bred to the imported dog Odds On. This bitch F.T.Ch. Decoy of Arden, and her brother, F.T.Ch. Blind of Arden, had great and continuing influence for the good of the breed.

With the arrival of Raffles from Wales, the Earlsmoor Kennels of Labradors was founded, and added interest in shows and field trials. The impetus here was given through the breeding of F.T.Ch. Decoy of Arden to Ch. Raffles of Earlsmoor and resulted in production of the most famous litters in this country. Included were seven champions among them Dual Champions Shed, Gorse, and

CH. BAROKE'S YELLOW JACKET 1967 By Ch. Lockerbie Kismet ex Ch. Sandylands Mona Lisa. Bred and owned by Dr. Keith S. Grimson.

Braes of Arden and Ch. Earlsmoor Moor, the first bench champion to build up a five Best in Show record, not to be beaten for many years.

With the intelligent breeding of F.T.Ch. Tar of Arden at Deer Creek Kennels in St. Louis, a long line of excellent working Labradors of attractive appearance was produced. Two Dual Champions were developed at this kennel: Shed of Arden and Little Pierre of Deer Creek and resulted in the establishment of an important breeding kennel of that era.

At Grangemead Kennels in the Chicago area, the line of Dual Champions through Shed of Arden was developed and established what may be an all-time record of four dual champions descending in a direct line. Wonderful brood bitches were intelligently bred at this kennel, with Grangemead Sharon and Caunsett Chippie leaving their mark on the future. The bitches at both Deer Creek and Grangemead can be traced back to the great beginnings in this country with imported stock at Timbertown and Wingan Kennels on Long Island. Marvadel was another important kennel at this time on Long Island and possessed two outstanding bitches, Marvadel Cinders and Marvadel Topsy; both became great producers. This kennel also had some of the early imported yellows.

Wardwyn Kennels was producing on Long Island some of the first chocolate Labradors in this country through the line from Dual Ch. Bengal of Arden and his sister, Buddha of Arden. Two important bitches at this kennel were Wardwyn Welcome and Wardwyn Windbound and both were to leave their marks on the future of the breed. This kennel had great interest in showing their Labradors, as did Catawba Kennels. Through the use of the stud dog Mint of Barrington, the bitches Mathematition of Catawba and Marvadel Black Ash of Catawba arrived.

Chidley Kennels has upheld the standard for show type Labradors for many years. Joan Read (then Joan Redmond) started as a child with Ch. Bancstone Bob of Wingan. This dog came from that great litter produced from Ch. Drinkstone Peg, coming over in whelp to Lady Howe's Dual Ch. Bramshaw Bob, and most of the litter became champions in this country. When the bitch Marsh, a

CH. GENERAL OF GARSHANGAN 1951 AL By Ch. Poppleton Lieutenant ex Gigha of Garshangan. Bred and owned by Lt. Col. and Mrs. Hill.

daughter of Ch. Earlsmoor Moor, was bred to Ch. Bancstone Bob, the bitch Down II and the great winner and stud dog, Ch. Hugger Mugger, arrived on the scene. Later Ch. Chidley Spook, a daughter of Ch. Hugger Mugger, was to dominate the show ring along with many of her progeny. The yellow Labradors began their rise through Chidley Kennels with the first yellow American-bred champion being Ch. Chidley Almond Crisp.

LABRADORS RECOGNIZED IN THE U.S.A.

It was during 1931 that persons interested in the breed organized the Labrador Club and influenced the American Kennel Club to recognize Labradors as a separate breed. Field trials were held before interest in shows developed, and the first Labrador to win a field trial was an imported yellow, Carl of Boghurst. Labradors in those days were entered in both trials and shows and were used as retrievers through the duck season. They were rather closely held among a group of affluent friends who enjoyed working with their dogs in trials but also showed them.

SHOW VERSUS FIELD TRIAL

After World War I, separation began between the show and field trial enthusiasts, with Long Island owners providing most of the competition for the show part of the game. The Labrador Club group chose field trials as their chief interest and there appeared shortly thereafter two rather different types of Labradors, particularly in temperament. Field trial dogs, being bred for speed, became high-strung; show dogs stayed beautiful but many had no interest in hunting.

It was not long before rivalry became so extreme in both fields of competition that professionals slowly entered both sports. National and National Amateur championship awards became the supreme annual prizes for trials competition, and adding up Bests in Show wins to best previous records became the aim of those interested in dog shows. However, the great majority of Labradors were kept by persons satisfied with lesser triumphs, who enjoyed smaller trials, shows, hunting, and above all having their Labradors as members of the family.

In 1953 the record for Bests in Show, held for many years by Ch. Earlsmoor Moor, was broken by Ch. Dark Star of Franklin.

MARVADEL CINDERS 1938. Bred and owned by Eleanor and Gould Remick. Black bitch by Ch. Raffles of Earlsmoor ex Marvadel Topsy. Gould Remick was one of the early presidents of the Labrador Club. Cinders made a great name for herself as a brood bitch, in particular when bred to Mint of Barrington and Dual Ch. Little Pierre of Deer Creek. What a lovely head she had!

ROBERTA OF COOHOY 1951 AP 1951. By Whatstandwell Ballyduff
Robin ex Wanda of Coohoy. Bred by Mrs. Cliffe and Miss Hoyland.
Roberta is a sister of Romantic of Coohoy.

This dog, bred and owned by the Ziessows of the Detroit area, won
eight Bests in Show and also won a Labrador Specialty show. This
record was held until Grace Lambert's import, English, American,
and Canadian Ch. Sam of Blaircourt beat it with nine Bests in
Show and Labrador Club Specialty wins. In 1968 the record was
beaten again with twelve Bests in Show by the first yellow to reach
the heights, Ch. Shamrock Acres Light Brigade, bred by Sally
McCarthy and co-owned with Mrs. James R. Getz.

Members of the Labrador Club, realizing the danger of the keen
interest centered in the developing of a show type Labrador with
the possiblity of the loss of hunting ability, incorporated in the
standard for the breed the rule that a member of the Club having a
dog with an AKC champion record must not use the title until the
dog had passed a working test. Yet they made it so difficult in the
beginning for owners of bench champions to take the simple test,
and forgot to list in the Club records those dogs which had

acquired the working certificate, that few persons bothered to take these working tests for champions and many show-interested members resigned from the Club Recently the rules for judging the tests have been changed, but with few show people belonging to the Club and the habit formed of not bothering about field tests, it does not amount to much. In spite of this, some show kennels are obtaining field trial titles and some field trial kennels are insisting on producing dogs of attractive appearance.

Nilo Kennels and Harrowby Kennels are trying to close the gap that separates the trial and show Labradors and bring the breed back to a truly dual-purpose breed. As examples, Whygin, Shamrock Acres, and Franklin Kennels are proving that well-bred show dogs can compete successfully in field trials.

PROFESSIONAL VERSUS AMATEUR

The trend towards the separation between the professional and amateur is widening in both show and field trial competition, no

CH. SHAMROCK ACRES LIGHT BRIGADE 1964 By Ch. Shamrock Acres Casey Jones CD ex Ch. Whygin Busy Belinda. Bred by Mrs. James McCarthy owned with Mrs. James Getz. Twelve times Best In Show. Top Sporting Dog 1958 (Phillips system). (Pedigree 34.)

CH. WHYGIN GENTLE JULIA OF AVEC 1959 By Whygin Gold Bullion ex Ch. Whygin Black Gambit of Avec. Bred by Barbara Birdsall, owned by Sally McCarthy. Dam of 12 champions and one Amateur F.T. Ch. A great brood bitch.

INGLESTON NITH 1927 KK By Lochar Mac ex Kinmount Juno. Bred by Mrs. Crabbe, owned by K. Dobie.

CH. EARLSMOOR MOOR OF ARDEN 1937 By Ch. Raffles of Earlsmoor ex F.T. Ch. Decoy of Arden. Bred by The Hon. W. Averill Harriman, owned by Dr. Milbank. Three times Best in Show. A great stud dog. (Pedigree 29.)

LENA 1941 By F.T. Ch. Timbertown Clansman ex Wingan's Primrose. Bred by Mrs. Gavan, owned by D. Howe. Foundation bitch of Rupert Kennels. All breeding stock goes back to this bitch.

doubt due to the tremendous increase in the number of puppies being produced and the lack of knowledge among the general public regarding how much work and time is involved in "making up" a champion or field trial champion. With the price range for Labradors showing as much disparity as the quality of the stock, the professionals are handling many of the superior dogs in both fields. These animals must be continually campaigned all over the country if they are to become famous. These celebrated few are constantly being used at stud to a variety of bitches, resulting in the overproduction of so many different types of Labrador that it becomes difficult to find a typical one which conforms entirely to the standard. The throw-outs from those bred for field trials flood the market in

NATIONAL CHAMPION CORK OF OAKWOOD LANE 1951 by Coastal
Charger of Deer Creek ex Anoka Liza Jane of Kingsdale. Bred by Bill
Rook, owned by Dr. A. Harold Mork. This dog not only won the National
two years, but many of his progeny qualified for the National and some
won it.

some areas and many display such nervous temperaments that the
public is losing faith in the breed as a whole.

The gap should be closed between those dogs called Labradors
but having nothing in common with the standard for the breed and
those that are good-looking typey dogs but have temperaments so
timid that they jump at the slightest noise and are often inclined
to bite. The breeders must dedicate their enterprise to the long-
range purpose of mating together only those Labradors that appear
and act as really good ones, which have at least five generations of
important Labradors behind them to prove there is some chance of
getting equally fine progeny. This must be accomplished regardless
of the temporary reputation of the individual dog or bitch. It is
important to realize that a brood bitch or a stud dog is only as
important as its ancestors, and it requires tracing many generations
back of the Labrador under consideration to be certain of its lasting
value to the breed.

Labradors have climbed steadily in popularity and are among the top ten in registration with the AKC, and higher than that in Britain. Unfortunately this situation in America has produced "in and out" breeders who have little or no interest in producing anything but more puppies for sale and has led to an over-production of inferior stock. In England, breeders seem to survive miscalculations better than we do, and British breeders persist longer in pursuing perfection. It remains to be seen what will be the next turning point in the history of Labradors, but it must come through an increase in the number of intelligent, dedicated new breeders. The future of the breed depends on the appearance of breeders who are dedicated to high standards and they must be able to withstand the inevitable mistakes that will occur. The fascination of anticipating how puppies will turn out as grown Labradors and the resulting stimulation in trying to determine what best to do next is bound to produce interesting consequences.

The beginner may think that investigating what has happened in the past is outside his field of interest, or that this can be gone

CH. KINLEY COPPER 1962 AW By Ch. Kinley Skipper ex Kinley Tango. Bred and owned by Fred Wrigley. Twice winner of CCs at Crufts with many other wins to her credit.

into later when he has produced some puppies and is well on his way. It should be remembered that trying to discover what has produced success in the past can have great influence on what is to be done in the future. The true long-time breeder understands that breeding one outstanding dog is a tremendous step forward but that true success depends on the ability to produce such animals consistently.

It takes time to develop records and the sooner a breeder starts collecting photographs and pedigrees, along with names of both typical and untypical specimens of the breed, the quicker he comes to understand the possible cause for what he sees before him. Developing one's own record system wherein lists of names make sense is a good practice, and various parts should be available for instant use.

Such things as show and field trial catalogs not only give the breeding of various dogs but show the competition what a prospective winner is up against and as such should be kept for reference. Reading and filing judges' critiques of dogs on the way up is very instructive, and very interesting material to return to after a dog has become famous. This British custom of recording judgments should be adopted elsewhere but it takes courage and knowledge on the part of a judge.

Going back over old records and registrations helps to establish trends, as through the extensive use of such a stud dog as National Champion Cork of Oakwood Lane. The tremendous use of this dog (with nobody knows how many puppies raised to maturity) produced progeny that for many years dominated the National. Among show dogs in England, Ch. Sandylands Tweed of Blaircourt is the stud dog that is producing more than the normal number of winners at shows.

When a popular stud dog is found, it is more important than ever to notice the bitches serviced by him. In future generations it will be the best bitch line from this stud dog that will survive the tests of time.

Through the history of Labradors and the study of pedigrees, certain bitches stand out. Birkhill Juliet, the dam of F.T.Ch. Peter of Faskally, and her two sisters (see pedigree #3), and later Kirkmahoe Dinah and Brocklehirst Nell (pedigree #8) have had lasting influence. The fact that Dual Ch. Banchory Bolo was a prepotent

38

stud dog, alive at the same time as these last mentioned bitches was very fortunate. The progeny resulting from Bolo's being mated to Dinah and Nell were to a great extent responsible for a great period in the history of Labradors after the first world war.

YELLOW LABRADORS

It was after the second world war that yellow Labradors started an upsurge in popularity. The proportions of good otter tails,

CH. LOUGHDERG STROKESTOWN URCH 1954 AR By Ch. Strokestown Duke of Blaircourt ex Lisroyan Lady. Bred by Major S. Hales Pakenham-Mahon, owned by Mrs. J. Sim. One of the few Labradors to go Best In Show in Great Britain.

double coats, and the increase in bone in the yellows became popular. A recent critique of judge and breeder written by the late Dr. Acheson (Ballyduff Kennels) gives this influence to Poppleton Kennels. For years the yellow color has had control of the show ring in England but has been much slower in gaining popularity in this country. However, with the increase in use of imported stud dogs in this country (particularly on the East Coast), yellow Labradors have come into great demand and we see whole classes of yellows at some shows. In fact, it is becoming difficult to find a black stud dog that does not carry yellow genes.

CHOCOLATE LABRADORS

At present it seems to be the turn of the chocolate Labrador to struggle to the top. It becomes very important that breeders not become so interested in a particular color that they forget to notice the rest of the dog. Such things as light eyes and an unattractive coat of mixed color seem to create the challenge here.

It should be understood that both the yellow and chocolate colors have been in the breed almost from the beginning. There is a record of Dual Champion Banchory Bolo having produced a yellow and, since so many of our present Labradors go back to this dog, we can understand how the yellow genes might turn up anywhere in a black line. It is more than probable that FT.Ch. Tar of Arden received her yellow genes through Bolo.

Another interesting discovery behind F.T.Ch. Tar of Arden (pedigree #26) is the registration of a bitch named Duchess of Millichope (LL British stud book). This bitch was whelped the same day as Peggy of Shipton, the dam of Tar. In this country, Peggy's dam was always listed as Gehta unregistered. Yet the dam of Duchess of Millichope is registered as Gehta of Sigeforda. It turns out to be an important pedigree, Ch. Banchory Bluff ex Champion Balbeardie.

When going over old records, one never knows what will turn up of interest in the development of the breed. It is the discovery of things in the past that could have vital influence on the present and future of Labradors and as such is a constant fascination to those interested in searching records. Such data, the critiques on famous dogs written while they were still alive, and the recorded remarks of judges regarding trends during certain eras make delightful as well as instructive reading.

The future development of Labradors will continue but we must have dedicated breeders to steer it in an undeviating direction based upon the principles on which the breed was founded.

3. PET, COMPANION, OR WORKING DOG

PET

The need for a pet is strong with many people. Children in particular find satisfaction in any small creature, even a frog or a snake, but there comes a time when the demand is for a puppy. Certain qualities must be present if a dog is to become the ideal family pet. He should be adaptable, be willing to please, gentle yet courageous and dependable. A Labrador has all of these qualities plus intelligence which enables him to learn easily and meet new and different situations with suitable reactions. He is instinctively clean, which pleases the woman of the house, and is not the nervous jittery type that can be such a nuisance around the home. He would like to be with members of the family, yet will be quiet when left alone and can be easily taught not to bark unnecessarily. There is no problem with feeding him.

COMPANION

As distinguished from being merely a pet, a Labrador is capable of becoming a wonderful companion if handled in such a way that he loves and trusts his owner, gains an understanding of what is expected of him and is permitted to cooperate in various enterprises. The idea that obedience is forced on a dog through commands is not the approach if companionship is to be the end product, rather requesting a Labrador to perform some function, realizing he will do it happily through love and respect, is the better way. We all abide by certain rules and a dog should be no exception to this custom and should know the regulations that apply to him. It should be insisted upon that he conform to the rules once they are thoroughly learned, without having to continually repeat requests. The mentality of a Labrador develops and improves with learning and gradually he is able to understand whole sentences and in some cases make known his own answers. The dog in his own way transmits his requests to a sensitive and understanding person with whom he is in constant association. This mutual sensitivity between a person and his Labrador makes for the ideal companionship but takes patience and understanding.

Although a Labrador focuses his attention continually on the person who trains him he loves nearly everyone. He quickly acquires the habits of those surrounding him and fits into their life patterns as best he can. He will listen to the conversation of his master, ready to jump to attention when sentences he understands are heard. He conforms to the wishes of the family but at times is capable of working independently, a trait that is important when it comes to dangerous situations or when out hunting. As he develops, he becomes sensitive to the atmosphere around those he loves and is quick to sense danger and react to it by trying to protect them. His highly perceptive sense of hearing distinguishes between motors of automobiles and the resonance of footsteps; this ability helps him alert the family to the approach of friend or stranger.

The temperament of a Labrador with his quiet yet forceful reaction to situations makes him an ideal guard dog since he can be trusted to corner and hold a criminal yet not injure him unless it is necessary. Many are the cases of warning of fire and saving from drowning accomplished by Labradors. He can be depended on to protect children and be gentle with babies. If teased beyond endurance he will just walk away.

He thrives on affection and rarely needs physical punishment. A scolding is all that is necessary except in extreme cases, at which time tapping the side of the muzzle will be all that is needed. This hurts his feelings and teaches him to change his ways. He is a happy dog and can be depended on for his loyalty and courage.

WORKING DOG

With many sportsmen Labradors have gradually replaced other retriever breeds as hunting dogs. This has come about for several reasons, one of which is their short dense coat which sheds water and to which ice does not cling. Hunters have found they will retrieve woodcock, which some other breeds disdain. The family pet which has developed the mutual understanding with his owner and been trained by him makes an ideal hunting companion. They have been bred to please people and have the necessary patience and

CH. ANNWYN'S TRIC OR TREAT By Am. Can. Ch. Knoll Tops Cloud of Annwyn ex Ravencamp Grebe with Tom Murphy whose life he saved towing an oarless boat ashore by its rope for $3\frac{1}{2}$ hours in heavy winds and rough water, while duck hunting at Wolfe Island.

perseverance to keep on trying to solve problems asked of them.

The fields of endeavor in which Labradors shine are increasing continually. During wars they have been used to carry messages and detect mines and booby traps. Recently it has been found that their exceedingly sensitive noses can detect drugs, and more and more of these dogs are being trained both overseas and here for this purpose.

The great contribution they make in helping sightless persons is one of their most important functions. It has been found that they are more suitable for this than most other breeds. In England under the prefix of GUIDEWELL, Labradors are being bred for leading the blind and are of such excellent type that a yellow bitch GUIDE-WELL HAPPY has also a Best in Show to her credit. Another GUIDEWELL dog was used in a television series on BBC.

In America under the registered prefix of GUIDE DOGS Labradors are bred for leading the blind and have proved excellent. These dogs are brought up during their first year of life in families with children, many of whom are in 4H programs. These children with their dogs are under the supervision of trained GUIDE DOGS personnel and after the first year, if the dogs meet specific require-

Blind man descending from a bus.

GUIDEWELL HAPPY 1962 By Candlemas Sandylands Timber ex Guidewell Misty. This bitch was made Best In Show by Mary Scott as well as performing her duties at Guidewell Kennels in England.

LABRADORS FOR THE BLIND at GUIDEWELL KENNELS England testing for dog distraction.

A yellow Labrador in the USA guiding a student from the school bus after a day's training.

CH. RUPERT COUNSELLOR By Ch. Glenarvey Barrister
ex Ch. Rupert Marleigh Bingham advertising CBSports.

ments, the bitches are spayed and they start their serious training
for guiding sightless persons.

The Labrador is a versatile dog, and a yellow Labrador was used
in the filming of THE INCREDIBLE JOURNEY. A group from
National Educational Television filmed THE ESSAY ON DEATH
in Vermont the summer following the assassination of President
Kennedy. The film was given national coverage on the first anniversary of the President's death and was repeated the night after the
assassination of Reverend Martin Luther King, Jr. In this film
two black Labradors were used as Champion Scawfell Seekon
handled certain problems very well and Rupert Comet was more
dependable in other situations. They appeared so much alike that
the actions of one dog called for in the script could be divided
between both dogs without it being detected.

Many of us believe that once having had a Labrador no other
breed could be completely satisfactory.

4. YOU AND YOUR FIRST LABRADOR

Why have you decided to own a dog? No one should just bring a live thing into the home without a logical reason, whether it is just to befriend a stray, have a pet for the children, a dog for hunting, or to guard the family. Perhaps the reason is the desire to breed Labradors.

Before accepting a stray, it would be well to consult your veterinarian about its health. He might also have ideas as to whether as a grown dog it would be safe with children and neighbors. As pets, guards dogs, and hunting dogs, Labradors serve well. The good ones love people and are so intelligent that they know the difference between friend and foe and will not hesitate to forfeit life to guard their families.

PERSONALITIES

Another question is—How well do we understand ourselves in relation to our desire for a dog? First you should determine what kind of a person you are. Are you the dominating type? Do you like to get your way by quiet persuasion? Do you easily lose your temper, or do you sulk when things go wrong? Then figure out which traits a dog should possess to suit your personality.

If you are the dominating type and have the same type of dog, there will be a battle of wits to find out which wins and it will be a fascinating game of constant interest. If you allow the dog to be an individual and not cower into submission, you will develop mutual respect for each other with allowances made for individual accomplishments. If you are the kind of person who is not equipped to force your way on others but get what you want through subtle persuasion, you should have that kind of temperament in your dog as well. The danger here lies in spoiling the dog, giving in to what he wants, and asking nothing or not enough in return. The interest here lies in mutual adoration and an understanding that makes for cooperation without any commands being necessary.

Do you lose your patience and fly into a temper easily? Then observe the effect on your dog when this happens. Does it become confused, frightened, stubborn, or run away? At some time we all lose patience with people and dogs. Perhaps you are the type who throws up your hands in frustration, puts the dog out, and says "Why did I ever get a dumb one?" In other words, you sulk because you cannot make the dog understand what is expected; you are trying to get him to do something against his natural instincts or beyond his power to understand. Remember that it is the privilege of a dog to sulk or rebel against authority when you handle situations in the wrong way. It should be easier for you to understand him than for the dog to comprehend your wishes.

It is not easy to have mutual understanding between dog and man. Among many things, it takes being constantly together. Some individuals are better at it than others and some people never get the idea, in which case they should not have a dog.

PUPPY OR OLDER DOG?

The next problem might be deciding between puppy and older dog. There are advantages and disadvantages to ownership of both. An older dog is usually housebroken, and, if a kennel dog, becomes very appreciative of belonging to a family. However, an older dog has usually acquired bad habits which may be the reason you are able to get him. Most people prefer a puppy because there is always an appeal about a young thing. However, a puppy can be ideal or turn out to be a great mistake depending on the type of person who acquires him. It is easy to believe any Labrador puppy will turn out to be that perfect companion the whole family has been waiting for. It is well to remember that the fascination of a puppy does not last long and that it is the grown dog which will be with you for many years.

WHO'S IN CHARGE?

Who in the family is going to be responsible for the care and training of the puppy? Since a Labrador thrives best on love and affection, and gives it in return, he will depend on at least one person in the household for this. A Labrador does not do well away

MALLARDHURN COUNTESS OF KEITHRAY (on the left) By Ch. Sandylands Tandy ex Ch. Hollybank Beauty. Owned in USA by John Olin.

from contact with people and should at an early age learn to be a a house pet whether or not his future involves showing, hunting, or breeding.

TRAINING FOR THE HUNTING DOG

When looking for a future hunting dog, the problem involves whether or not you are capable of training a dog. There are professional trainers, but it is generally the human being who needs the training more than the dog. All the professional training in the world will do no good, and probably a great deal of harm if a person does not have the right instincts and relationships with his dog whether bought for hunting or just to have a well-behaved dog around the house. Obedience class conductors and dog psychologists do a rushing business in readjusting dogs to given situations where it is not the dogs but their owners who are in trouble. To change a relationship between a dog and a human being that has gotten off to a bad start usually ends in failure, as it is the rare person who will admit to being at fault. A Labrador to be used for hunting should be a faithful companion to a thoughtful, kindly master who understands and cooperates with his dog.

SEX

Male or female is another question to be decided before buying a Labrador. For those who want above all a hunting dog, a male is preferable because a bitch may come in heat just when she is needed as a retriever. In other circumstances, there is really not much difference; each sex has advantages and disadvantages. Either will wander if enticed away by neighboring dogs, or stay at home to be with their well-loved family where life is never dull.

START WITH THE BEST

If your interest is in raising puppies, you should start with the best bitch you can find. If you cannot afford the best, wait until you can. Make sure that you do not get involved in a so-called "puppy mill" or "back yard" breeding of inferior puppies. There are persons who care only about making money and "farm out" bitches for mass production of inferior puppies with no interest in the future of the breed. Of course, good things come high in price, but the bargain often turns out to be more expensive in the end when you figure veterinary expenses among other things. The initial cost of a puppy when spread over the twelve or fourteen years of life expectancy does not seem like much. Even if you only want a family pet and never intend to breed, show, or hunt, why have to apologize for a dog all the rest of its life because you bought it at a "bargain basement" price? It is always a surprise to find persons rather proud of the fact that their dog has some imperfection; whereas everything else they possess has to be relatively perfect. This seems rather like buying a fake antique for a real one and telling the world it was a bargain.

FINDING YOUR LABRADOR

Assuming that the decision is finally made that a Labrador is the only dog for you and your family, and that less than the best puppy will not satisfy you, the search begins for a puppy that will hopefully be an ideal pet for the family, will be fun training to retrieve and can be used as such during the hunting season. If the desire is to raise puppies, the demand is for a bitch and a good one.

LEARNING ABOUT DOGS

For the average person, a good way to find the right Labrador is to go to dog shows. The dog magazines list the shows with dates and where they are to be held. At a dog show, talk with as many people as possible, especially with those who will put you in touch with active breeders. Unfortunately, many successful breeders are "kennel blind," believing so strongly in their own type of Labrador that they do not see the faults in their stock. However, breeders are flattered when a serious beginner asks their advice; and the more intelligent the questions asked, the more interest there is in helping the new breeder to get started. The successful breeder is the one with many satisfied customers, and it becomes important for the beginner to talk with owners of Labradors from some of these kennels before visiting the kennels or starting a correspondence. This is a big country, and you may end up buying a high-priced puppy

PUPPIES AT NILO KENNELS 1969 By F. T. Ch. Ace of Garfield ex Mallardhurn. Countess of Keithray (leading the puppies).

from a person you have never seen, so you must make certain that you will get what you are paying for. This involves talking with a great many Labrador owners and breeders and eventually deciding upon a breeder whose advice you believe to be trustworthy. No one is infallible; miracles rarely happen and we never get perfection, but with an intelligent approach such as is used in acquiring other important possessions, mistakes can be minimized when buying a puppy which you hope will be a superior, all-purpose Labrador.

At first, the beginner can rarely see the difference between one puppy or dog within a breed and another, especially if they are all-black. It takes constant training of the eye to distinguish various differences between the Labradors one has the opportunity to see. Also, there is more involved than visual appearance in selecting the ideal one (more about this later). A beginner will be more capable in choosing the right breeder than the right puppy and should rely upon the breeder to make the selection.

PRICE

As with any animal, prices for the young vary according to the performances of the ancestors, whether it be milk production in cows, number of eggs per hen, or winning of races by horses. It also takes understanding of how to combine pedigrees of the sire and dam in order to stand a chance of producing superior young from a given breeding. A person who has raised many litters of puppies from his own line of bitches learns many things about these bitches and slowly tries to eliminate faults while holding the good points from generation to generation. Experience should have a cash value, and the intelligent beginner should understand that top prices are asked and received by good Labrador breeders. As with other rare products, when a top-quality puppy for breeding is wanted, it should be reserved well in advance of whelping, sometimes necessarily as much as a year or two ahead. However, a good pet can sometimes be bought fairly reasonably with or without registration papers from an established breeder.

Remember that a puppy is so classed up to a year of age. Breeders vary as to when prices go up and down in relation to the age of the puppy. Since the major demand is for puppies of eight or nine weeks of age, prices often go down as soon as the puppies start

RUPERT CEDAR OF BIRCHWOOD 1969 at eight weeks of age. By Ch. Nokeener Pinchbeck Seafarer ex Rupert Due Process. Bred by D. Howe, owned by Barbara Ganley.

getting "all legs and arms" and too lively for the average person. On the other hand, for breeding stock after an X-ray for hip dysplasia at six months of age, the price may suddenly go up or way down. Since diagnosis of being free of hip dysplasia is not accurate until at least a year of age, prices will again fluctuate at the age of a year, especially if the puppy has been shown and has won points and/or is a good hunting Labrador. Prices between males and females also vary with the breeder. In some cases, males are more expensive and at other times the females are more valuable, depending on various circumstances. Pets can often be picked up cheaply as a result of a first-time litter kept too long and becoming a nuisance. In such case, the owner of the bitch and the bitch herself are fed up with the *brats* and anyone who will take them away at this age need not pay much. However, beware of taking home wormy, sick, malnourished puppies only to have them die on your hands or introduce fleas. Understand that the bargain puppy is sold "as is" and any "livestock" on them is thrown in free! You

53

CH. CANDY STOMPER CD By Chipsdale Early Win ex Black Stomper. Owned and handled by Mrs. Toth. Top winning bitch 1963 (Phillips system).

may also find that your cute puppy grows up to look more like another breed than a Labrador.

SHYNESS

When buying an older puppy from a kennel, you may run into "kennel shyness." This may be inherited timidity or be acquired by the puppy becoming so used to being behind wire that it is frightened of the big, wide world outside. Another reason for acquired shyness is being dominated by a litter mate or an older dog. I have also been told that among litter brothers brought up together to breeding age, sterility may result in the dominated individual. Inherited shyness is another matter, and the experienced and ethical breeder will know the difference. Often a shy one is best for an older person as this one is apt to be a "one man dog" and stay close to his owner. An extrovert, highly strung dog might tend to wander off unless given proper training.

QUALITY IS NOT INSTANT

With the population explosion in Labradors we often find persons with an inferior bitch which they have bred to a top quality stud dog. Perhaps they started with a pet bitch and decided to breed her to the popular stud dog of the moment believing that the puppies would take after their sire. This supposedly quick approach to breeding succeeds but rarely, and more often than not the puppies are just mediocre specimens and a great disappointment to the owner of the litter. These persons do not realize that the breeding of superior stock is a long, slow process and starting with inferior stock makes the process even slower and may never yield any good results.

Some owners of superior stud dogs are after the "fast buck" and will encourage the use of their studs on any bitch that happens along. The resulting puppies mean nothing to them, and they do

CH. CEDAR WOODLAND 1952 AL By Sandalwood ex Susan of Haywood. Bred by Mrs. White, owned by Mrs. Morton Ball. CC Crufts.

not realize that they are downgrading their stud dogs as well as any puppies that might have resulted from their being bred to superior bitches. Sincere owners of stud dogs usually refuse to let their dogs service inferior bitches (either from type or pedigree) because of a genuine concern for the breed. However to those interested in buying an especially fine type, care should be taken to investigate the quality of both sire and dam of the Labrador they are interested in.

HOW TO INTERPRET ADS

Advertisements in newspapers give some idea of what not to buy; for instance, beware of puppies at very low prices or under eight weeks of age. Paper training means only that papers have been laid down where the puppies have been brought up (which is customary anyway) and might by habit entice a puppy later on to "go" on a newspaper rather than the rug. Good kennels teach their puppies to be "housebroken" at an early age by slowly removing the newspapers from the area around their "nest."

The aim in answering advertisements in magazines or newspapers is to tactfully find out how much experience the breeder of the puppies has had and whether or not you think you can trust him. You also want to find out the background of the puppies and be careful that you do not treat the experienced breeder like a beginner. The novice can often be spotted through an air of over-confidence, but the novice who can be trusted is modest in his approach, explains that this is his first litter and that he has bought his bitch from such and such a kennel and is taking the advice of that experienced breeder. He would be glad to have you come and take a look and will send a copy of the pedigree of the puppies if you are seriously interested.

When you write or talk on the telephone with the owner of a litter that you may be interested in, one of the first questions might be, Have the parents of the puppies been X-rayed for hip dysplasia? If HD was never heard of or the answer is "No" or "I do not know," hang up as soon as you can do so politely. Another leading question might be to ask for the registered name of the dam of the litter and where she came from. Be wary of silly-sounding registered names, also of offers of free gifts. At about this time the breeder who is a novice will tell you the number of champions that are listed in the

Labrador puppies need human love and affection in order to take their place in the home and develop into lifelong companions.

pedigree. Your questions here might be in relation to how many in the background of the puppies are bench, field, and dual champions. If the number of champions in the pedigree is not brought up, this is better. Here the intelligent owner of a well-bred litter will probably mention that the sire, dam, or both are champions and perhaps give the name and show record of some outstanding dog or bitch close-up in the pedigree. He might also give some indication of the quality of one of the parents of the puppies. When buying a puppy, only famous names close-up in the pedigree or in duplicate are of importance; but for breeding stock, it is a different matter and it is the combination of pedigrees that denotes superior stock. In this connection, discussion is purely about a pet or hunting stock and breeding stock is a different proposition entirely.

Temperament is the most important quality needed for pet, show, and hunting stock; in fact for *all* Labradors. The puppy should be neither timid nor aggressive and definitely never a "jitterbug." You should not expect everything in one puppy, and neither should you buy under false pretenses, as by ordering a pet for hunting and telling the owner after all arrangements have been made that you plan to breed. One thing is sure, and this is that a good breeder does not sell his top-quality breeding stock solely as a pet.

JUDGING PEOPLE AND DOGS

The important thing in finding the right puppy is your judgment of people. The experience required in evaluating puppies and grown dogs will come later.

These suggestions can be used in reverse for those having puppies or grown stock that they wish to sell. Again it becomes a matter of judgment of people and trying to stay out of any arrangement wherein you feel that you cannot trust the prospective purchaser with one of your puppies. Also make sure that you are frank with a buyer about the type of puppy you have in relation to what he may want. There is no need to overdo describing faults in your stock when discussing a sale to a person who wants a pet. However, when it comes to breeding stock, be quite sure that you understand what you are talking about. Too many persons use big words without understanding the "meaning " and in trying to be impressive, they become ridiculous.

Good luck, and may there always be Labradors of the best to go around!

5. GENERAL CARE

One of the advantages of owning a Labrador is that the breed is normally healthy if given a good start in life and a certain basic care thereafter. A Labrador soon becomes a member of the family and often the most generous with love and devotion and the least complaining of all dogs. Be thoughtful of your dog and remember that it depends on you not only for physical needs but also for mental happiness.

A Labrador turned out the door to do as it pleases is a neglected dog belonging to lazy, irresponsible owners. Not only is he apt to be run over by a passing car, but children following the dog may also be injured. In the country, such uncared for dogs may join other dogs to chase game, and perhaps be shot or stolen. In towns, such dogs become a nuisance to neighbors, causing tighter enforcement of leash laws all over the country.

Your Labrador is bred to love people and to do what will please them. His capacity for understanding what you want him to do is limited only by your ability to communicate what you mean. Usually it is people who are responsible for the trouble a dog gets into and not the fault of the dog. The problem is that basically some people have absolutely no capacity for understanding what to do with animals, dogs in particular. Those who do have the ability to develop mutual love and understanding with a dog should make sure that they remember that they are dealing with a dog, with a dog's capacity to understand, and not to expect the reactions of a human being.

CONTROLLING THE LABRADOR

To develop a truly wonderful relationship with a Labrador, certain basic needs should be taken into consideration. Instinctively the dog lover will know what to do, but experience has taught some of us how to hasten the building of a relationship of mutual trust and understanding. Perhaps first in importance is the fact that a true Labrador practically never needs physical disciplining, and the hurting of a Labrador's feelings by tone of voice is often more effective anyway. It should be understood that the capacity of a dog to understand is rather limited to the present in spite of the fact that Labradors have remarkable memories for some things. Any discipline of a dog should be given during the act of wrong-doing. The person who finds his dog has run away and beats him when he returns could not be more wrong in the understanding of the mentality of the dog. To the dog, he has come home where he belongs. If he had been scolded while in the process of going, he would have understood but will not comprehend punishment upon coming back. The same holds true for coming when called. Many persons cannot understand why their dog will not come to them when asked to do so, not realizing that at some time in the past he has been called and chastised upon responding.

HOMECOMING

One of the first things to do when you bring home your puppy or dog is to let him investigate the house and become familiar with it. The intelligent puppy may stand still in the middle of the room, shaking with nervousness; but, if left alone and talked to quietly, will soon start investigating the surroundings. It is a good idea to follow him around from room to room, watchful for any signs of wetting. In such event, pick him up immediately and take him out-of-doors. Otherwise, leave him alone to investigate his surroundings. When his tail begins to wag, you will know he is beginning to accept his new home. Soon he will find a place where he can sleep; and, if this place happens to be a convenient one for the family, let it belong to the dog and be out of bounds for children and adults. Later a special blanket, chair, or cage should be designated as belonging to the dog. The convenience of a cage is that it can be moved to other spots and at night could be placed in your bedroom where a Labrador loves to be. This cage is very convenient when puppies go through teething and become so destructive in the house and car. Caging is also the quickest way to housebreak a puppy because he will not soil his cage if he can possibly help it.

WATER, BUT NOT IN THE EARS

A Labrador is instinctively clean and will stay that way with your help. The blanket he sleeps on should be washed often, and the

Since they are water dogs, Labrador puppies should be introduced to wading and swimming at an early age.

place chosen for his out-of-doors eliminations should be kept tidy. He need not be washed but a few times a year if you brush him often. A Labrador loves the water and a huge bath towel to roll him in when he comes out after a swim is delightful to him and fun for you. Watch out for the ears though; a dog's ears are different from ours. Water does not drain out as it does from our ears, and it is a good idea to wipe them out carefully after a dog has been in the water. If you see your dog constantly shaking his head, suspect trouble. Sometimes mites are present and should be taken care of soon or the infestation may become very difficult to eliminate.

EXTERNAL PARASITES

Since I have never had the problem of fleas and ticks on my dogs, I cannot give help based on experience; however, I believe in the theory that a healthy, clean dog is much less apt to get various troubles than a neglected one. Brushing a dog should be a great help in controlling fleas, as well as in hastening the shedding of old hair when the new coat is coming in. Fleas are also a great nuisance in the house, and much more difficult to eliminate from the house than from the dog. They are also the host for certain types of worms in dogs, so do not neglect a dog you suspect has these insects.

KENNEL CARE

If you have a kennel with several dogs, it should be disinfected once in a while to be on the safe side. There is just no excuse for an evil-smelling kennel. Twice daily removal of droppings and a daily hosing of the yard should be considered minimal maintenance. In cold weather, the hosing should not be done as a wet run surface in sub-freezing weather may pull skin from the pads of a dog's feet. In below-zero weather, you will see dogs picking up their feet and shaking them, which may be occasioned by licking sore pads and then going out into the cold where they stick to the snow.

Green soap, which is used in hospitals and has no strong odor, contains a certain amount of sterilizing material and is excellent for washing dogs and the kennel. However, make sure that it is rinsed away; it makes floors slippery; and, if licked from the coat by dogs, is apt to cause diarrhea. The floor where puppies eat should not be washed with anything but plain water; puppies pick up spilled food, and disinfectant of any kind getting to their stomachs may cause trouble. When you wash a dog, watch out, of course, for soap getting into his eyes and water in his ears. Most dogs will not mind being washed with a hose, if the introduction to this method is done carefully. Most dogs dislike or are apprehensive of the sound of a vacuum cleaner, but such an appliance is good for collecting loose hair before it gets to the rug, and if introduced carefully will be accepted. Both the hose and vacuum are convenient tools and save a lot of time and energy. Dog hair in the house can bother a great many persons and a healthy Labrador has a lot of it as there is an undercoat as well as an outer one to shed every year. Combing and brushing hasten the process of shedding and with a stainless steel screw-eye high on a wall or ceiling to which you attach a chain and snap-hook, the dog will be under better control. If he is on a table where the snap-hook can be fastened to the collar, he soon becomes used to the proceedings and likes the attention involved in all the brushing and combing. Bitches usually shed after they have raised a litter of puppies, so you can anticipate when they will be out of coat and won't forget to take pictures of them when they are in full coat and beautiful. You can tell when a Labrador is in full coat as the hair on the tail is the last to grow in.

DOG COLLAR AND TAGS

It is required by law in many communities that all dogs wear a collar on which are tags showing that they have had rabies shots. But if your Labrador is never allowed out alone and is under control, it is a mistake to insist on a collar at all times. Several dogs have hanged themselves by catching the collar or tags on something and the marks of a collar on the neck of a dog are very unattractive and not to be tolerated for a show dog. Incidentally, a metal collar is aggravating to a dog in winter and as for the chain lead so many buy, nothing could be worse for a person's hands and does no good in controlling a dog. Those made of nylon are much better and can be had in any good pet shop. Rawhide of latigo leather leads are also very good. The lead should be fitted with a bolt or seeing-eye snap.

NAIL TRIM

City dogs walking on hard pavement usually have no problem with nails that grow too long and result in feet getting out of shape and losing the compact form required in the Standard for the Labrador. Country Labradors run on soft grass in summer and snow in winter and their nails should be taken care of regularly. It is a tricky job, particularly on a black Labrador, to cut nails without cutting the flesh as well. With show dogs, this should all be done well in advance of a show, and a kennel owner will find it worth-while to get an electric file. Since the nails of a dog are different from those of a person, the filing should be a down-stroke and not back-and-forth. Be prepared for a wiggling dog, as most dogs do not like to have their nails touched. The best procedure is to place your dog on a table, restrained by a chain attached to a ceiling hook.

BRED UNSCHEDULED?

For anyone keeping both a dog and bitch puppy from a litter, which in general is not a good practice, care should be taken that the bitch does not get bred unscheduled. This can happen occasionally in the best regulated household, but can be prevented with a certain amount of caution. Puppies start mounting one another at very young ages and this is no indication that a bitch is coming in heat. Neither is it safe to wait for drops of blood to be seen on the floor as indication of estrus because Labradors usually keep everything cleaned up at first. The only safe procedure is to institute a routine of wiping the bitch clean and watching for any swelling of her vulva. I was told that Dual Champion Grangemead Precocious got his name from having bred a bitch at the tender age of six months. Aside from the fact that inbreeding done by mistake is thoroughly bad, a bitch should be allowed to develop physically and come to her second period of heat before being expected to raise a litter of puppies. If an undesired mating is discovered, a veterinarian can give an injection that will prevent pregnancy.

TRAVEL

When taking puppies in the car, it is important not to feed them for at least four hours before going and best to give them no water as well. Puppies in particular are less apt to be car sick on an empty stomach. If carsickness does occur the first time a puppy rides in a car, he may never get over the experience. Keep a puppy right in your lap during its first car ride; and, even if the drive is as long as four hours, he will probably go right to sleep with the motion of the car and not wake up until a stop is made. I am always amused at the precautions taken in bringing a box, lots of blankets, towels, and other items when most new owners come to take home a puppy. They usually telephone back "You were right, no trouble at all, and he slept all the way home."

On a trip, take a cage along even for a dog that lives in the house and is housebroken. Some dogs make mistakes when left alone in a strange motel and they may be worried about your coming back to them. Also in hot weather you can leave the cage any place that is cool. In their tour book, The American Automobile Association lists motels and hotels that allow pets. Some motel chains even provide free food for dogs. However it is better to take along the food your dog is used to as well as a supply of water, as a change may be upsetting. There is on the market a leak-proof drinking dish which carries the water and all you need do is tip it up to give your dog a drink. Station wagon barriers that keep the dog from

CH. KIMVALLEY CRISPIN AY 1963 By Ch. Sandylands Tandy AW ex
Kimvalley Guildown Cassandra AU. Bred by Mr. and Mrs. D. Beckett
owned in USA by Mrs. Robert Clark Jr.

jumping into the front seat are also available and many dog owners have found them useful. If by chance your Labrador makes a mess in the motel, clean it up as best you can. With the modern "in and out" carpet that is found in many motels, clean-ups are no longer problems. Before you leave, tell the motel owner what has happened and ask if there is anything else he would like for you to do. Persons who are guilty of running off in the morning after a dog has messed are the ones who make trouble for the rest of us and are responsible that many motels refuse to take dogs. Also, please train your dogs to stay off beds and chairs. Remember that not all persons love dogs the way we do. When staying in a motel, it is well to ask for a room on the ground floor; this makes it easier to take your dog out and to control barking if you leave him in the car.

When planning to take a dog into Canada or Bermuda, it is advisable to inquire beforehand what requirements are demanded. For instance, Canada is very fussy about proof that a dog has had a very recent rabies shot, and in both localities a health certificate is necessary. Coming back into the United States with your dog from Canada may entail difficulties unless you can produce proof of ownership.

The principles of general care involve thoughtfulness on your part as well as observation. We should all realize that our dogs will forgive us the mistakes we make but we should never, through carelessness or thoughtlessness, require them to do so.

6. FEEDING ADULT DOGS

The theory that dogs in the wild subsist on a diet of meat and that domestic dogs therefore should be fed exclusively upon meat has been discarded. In this age of diversification, large companies dealing in foods and seeking markets for byproducts have gone into the dog food business. Having spent years experimentally feeding groups of dogs under controlled conditions, they have developed balanced formulas for keeping the average dog healthy. Various companies have different formulas for what they consider the essential ingredients, all in proper nutritive balance. Although the end products may appear to be alike, the formulas and contents may be quite different.

OMNIVOROUSNESS

Because dogs are not people, it should be understood that a Labrador can live, thrive on, and enjoy the same basic food all its life. However, under certain conditions, such as bitches in whelp, growing puppies, over- and under-weight dogs, or animals being worked during hunting season, additions can be added to the basic food. Fat in the form of suet can be fed during cold weather, but care should be taken to see that it does not become rancid. Puppies, as well as older dogs in new surroundings, are apt to get diarrhea and the addition of cottage cheese to the diet tends to control the situation.

VITAMINS

In this *age of the vitamin*, we are apparently beginning to make a more sane approach to handling various situations. It has been found that too much vitamin supplement is bad for dogs, and most dog foods have an adequate supply. The belief that all dogs, particularly puppies, need vitamin D (cod liver oil) and dicalcium phosphate in addition to that contained in prepared dog foods has

CH. DIANT JULIET AP 1954. By Ch. Diant Swandyke Cream Cracker AJ ex Diant Reflection. Bred by Mrs. J. M. Steeds, owned by Mrs. L. Wilson Jones.

been changed. The new theory is that 15 minutes of sunshine a day is enough to replace artificial vitamin D and overdosing with dicalcium phosphate has proved to be detrimental to some bone formations in dogs. This has changed the feeding procedures of many breeders. However, under certain conditions dogs could have vitamin supplements in tablet form. Powdered vitamins should be given with care as the heavier elements in the mixture tend to sink to the bottom of the bottle, destroying the balance of the formula. Then too, we do not know how quickly various elements in the vitamin products deteriorate or how long the bottles have been sitting around waiting for our dogs to use their contents. If a veterinarian prescribes vitamins for a definite condition, the tendency is to feed too much and to continue indefinitely on the theory that the dogs love them. Some owners thus keep on giving what the dogs seem to like and what the veterinarian has said is good for them, forgetting that it was for a certain condition that the vitamins were prescribed in the first place. When the temporary condition is taken care of, be sure to go back to the regular diet on which your dog has previously thrived.

There are various methods of feeding dogs and the shelves at supermarkets are so full of different brands of packaged foods that the average person has no idea which to buy. There certainly are differences between brands, and advertising seems to pay off for the dog food business. Just about any product can get off the ground with plenty of advertising, to the confusion of all of us.

Nobody owning a dog should try to economize in feeding; however, all things being equal, we can bring this to the extreme and feed prime tenderloin when a cheaper form of meat is just as good or better as far as the dog is concerned. Many kinds of canned dog food are comparatively inexpensive because they contain a high percentage of carbohydrates in the form of cereals. If you read the labels you will see that about seventy percent of the contents is in the form of liquid, this being necessary for the sterilization of the contents of the can. After paying for the can, the moisture, the cereal, and the processing, you will find the nutritive value for your Labrador quite low in relation to the cost. It is far better to feed the cereal separately, adding moisture and using this as the

AMERICAN CHAMPION SCAWFELL SEEKON 1962 By Ch. Landyke Lancer ex Bellheather. Bred in England, owned in USA by Mr. Propst.

main diet with addition of other products where necessary. Milk and table scraps are all right if not added to excess, but skip starchy products. Always have in mind that the dog food company has put out its product in the ideal balance of nutritional essentials for the average dog.

By watching the droppings from your dog, you can keep track of whether or not you are feeding too much or too often. If there seem to be too many stools from your dog, being fed too often may be indicated. However, some types of dog foods produce more droppings than others, and it is not necessarily the cheapest per pound of food that is in the end the least expensive way of satisfying the requirements of your Labrador. We also find many "soft-moist" dog foods on the market today. This food is processed and packaged to resemble real meat, which it is not. Consider the nutritive value of these foods, but remember that meal or kibble mixed with meat makes the most satisfactory diet.

If you are confused about all the advertising, the best thing to do is to trust the experienced breeder of your puppy and follow the brand used by him. Unless your veterinary bills go up and the health of the dog goes down, hesitate before changing to another brand. Another safeguard is the federal government stamp of approval of a product (printed on dog food labels). The formula in this case is registered, and if one of the ingredients becomes in short supply, and hence up in price, the company may not substitute a cheaper product. To repeat, we may get bored with our food, but dogs can eat the same thing every day of their lives and enjoy it, so do not keep changing dog food without good reason. It is also well to keep to regular feeding hours if possible.

When taking your dog on a trip, do not feed it for at least four hours (longer for puppies) before leaving. Take along the dog's daily ration which can, for convenience sake, be measured into separate bags for individual feeding. In feeding a dog, it is well to always measure the food dry and in the same cup each time so that you can add or subtract with more accuracy if you want to change amounts. Do not risk taking meat as it might spoil, and for a while a Labrador can get along very well without anything but kibbles and water. Try to take along water from home as many Labradors will not drink the chlorinated water so often found in overnight lodging places. The excitement of new surroundings and the change of

(Left to Right) CH. KINLEY CURLEW OF ULPHATHWAITE By Ch. Kinley Comet ex Oriole of Ulphathwaite; KINLEY MARKSMAN By Ch. Whatstandwell Coronet ex Ch. Kinley Charm; CH. KINLEY MATADOR By Poppleton Beech Flight ex Kinley Sparrowhawk; CH. KINLEY MELODY, sister of Kinley Marksman. All at Kinley Kennels.

water may upset a dog and possibly bring on an attack of diarrhea. In such case, the addition of cottage cheese to the diet will help.

WEIGHT-WATCHING

A healthy Labrador will eat everything put before him or anything he can reach in the kitchen unless taught not to steal. One bitch of mine even cleaned up a whole bowl of strawberries I had just prepared for a party. Weight-watching for Labradors usually becomes important. A test for over- or under-weight is to feel along the backbone; if the vertebrae stick out, the dog is too thin and you should increase the amount of food at each feeding or better still add another meal each day until the correct weight is attained. If the dog is too fat (not unusual with Labradors), cut down the amount fed and give nothing between meals. If all else fails, there is a product formulated for maintaining ideal weight and it is supposed to be a balanced diet; this is obtainable through veterinarians and is based on cottage cheese. You might try substituting cottage cheese for part of the kibbled meal but remember that cottage cheese and meat alone are not a balanced ration. Go back to the regular kibble feeding as soon as possible when the temporary situation is under control. If by any chance your Labrador will not eat and your veterinarian tells you there is nothing wrong, try adding tuna fish to develop an interest in eating.

THE SWITCHOVER

If you have been feeding your Labrador a diet composed mostly of meat and decide to change to a more balanced diet, your Labrador will probably not cooperate as he will prefer the meat. However, by adding the kibbles slowly and reducing the meat gradually, he will eventually eat what is offered.

DIET STATUS

Be suspicious of a breeder who demands a complicated list of items to be fed a Labrador; such a variegated diet just does not make sense in this day and age. Some breeders believe that a long list of things to feed gives a dog status and that it will be better taken care of as a result.

BONES

Giving bones to dogs is very risky as pieces can be broken off even the biggest knuckle bone. However, if you must feed bones, make sure that you sterilize them first. For sale in many stores are bones, already sterilized, that are very difficult for dogs to break apart no matter how much they try and they will try all day long. Bones of rawhide or nylon make good tranquilizers and save your furniture as well.

7. AILMENTS

Labradors are one of the healthiest of breeds if properly cared for. The prime requisite for keeping a dog healthy is keeping his surroundings clean and not allowing him to wander away unattended. Labradors love to eat and if allowed to go where they please will become garbage hounds, find dead animals in the woods, and in general get into trouble. The owner of any animal has the definite responsibility of noticing indications of trouble and doing something about it.

TAKING TEMPERATURE

Veterinarians are busy people and their time should not be wasted. One way to help is not to wait until the dog is desperately sick before calling the vet; and, if you suspect something wrong, take your dog's temperature before calling your vet on the telephone.

A rectal thermometer dipped in vaseline and inserted about one inch into the rectum and held there for about three minutes will indicate whether or not your dog has a fever. After removing the thermometer, wash it in warm water, shake it down, and let it stand for about half an hour in alcohol before returning it to its case. The following are some temperatures to interest you:

Puppies—101.5 (a few points more or less) normal.

Mature Dogs—101.2—normal (a bit higher after whelping—not unusual).

102.5—slightly high temperature

102.5–103—call the veterinarian

104—high temperature

104–105—possibly mastitis (caked breasts) involved.

105–106—dangerous

A marked rise in temperature with a vaginal discharge and lack of appetite is an indication of the inflammation of the uterus after whelping. A temperature drop to 99 with a pregnant bitch indicates that she will produce her puppies within 48 hours. A hot dry nose is not necessarily an indication of sickness, contrary to what many persons believe. However, loss of appetite in a Labrador certainly indicates that something is wrong.

DIARRHEA

The cause of diarrhea in young puppies should be diagnosed as soon as possible. Diarrhea is usually a sign of real trouble and the sooner the cause is discovered the better chance there will be of saving the puppies. With older dogs it is not as serious and could be caused by change of water or food. In any case it should be diagnosed; if the condition is allowed to go on too long, the dog will become dehydrated and this is a problem. With young puppies it may be a sign of coccidiosis; with older ones, the indication may be of some sort of poisoning, such as from licking disinfectant off the floor in the process of picking up scraps of food.

DAMPNESS

Dampness is one of the causes of trouble among dogs, especially puppies. Newspapers that have been allowed to thoroughly dry out, the older the better, should always be kept in a convenient place in a kennel. It is difficult to keep the surroundings of puppies clean and dry but sanitation is made easier by continually placing dry newspapers on top of soiled ones. Removing the whole lot once a day is generally sufficient.

Dampness is usually the cause of "hot spots," the runny sores that appear in hot weather on some dogs. Hot steamy coats that are never allowed to become thoroughly dried out not only cause hot spots but provide excellent conditions for propagation of fleas and other pests. Labradors love the water and lying around on wet ground is nice and cool in summer but is not good for them. The ears should be dried out after swimming as water does not drain from them naturally. Nothing stiff should be inserted into a dog's ears but a soft absorbent piece of cloth may serve to remove excess moisture. Consult your veterinarian if your dog continues to shake his ears.

BOWEL MOVEMENTS

Dogs will choose one particular spot for their eliminations. If your property provides space enough around your house, a Labrador will defecate at a distance and there will be no trouble. However,

CH. HARRIS TWEED OF IDE By Ch. Sandylands Tweed of Blaircourt ex Cindy Sue of Ide. Bred by Joe Braddon, imported by James Lewis III.

AMERICAN CH. STROKESTOWN TRIGGER By Dual Ch. Staindrop Saighdear ex Ch. Strokestown Sulia. Bred by Major Pakenham-Mahon owned in USA by Mrs. Austin. Shown at Labrador Specialty show.

since most of us have kennels and yards for confining our dogs, it is important that these be kept clean. Stools should be picked up at least once a day and preferably as soon as they are dropped. Learn the habits of your dog and keep the yard clean at all times. This will solve another problem too, as some dogs get into the habit of eating their stools. This is a digusting habit and hard to correct. In fact, I know of no way it can be corrected except by having a clean yard. However, this habit is sometimes caused by the dog having worms or because it is just bored with existence, and is looking for something to do. Perhaps a nylon bone will prevent starting the habit. Sterilized shank bones are on the market for dogs to chew on, but be careful about bones from the butcher shop. Most of them can be broken and are then potentially dangerous to your dog.

EARS, EYES, AND FEET

One sign of ear trouble is that a dog shakes his head or holds it to one side. It is well not to let this go on too long as you may have real trouble in curing it. Also with the shaking of the head, the ends of the ears may fill with fluid and have to be drained. Mites thrive in damp ears and frequent examination should be made to prevent infection.

Pus in a dog's eyes or dryness of the rims of the eyes may indicate worms. However, in dry weather when seeds are blowing around or a dog is hunting through heavy cover the eyes often become irritated. They are also subject to irritation in hunting season.

The feet may also get sore if they are wet when the dog is let out in sub-freezing weather. It is difficult to keep a bandage on a dog's foot but stockinet can be purchased of the right tubular size for a dog's leg. Cut a piece about 20 inches long; draw its half it length up the dog's leg; twist it below the foot and then draw the rest up the leg. Adhesive tape around the top, about two inches below the end of the stockinet will hold it with the loose part folded back down over the adhesive. This stays on quite well in most cases.

THE MUZZLE

Every dog owner should know how to put on a muzzle, as you never know when you might need it. A Labrador will not bite unless

Puppies fed and cared for properly are the picture of health.

he is in real pain, though a bitch in heat may turn on the stud dog. If the owner of the stud dog in such circumstances is convinced that the bitch is ready to be bred, she should be muzzled. Otherwise the bitch should be taken away from the dog and the mating tried another day. When put on correctly, a muzzle of cloth or other type of material that will not dig into the skin and damage her does no harm and may also be needed when taking care of a cut or other situation.

GIVING MEDICINE

There are many times when it is necessary to give pills and medicine to dogs, and care should be taken not to get liquid medicine into the lungs. The best way to give liquid is to fill a very small bottle with the correct amount, draw the lower lip to the side and away from the teeth with one hand to make a pocket into which the medicine is poured with the other hand. If you cannot get help to hold the dog, you might try straddling and backing him into a corner or perhaps placement on a table for better control. Pour the medicine slowly into the pocket of the lip and hope that it is swallowed. Giving pills is much easier; I have never known a

Labrador that would not take them when wrapped in hamburger. Some smart ones will manage to eat the meat and spit out the pills and this poses a problem. To make sure that pills are swallowed instead of held in the mouth until you turn your back, give a drink of milk or water right after the pills. Another indication that the pills have gone down is given when the dog sticks its tongue out.

DOG FIGHTS

Labradors usually will not start a fight; but, if another dog starts one your dog will defend himself. However, stud dogs often fight one another, and some dogs become jealous of their owner to the point of fighting any dog that comes near the house or car. It is dangerous to try stopping a dog fight. While fighting, the dogs are emotionally out of control and may bite a person at this time. It is no use shouting at them to stop and you should not try to separate them, as the dogs are generally stronger than you are. The most effective way to stop a fight is a pail or two of water dumped on them or best of all a hose with spray nozzle attached and the water turned on full force. Since fights often happen near the house, it might be well to keep a hose in readiness if you have the bad luck of possessing any dogs that do not get along together. Labradors are not of mean temperament, and I doubt if any are born fighters; however, certain bitches (as well as some dogs) may form dislikes and it is usually rather hopeless to attempt reconciliations and more practical to prevent encounters which can lead to fighting.

FIRST AID

If your veterinarian lives at quite a distance, you might ask him what medicine and first aid articles you should keep on hand. Then, in an emergency, he can tell you on the telephone what to do. Make sure that medications are carefully marked so that you know what they are for.

PREVENTION AND RESISTANCE

Just because dogs do not complain is no reason for not thinking of their comfort. Always provide plenty of fresh water. See that they have shade in summer and assure warmth in winter, perhaps with a draft-proof shelter of some kind. Disinfecting their sleeping quarters at the end of the summer helps control fleas and other insects that tend to dig into the nice warm coat of your Labrador to spend the winter. However, make sure that the disinfectant or strong soap is rinsed away, especially any with a phenol base (the kind that turns white in water) as this is poisonous.

The normally high temperature of a dog as compared with that of a human being prevents many types of infections common to us. Ordinary wounds such as may lead to human infections will be taken care of in a dog by constant licking. However, any wound should be watched, and signs of swelling indicate that it should be inspected by a veterinarian. If a show dog gets a wound, the new hair which comes in will be white and is not attractive on a black dog. This may also happen when a Labrador wears the hair off the end of the tail by constantly wagging and hitting the end on a rough surface. When taking a show dog to the veterinarian and clipping off the hair may be involved, talk the situation over with him and explain that you wish to show your dog in the near future and you would prefer that he did not clip off any of the hair unless it is absolutely necessary to do so.

DISTEMPER

No dog today should ever get distemper; it is very easy to prevent. A few things about inoculations should be remembered. The most important of these is that in order to be made immune a puppy must be susceptible to distemper. Thus a puppy should be isolated during certain periods of life from all sources of infection, such as other dogs which may not have been properly inoculated. The only exception to the rule of it being necessary for a puppy to be susceptible before it can develop immunity is when previously having been given a measles vaccine. With the system wherein several inoculations of killed virus are given, the puppy must usually be susceptible after it leaves the kennel. With the modified live virus as a single shot between eight and nine weeks of age, after which the puppy does not leave the kennel until nine weeks old or five days after being given this shot, most puppies would be immune when leaving the kennel. A repeat booster shot at sixteen weeks of age should be given to be on the safe side. Certain precautions should be taken, such as making sure that the vaccine is not out-dated and has been kept at the correct temperature. It is up to the owner of a Labrador to make sure that the annual booster

RUPERT COMET By Eng. Can. Am. Ch. Sam of Blaircourt ex Ch. Rupert Aurora Borealis shown during the filming of *An Essay On Death*, by the National Educational Television production of a memorial to President Kennedy on the first anniversary of his death. Later also shown on TV for The Rev. Martin Luther King, Jr. after his assassination.

shots are given, and in some cases every six months is indicated for such boosters although once yearly is the usual procedure.

WORMS

Worms are a constant problem in some areas. Most dogs and puppies should have their stools checked for worms at regular intervals. A small sample of the stool placed in a bottle and kept cool until it reaches the veterinarian is all that is needed. However tape worms do not show up all the time in the stool, but appear as small white segments that can be seen by the naked eye once in a while in the feces. When an otherwise healthy dog becomes listless or thin or in general seems out of condition, very often it is worms that are causing the trouble. Since eradication of each type of worm requires a particular agent, it does not make sense to go to a chain store and buy a package that bears a "worm medicine" label. It is better for your veterinarian to tell you how to get rid of the particular worm your dog seems to have. If you see worms the next day, you can be sure that there was a heavy infestation and you had better find out the life cycle of that worm and repeat the worming at the proper time to get rid of the eggs that are probably still in your dog. Remember that practically all worm medicines are poisonous and should not be given indiscriminately. A bitch should be wormed before she is bred and not when she is pregnant. Piperazine, however, is non-toxic and can be given to puppies if necessary. Heart worm trouble has spread rather rapidly throughout the United States and is transmitted by mosquitoes. The disorder may occur in mature dogs of any age, but is most common in older dogs. Where dogs are kept out of doors a great deal of the time in heavily infested areas, there is a preventive system which should be started

CH. WHATSTANDWELL CORONET AM 1951. By F.T. Ch. Whatstandwell Hiwood Brand AD ex Ch. Honey of Whatstandwell AD. Bred by Mr. and Mrs. H. Taylor, owned by Mrs. E. W. Salisbury. CC Crufts.

at least a month before and continued for a month after the mosquito season. This would be particularly advisable for field trial dogs or dogs that travel.

A Labrador that has intermittent coughs and tires with mild exercise but shows no other signs of trouble should have a blood sample taken for diagnosis. Early discovery of heart worms permits easier eradication than if the condition is allowed to become chronic. Your veterinarian can give injections of a drug called diethylcarbamazine, which is recommended by the Cornell Veterinary Virus Research Institute. If heart worm is allowed to go untreated, the lungs, heart, and liver may become damaged and surgery may become necessary.

SKIN

The diagnosis of skin troubles should be determined by a veterinarian before becoming a major problem by being disregarded. Some types can be transferred to human beings but all are irritating to the dog. The wrong diet, dampness, and many other things may result in skin trouble and the sooner attended the easier a cure will be. Dogs will lick away almost any ointment, but a liquid called Blu Kote is distasteful and will be left to do its work. (However, this stains everything it touches, including the skin of the dog, and a show dog with a purple coat will get plenty of laughs.)

VOMITING

Do not worry if a dog vomits. As you probably know, birds predigest food for their young, and a bitch will often do the same thing for her puppies if she thinks they are not getting enough to eat. The worry should not be about the dog, but about your self because you have not started the puppies on solid food early enough. Dogs vomit very easily and regurgitation does not necessarily indicate that anything serious is amiss.

COUGHS

Kennel cough is not fatal but very annoying to dog and owner. It is rather similar to the human cold; nothing does much good in trying to cure it, and it will generally run its course in a few weeks. However, it is contagious and a dog with kennel cough should be kept away from other dogs.

POISONS

If a poison is suspected as being the cause of suddenly appearing distressed, call the veterinarian at once and find out what to do. Rat poisons should not be used around kennels and paints should be checked for poisonous ingredients before use.

HERPES VIRUS

A relatively new affliction of dogs, caused by herpes virus, is being studied at the Cornell Veterinary Research station. This virus attacks very young puppies, with trouble generally starting between the fifth and eighteenth day after birth. Seemingly healthy puppies will screech with pain, stop eating, and be dead within a very short time. This virus attacks the kidneys and is transmitted only by contact with an infected dog. Thus a sick puppy infects healthy ones and a whole litter dies. If a litter of puppies has passed three weeks of age, the chances are that they are free of contagion. It is currently believed that an attack in a kennel renders every animal present immune to herpes virus attack and each bitch passes on her immunity to the first generation of her offspring following exposure.

ORCHIDISM

A structural fault which is inherited as a recessive is that wherein one or both testicles fail to descend into the scrotum (monorchidism or cryptorchidism). It is questionable as to how widespread this condition occurs in the Labrador breed. Bitches may carry the genes and a stud dog may be a carrier but not show the fault. He may sire a great many puppies, and possibly throughout his life never produce an abnormal puppy. It is very difficult to discover whether or not the gene is carried because it must be carried in both parents, and at least four normal male puppies must be in a litter in order to be sure that neither parent has the gene.

Since the fault appears so infrequently, even a dog or bitch known to be carriers but which are otherwise outstanding representatives of the breed should not be considered as having a major fault and should not necessarily be discarded from a breeding program. The important point is that care should be taken so that two carriers are not bred to each other. Many outstanding stud dogs today are known to be carriers of the gene for this fault and breeding carrier

bitches to them will lead to widespread distribution of the malformation. A monorchid is not allowed to be shown in the ring, and
before the English Kennel Club will give an export pedigree for a
dog going to the United States, there must be a veterinary certificate
stating that both testicles are in the scrotum. However, this does not
prove that he is not a carrier of the defective characteristic gene.

SPAYING

Spaying a bitch is not the simple operation many persons consider it to be and the rush to have bitches spayed just to save a couple
of dollars at registration time is disgusting in my view. Experienced
veterinarians realize that a bitch should not be spayed before her
first heat, but some owners believe that the operation is less dis-
tressing to a puppy and the earlier it is performed the better. A
bitch puppy that has not been allowed to develop mentally and
physically before being spayed becomes a neuter, neither male nor
female, and may develop a strange personality. The idea that a
bitch is more apt to stay home if spayed is not a legitimate reason
for the operation, and dogs should not be allowed to wander
anyway. The nuisance to the owner of a bitch of having strange
dogs sitting on the door step and digging up the garden for three
weeks every six months will hopefully be taken care of by dog
ordinances which will prevent irresponsible persons from owning
a dog that is permitted to roam about and become attracted to a
bitch in heat.

CASTRATION

Castrating a dog comes under the same category and should not
be done unless there is a particular reason for it. Some persons
believe that castrating a dog will solve the problem of bringing a
too-lively dog under control, whereas the usual reason for lack of
control is that the person handling the dog lacks the ability to train
his dog properly, and it is doubtful that castration will prove at all
helpful.

GROWTH DIET

Thought should be used before trying any advertised new product.
It has been found at the Cornell Veterinary Research Laboratory for
Diseases of Dogs that the effect of "all meat" foods during the

DEVELOPMENT OF A PRIMORDIAL SEX CELL

MEIOSIS

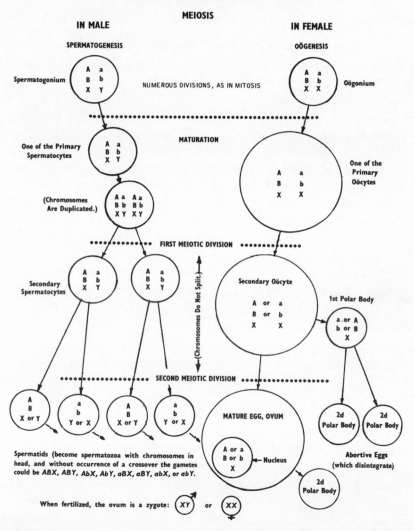

IN MALE

SPERMATOGENESIS

Spermatogonium

A a
B b
X Y

NUMEROUS DIVISIONS, AS IN MITOSIS

IN FEMALE

OÖGENESIS

A a
B b
X X

Oögonium

One of the Primary
Spermatocytes

A a
B b
X Y

MATURATION

One of the
Primary
Oöcytes

A   a
B   b
X   X

(Chromosomes
Are Duplicated.)

A a A a
B b B b
X Y X Y

FIRST MEIOTIC DIVISION

Secondary
Spermatocytes

A a
B b
X Y

A a
B b
X Y

(Chromosomes Do Not Split.)

Secondary Oöcyte

A or a
B or b
X   X

1st Polar Body

a .or A
b or B
X

SECOND MEIOTIC DIVISION

A
B
X or Y

a
b
Y or X

A
B
X or Y

a
b
Y or X

MATURE EGG, OVUM

2d
Polar Body

2d
Polar Body

Spermatids (become spermatozoa with chromosomes in
head, and without occurrence of a crossover the gametes
could be *ABX, ABY, AbX, AbY, aBX, aBY, abX,* or *abY.*

A or a
B or b
X — Nucleus

Abortive Eggs
(which disintegrate)

2d
Polar Body

When fertilized, the ovum is a zygote: (XY) or (XX)

85

early growth period indicates that they are incomplete diets. Very important is the variable calcium content of prepared foods, some of which result in adverse calcium to phosphorus ratios in the diet.

HEREDITARY FAULTS

The morally responsible breeder must face up to the fact that certain matters of health are his responsibility. Such a breeder should do everything possible through his breeding to keep certain known inherited serious faults from becoming widespread in Labradors. He should also try his best to understand what to do about inherited faults detrimental to the breed that have already become widespread within the breed.

There seems to be two extremes among persons interested in breeding dogs. There are those who are over-cautious and others who will breed anything to anything and trust to luck. The more intelligent approach is to investigate and leave the final decision to the weighing of various aspects of each particular problem. Elimination from the breeding program of every dog falling the slightest bit below perfection is not the intelligent approach.

Various breeds of dogs have their own particular inherited problems, some of which (as color of eyes) are a matter of physical beauty. Light eyes in Labradors are frowned upon, but since there is no basis in fact that the color of eyes in a dog has anything to do with his vision, color becomes an esthetic choice. Dark eyes are dominant in inheritance in most breeds; if a breeder prefers not to have that color, he should take care never to breed to a yellow-eyed dog or he will develop "carriers" for light eyes in his strain, if not light eyes themselves. This fault of appearance is not widespread in the Labrador breed and is a far lesser fault than progressive retinal atrophy (PRA).

Progressive retinal atrophy leads to complete blindness and is widespread in many breeds, including Labradors in England. It is not a serious problem at the present time in this country but any signs of it becoming on the increase should be watched for by breeders. The danger of its becoming widespread in this country is the fact that blindness develops slowly and a Labrador cannot be declared free of affliction until he is four years of age. This age factor varies with different breeds. Any case of blindness should be diagnosed by a qualified doctor or veterinarian.

CH. PUHS CHOCOLATE PRINCE By Int. Norwegian Ch. Cookridge Roamer ex Int. Norwegian and Swedish Dual Ch. Kamrate Careena. Owned by Fru Brit-Marie Brulin.

Kennel owners in Britain are taking their Labradors and other breeds to Dr. Keith Barnett. Temporary certificates are issued for those dogs proved clear under four years of age and permanent certificates after that age. The British Kennel Club lists all dogs holding such types of certificates in their monthly official magazine. They also do this for their hip dysplasia program. A real effort is being made to bring progressive retinal atrophy under control over there, but it will be difficult since many dogs and bitches will be bred from under four years of age without knowledge of whether or not they are passing on the genes of inheritance for this blindness. For those working four or five years training or hunting with a Labrador only to have him go blind is upsetting, to say the least.

An article by Dr. Barnett on the subject is here reprinted by permission from the 1970 yearbook of the Labrador Retriever Club of Great Britain.

"Progressive retinal atrophy, often referred to by the initials P.R.A., is an inherited form of blindness in dogs, as well as in man. The retina is the lining membrane at the back of the eye and is composed of nerve cells sensitive to light. Atrophy means the degeneration, or wasting away, of these cells and it is accompanied by impaired function. The result of P.R.A. is, therefore, gradual blindness.

"The condition has been described in many breeds but is far more common in some than others. A few years ago it frequently occurred in the Red Setter but it was successfully eradicated and it is now rarely, if ever, seen in the breed. At the present time P.R.A. is a serious condition in Miniature or Toy Poodles, Cocker Spaniels, and Border Collies, as well as in Labrador Retrievers and a few other breeds. However, it is very rarely seen in some popular breeds e.g. Alsatians and Boxers. It also occurs in certain strains within a breed, while other strains remain clear, and it is these facts which indicate that the condition is inherited.

"In the dog there are two forms of P.R.A. They affect different breeds, different parts of the retina, and their diagnosis depends on different signs apparent at the back of the eye when viewed through an ophthalmoscope. In the Labrador it is the central part of the retina which first degenerates, the periphery remaining normal until, with progression of the disease, the central blind spot becomes larger and finally the whole retina is involved. The animal is then completely blind. This central type of P.R.A. gives rise to the typical signs of defective vision usually noticed by owners. These include the inability to see stationary objects although a moving object can often be followed. The pet dog may catch a ball but bump into a bucket or large toy left in its path. Near sight is also defective and objects held near to the animal's head, for example a piece of food, are not seen. The gundog may see a shot bird fall but have difficulty in marking accurately, finally retrieving by scent. On return to a handler who is standing still the dog may have difficulty in locating him. Hand signals may also be missed and thick cover is disliked.

"In P.R.A. both eyes are affected equally and in the early stages look perfectly normal, also the condition is painless, the loss of sight is gradual, and in every other respect the dog is in perfect health. Because of these facts dogs with P.R.A. are often not suspected by the owner until middle age and therefore may have been bred from before the condition has been diagnosed. The examination of all breeding stock by a veterinary surgeon qualified to issue official P.R.A. certificates is a vital part of any plan to eradicate the condition. In this way many cases of P.R.A. will be discovered before they are suspected by the owner. This is because the ophthalmoscope examination of the retina will reveal the tell-tale signs early in the course of the disease. Consequently affected dogs will be revealed prior to breeding and in many cases before training has been completed.

"In the Labrador, as well as in other breeds, there is some variation between affected dogs, particularly regarding the age at which an animal is first affected and the speed at which the disease progresses. It has been possible to diagnose cases with an ophthalmoscope soon after the animal is one year old but usually it cannot be done before the age of two and sometimes not until four years old. Such is the variation in this condition that some dogs may be blind by two years, while others may retain their sight until perhaps 10 years of age. It must also be realised that some of these old dogs may breed animals affected much earlier in life. In the Labrador both dogs and bitches, of both yellow and black coat colors, are equally affected.

"The soundest advice that can be offered at the moment is that Labradors, particularly breeding stock, should be examined under the British Veterinary Association and

Kennel Club P.R.A. scheme. The owner of a bitch wishing to use any particular stud dog should only use a dog that has received its permanent certificate of freedom from P.R.A. When buying a puppy try to buy from cleared stock. In this way and with the continued sensible support of Labrador owners and breeders this serious hereditary defect will finally be eradicated."

Another major fault of structure which appears worldwide in all breeds of dogs and in human beings is hip dysplasia. In this country, Dr. Gerry B. Schnelle was responsible for bringing the problem out into the open and convincing breeders that they should do something about getting it under control. He was head of the famous Angell Memorial Animal Hospital in Boston until his retirement and through his wide experience with animals, and particularly his knowledge of radiology, has come much benefit to breeders. He has generously taken the time to write for publication herein the discussion of congenital hip dysplasia that follows:

"Hip dysplasia is not uncommon in the retriever. The term 'hip dysplasia' (HD) means faulty development and it has been quite well-established that it is hereditary. The hip is the only 'ball and socket' joint in the dog's body and it is this construction, combined with the importance of the hip to locomotion (the dog has 'rear engine drive') that make the faulty growth (HD) very important. Simply speaking, in HD the socket is shallow, or the ball does not fit the socket, or the joint ligaments are loose, allowing the ball to wobble rather than functioning smoothly. Any of these conditions can cause pain and instability during adolescence and arthritis in the ageing. It is important that a working dog like the Labrador Retriever not have HD.

"HD is inherited as a genotype, meaning that certain type parents produce pups with it. It is not hereditary from a single gene and so it cannot be eliminated by sharp segregation of certain individuals, who by pedigree study could be determined as carriers of the gene. It also differs from a hereditary fault like progressive retinal atrophy (PRA), which also exists in the Labrador, in that the occurrence of lameness as a result of HD is not nearly the tragedy that is the blindness that develops from PRA. HD is diagnosed by

FOXHANGER MAJOR, London Metropolitan Police Dog, was bred by Lady Simpson, wife of the Commissioner for Metropolitan Police. He was a charming dog.

X-ray of the pelvis and its severity is also defined by this procedure. It is graded from 'marginal,' which defines itself, to grade 4 in which the ball is completely out of the socket. Dogs with the lesser degrees of HD can be shown, can hunt, and can even live a lifetime with a family without their knowing that the trouble exists.

"The arthritis which develops in the mildly dysplastic dog may not show up until it is three or four years old. Both the adolescent and the ageing dysplastic show somewhat similar signs which are principally difficulty in rising, particularly on a slippery floor. Once up and moving, they get along quite well although an observant person can usually detect a widening across the rump and a shortened gait in the hind legs. An aging dog will often gallop, bringing both hind legs forward at the same time. This gait does not require maximum length of stride of the hind legs, a motion which causes pain in the hip joints. Dysplastic Shepherds that show nothing at all visibly, even to the expert, in their gait, have been shown by slow motion movies of their hurdling, to avoid in every way possible catching their weight on their hind legs. If dysplastic dogs could talk there is no doubt but that we would hear many complaints about their uncomfortable hip joints. A hunting retriever may become quite lame after being in the water during cold weather, especially if it is put in a crate or in other cramped quarters for the trip home. Aspirin and warmth are both very comforting to an arthritic dog when painful episodes occur. Understanding of the underlying condition and thoughtfulness with regard to it can ease the uncomfortable episodes a great deal.

"To the breeders: remember that excellence in other qualities can surely outweigh minor degrees of hip dysplasia, but it does not make very good sense to take an 'ordinary' Labrador with the added unsoundness of HD and use it for breeding."

John Olin has founded an organization for the registration of dogs designated as free of hip dysplasia. These dogs are given an OFA number (Orthopedic Foundation For Animals Inc.), which is certainly a step in the right direction. More information on this Foundation can be acquired through the University of Missouri, St. Louis.

The Cornell Research Laboratory is working on this problem too and it has been found that feeding vitamin supplements and hormones caused changes in certain functions in hip joints of both young and mature Beagles. They are now working on a breeding program with Labradors, both normal and dysplastic, in a controlled kennel and trying to find more information about malformation of the hips.

The majority of breeding kennels of show Labradors in this country are only using for breeding purposes such dogs as have been X-rayed and found clear of hip dysplasia.

A kennel run is made attractive with the addition of an old iron fence. This one is big enough so that several Labradors can exercise together.

8. PLANNING YOUR KENNEL

There are many decisions to be made before planning a kennel. One of these should be how many litters you plan to raise each year. The chances are that you will begin with a litter or two, in which case you will have one or two bitches of breeding age and a small number of puppies growing up. You should allow for changing your mind later on when you may keep more stock, but some of these will be in the house from time to time. At least four runs of different sizes would be about right. If you are lucky, your bitches will all get along well and they can be kenneled together for convenience and mutual warmth in winter. However, it is surprising how many times you will need all the runs so you had better plan for them in the beginning even if you do not build them at first.

Separate runs for each dog are a necessity when bitches come in season. Built-up foundation is to keep snow from blowing into the runs.

ONLY YOUR OWN DOGS

It is well to decide in the beginning that under no circumstances will you take in dogs owned by other persons, even those you have raised yourself. The problems involved with outside dogs are endless and an unnecessary risk and responsibility for a breeder. By making a hard-and-fast rule for yourself in the beginning, you will save yourself a lot of explaining. There are numerous boarding kennels maintained by persons trying to make a living by helping owners with their pets, so keep on hand a list of those which you have inspected and make it available to persons trying to impose on your good nature.

LAYOUT

The most important part of planning the kennel is to make it convenient for yourself by attaching it to the house in some way so that you do not have to put on boots and all sorts of foul-weather gear before letting the dogs out into their yard or the kennel. A covered archway between the house and kennel would serve; if there is an attached garage, the whole thing could be arranged there. If possible, have the runs where snow will not slide from the roof and make extra shoveling, and don't overlook provisions for shade in the heat of summer.

The size of runs depends a great deal on your situation, but a long narrow run is better than a square one as dogs rarely use the center and generally run along the fence. The rest of the time they will sit or lie at the gate and will use for their eliminations the area farthest removed from this gate. It is important to have a double entrance arrangement. You will likely be surprised how many times a gate will be left unlatched, but seldom will two gates be left

Light-weight swinging door for puppies exits to cleated ramp with sides so that puppies will not fall or jump off when playing and injure their shoulders.

open at the same time. Thus a double-gate system is a safeguard against a dog wandering away and perhaps coming to harm. Single runs can be four by sixteen feet, and those made for several dogs can be made any size and might go around a corner of the building for providing shade in summer. If there is land available, instead of the double entrance to the outside runs, there might be a large, fenced-in exercise area.

FENCE AND GATE

Chain-link fencing is attractive, but expensive. Turkey wire is practically as efficient, much less expensive, and does not require pipe at the top. It is more difficult for a dog to get over a fence that does not have such a rigid top, but if luck is against you and you have a dog that can get over any fence no matter how high, the solution is eighteen-inch brackets at the top of the posts bent towards the inside so that a chicken wire baffle can be affixed. All posts should be set in cement, with gate posts high enough for the tallest man to go through, making allowance for the build-up of

To avoid "kennel shyness," puppies should be exposed to children and adults in order to develop human relationships at a tender age.

A simple dog-proof latch. The piece of metal above drops down to prevent the dogs from lifting the latch. This can be opened by people from either side.

snow in winter. The turkey wire should be galvanized and about two by four inch mesh and six feet high. One foot of the fencing goes in the ground and is attached to pipe. The latch is very important as a Labrador can open almost any gate except one fitted with a positive-closure latch. Make sure to provide one section for small puppies with a wall between this run and the others to isolate them from the older dogs. Also, when planning the kennels and runs, put the single ones in the center between the larger runs so that bitches in heat need not be in outside runs where visiting males might bother them.

Puppies soon learn to go in and out of their swinging door.

PAVING

There are several materials that can be used as a base for the runs. The best, I believe, is macadam (commonly called black-top) sloping towards a drain in one corner. With such construction, droppings are picked up at least twice a day, put in covered pails lined with newspaper for easier cleaning, and the run is washed down every morning after the dogs have had a chance to relieve themselves. Macadam is expensive as it requires cement retaining walls, as does washed gravel, the next best material. Washed gravel should be laid at least two feet deep so that there will be good drainage. The reason for using washed gravel is that it is less apt to freeze to a solid mass in winter, and it is easier to pick up the droppings than from hard-packed ground or grass. When droppings are picked up, some gravel comes up with each shovelful, which makes the pail heavy to carry, but is a quick method of cleaning yards. Cedar posts are attractive, but pipe makes for a straighter fence.

KENNEL IN GENERAL

The entrance ot the kennel should be raised above the dog yards, especially if you live in a heavy snow area. If a cleated ramp or runway is used, the sides should be built up so that puppies will not fall off. The sides can be of cement blocks, but they should be placed so that no legs are broken in the holes. The opening into the kennel should be about fifteen by twenty-four inches with a door swinging on barrel bolts. Over this, on the inside of the pen, is a solid door hinged at the top, to be hooked up and out of the way when not needed to confine the dogs either inside the kennel or outside in the runs. I do not like the arrangement used at many kennels wherein a rope to the outside of the gate raises and lowers the dog door. The more often we come in contact with our dogs, the better for the Labrador, and going in and out of the kennel provides contacts denied by an owner who remains outside pulling a rope. Doors hung on barrel bolts allow them to swing in and out and can be made of various materials. A "see through" material will housebreak puppies about as soon as they can walk and, if constructed of light material with a strip of canvas at the bottom, will prevent damage to tails. Since a puppy's tail outgrows the body at times, it can be easily caught and broken, so allow space at the bottom of the door with a canvas strip for closure to keep out the cold in winter. Flies are not a problem if the kennel is kept clean but, if necessary, screens can be used in place of a solid door in summer. On the outside of the kennel, the opening should be above ground level with stepping stones of removable cement blocks placed so that the openings are on the sides. The floor on the inside should be of a material that is nonabsorbent and not slippery.

HEATING AND COOLING

The amount of room on the inside of the kennel depends on what yard area is available, and, to a certain extent, on weather conditions. With the long winter of November to May in many areas, more space is needed than in milder regions, and it is well to plan to kennel as many dogs together as possible for mutual warmth in winter. There should also be space for removable wooden sleeping boxes in winter and wire cages in summer, allowing space to walk by these to close the dog doors and for cleaning. Four feet wide is minimum, with more space allowed when several dogs are kenneled together. Plan an area for a pail of water in the run. An eye hook in the wall with a double-ended snap hook to attach to the water pail works well and can be moved out-of-doors and attached to the fence in summer. For puppies, a pail set in a rack of two by fours is prevented from tipping over and provides for the puppies to drink. In warm weather, a pan of water left in the outside yard for puppies to walk through gets them used to being the water dogs they are bred to be.

Whether or not you heat or cool your kennels is your decision. However, puppies must have heat at least until they can move about well, and they cannot be moved in cold weather from a heated house to a cold kennel unless done gradually. This is also true regarding bitches coming in heat in winter. They must either be left in the cold kennel in the fall until after their heat period before bringing them into the house, or the kennel must be heated. If the kennel is heated, you can have running water, which is very convenient for mixing food and a must for washing down the outside yards. For washing dogs, a minimum of mess is caused by doing it in the outside yard with a hose; or they can be soaped, rinsed a bit, and then put in a brook for rinsing. If there is likely chance of a dog fight, leaving a hose connected to a water faucet ready for use is necessary and a quick and easy way to end the trouble. Labradors are not fighters, but it is difficult to keep two stud dogs from fighting and jealousy among some Labradors sometimes creates a problem. Fighting also happens once in a while with bitches, and there is not much to be done but to keep them separate. Another use for a hose is on stray dogs that can become a real nuisance if your neighbors are not able to keep them at home. Remember that the cleaner you keep the dog yard, the less trouble you will have in keeping the kennel and dogs clean and free from parasites. However, a Labrador needs very little bathing if the surroundings are kept clean. Admittedly, Labradors that are kept in a city and exposed to dirty environment require more frequent bathing. Labradors are instinctively clean and will keep themselves groomed if you help them by keeping their surroundings clean. Dogs will endure and survive under all sorts of bad conditions without complaining, but should they be made to do this? Thoughtful kindly persons will consider the comfort of their dogs and take care of them without pampering or treating them like human beings. There is a difference between cruelty at one extreme and silly babying at the other. Common sense, observation, and thoughtfulness should direct the proper course of treatment.

INDIVIDUAL QUARTERS

For those building a house for a single dog to be placed in a yard, there should be shade of some sort so that the dog can get out of the heat of the sun in summer yet have plenty of sunlight in winter. The entrance to this house should be off-center to prevent a direct draft on the dog, and should be insulated all around and on the top and bottom. It should have a floor to keep out dampness and be provided with a porch or flat roof to permit the dog to get off the wet ground in winter or stretch out for sunning. A barrel, braced with a board across the lower part of one end to prevent rolling, makes a good dog house. Such a house should be made using a wooden barrel, not a metal one, and a piece of canvas hung for a door completes it.

9. ON KEEPING A STUD DOG

I have purposely not mentioned a yard and kennel for a stud dog because I am aiming this book at the new breeder in hopes of encouraging more of them to appear. Therefore I will not go deeply into the subject of stud dogs.

DOGS OR BITCHES?

The principal reason for a breeder keeping bitches rather than dogs is that it is the owner of the bitch, not the owner of a stud dog, who has control of future puppies. In the first place, the experienced breeder knows where the top quality stud dogs are, and owning a fine brood bitch has the choice of practically any stud dog in the country for servicing her. The owner of a stud dog cannot choose the bitch; he must present proof of the value of his dog before good bitches will be sent to him, and this involves time and expense.

The beginner has no idea of how often the mating of a dog and bitch does not take place as expected. There are many reasons for this, but misses are usually caused by coupling on the wrong date for the bitch. The beginner does not know the in-heat cycle, and even the most experienced person may miscalculate. Having bitches being sent to be bred to a stud dog involves accepting a real responsibility and may be very upsetting to your own dogs. Neighbors are also apt to complain about the barking that goes on.

Here in the east, many of the Labrador studs being used are imported and results in there being very little demand for services of American-bred dogs. An American stud must be of much higher quality than an imported one or his stud services are very unlikely to be requested.

INTRICACIES OF PREPARATION

If the owner of a stud dog agrees to a mating, the assent becomes almost a contract to honor it, and may entail a change of plans for your vacation. Bitches do not always come in heat on schedule,

IRISH, CANADIAN, AMERICAN CH. CASTLEMORE SHAMUS 1958 By Ch. Strokestown Duke of Blaircourt ex Ch. Hilldown Sylver. Bred by Mrs. Eustace Duckett, owned in Canada by Hugh Crozier. Sire of Canadian and American Dual Ch. Happy Playboy. From a famous line of producers.

and to upset a breeder's carefully laid plans by not having the stud dog available is both unfair and unethical.

You may think it would be easy to buy a nice dog and put him up for stud, but things do not work out that way. In the first place, it is customary that a given dog is not advertised at stud until he has actually sired puppies. Then the owner of the bitch chooses the stud dog, and a breeder is usually extremely fussy about the appearance of that stud dog, as well as to what the combination of the stud's pedigree promises in being joined with that of his bitch.

The owner of a well-bred, typey stud dog must spend a great deal of time going to shows or field trials in order to establish a good win reputation and thus create a demand for stud services. Travel costs and entrance fees mount up. If the dog does not become a well-known winner in any field, it is doubtful that there will be much chance of his being used at stud, at least not on good bitches.

Another problem develops if the owner of a bitch does not telephone until she is ready to have her bred. This is very discourteous, and gives you no time to look at her or the pedigree, and very often no x-ray has been taken. In such case, there is usually not time to arrange for an x-ray and to get a proper written diagnosis from the veterinarian. It is important to have this written diagnosis before allowing your stud dog to be used; if the bitch is not definitely proved to have no indication of hip dysplasia before allowing stud service, the owner of an afflicted bitch may place blame for defective pups on the stud.

COLOR

Another problem with a stud dog is the matter of color. The owner of a bitch may want an all-black litter or some yellow

CH. GARVEL OF GARSHANGAN 1960 A V By Ch. General of Garshangan AL ex Ch. Gussie of Garshangan AR. Bred by Lt. Col. and Mrs. Hill. Owned by Mr. and Mrs. F. Whitbread.

puppies; and, unless you know the background of the bitch, you will not be able to conjecture what the chances are for yellows. Again, if a chocolate puppy should turn up unexpectedly, you may be in for trouble as many persons do not know about this color and will think that there is something wrong with your dog, tell the world about it, and thus cast suspicion on your dog. In some sections of this country there is no demand for yellow puppies; in others, there is a great demand for that color, and as the keeper of a stud dog you should determine which color is preferred in his locality. If you have a yellow dog and he is bred to a black bitch and you do not know whether or not she carries yellow genes, the whole litter may be black when the owner of the bitch has his heart set on yellow puppies. Again, everyone involved is unhappy through a misunderstanding of what happens.

THE NATURAL WAY

A dog should be used at stud for the first time rather young (but not usually at less than a year of age), or there is a possibility that he will not understand what is expected of him. On the other hand, he should not be used too often and your veterinarian should be consulted about this. Incidentally, many veterinarians do not understand about the mating of a dog and bitch as veterinary schools teach artificial methods but seldom consider the natural way. Never have your bitch bred artificially; the AKC is very fussy about registering artificially-bred puppies, and it is a complicated procedure to register them. It is also bad for the breed to take the chance of introducing genes for sterility which may be, and probably is, the reason for the artificial breeding. To begin with, artificial breeding in dogs is practiced in completely different circumstances from such insemination of cows to make use of outstanding producing bulls in situations wherein bringing a cow and bull together is impractical.

If you insist on keeping a stud dog, you had best consult an experienced breeder and, if possible, observe the process of mating a dog and bitch. When the time comes for a mating among your dogs, arrange for the help of some person who understands the difficulties that may turn up.

10. THE BROOD BITCH

For those interested in breeding Labradors, as distinguished from just raising Labradors, the most important factor is the choice of the first bitch. Then the exercise of keen observation and study is necessary if there is to be a continuous line of superior bitches descending from outstanding litters.

It has been proved through the years that it is through the influence of the female that great strains of Labradors have been developed; and, without top-quality, typical bitches to breed to excellent males, no continuous and permanent progress can be made. Breeding means the developing of a line of Labradors descending in steady progression from your bitch by keeping at least one bitch puppy from each litter which is considered successful, and possibly also from a litter that has not turned out as fine as anticipated. Along with this, intelligence and patience must be used to overcome mistakes and setbacks that inevitably show up. The tendency of some persons is to start with another bitch from a different line as soon as a litter, or perhaps two, has produced no sensational winner. This shows lack of understanding of the problems involved with becoming a breed of Labradors. If care has been taken in finding the best bitch (of course she is not perfect, as nothing is) and her "blood" lines are outstanding, you should eventually win out with patience and careful choice of the stud dog used to mate to her.

STUD'S CLAIM TO FAME

In the study of pedigrees, it is easy to see where the influence of outstanding males has produced superior stock. Since a male can sire hundreds of puppies, it may take only one superior puppy of his to bring every owner of a bitch rushing for his services. Or he may make his reputation in the show ring or field trials and start such a line-up. In almost every case, the male is given the entire credit for upholding the continual line of superior Labradors. When we realize how few puppies a bitch can produce in relation to the number sired by a popular male, it is more easily understood why famous bitches have been lost sight of and can only be found through the study of pedigrees down through the years.

READING THE PEDIGREE

An outstanding brood bitch is the result of what she looks like and the unseen genes of inheritance that can often be anticipated through the study of her pedigree. At first the novice has no idea of how to read a pedigree, and it might just as well be held upside down insofar as concerns his understanding the implication of all that stands behind the registered names. Until the names start to mean something, no one can qualify as a breeder.

Understanding involves study of pedigrees of a meaningful number of outstanding, present-day Labradors. What you are searching for are names of dogs, and in particular bitches, that keep repeating themselves in different pedigrees of outstanding Labradors. Just three or four generations are not enough, especially if

RUPERT DAPHNE 1947 By Dauntless of Deer Creek ex Lena. Bred and owned by D. Howe. All breeding stock at Rupert Kennels goes back to Lena.

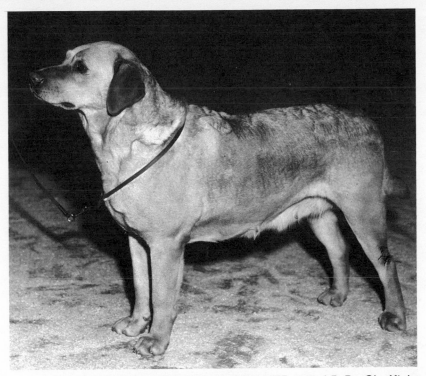

CH. KINLEY CURLEW OF ULPHATHWAITE 1955 AP By Ch. Kinley Comet AM ex Oriole of Ulphathwaite AM. Twice CC winner at Crufts. Bred by Mrs. Cooper, owned by Fred Wrigley.

you want to establish the great ones that have probably been the important influence behind the one in a short pedigree. When certain names in a present-day pedigree begin to mean the production of other important names, they start to have personality. For instance, Olivia of Blaircourt was the dam of both English, American, and Canadian Champion Sam of Blaircourt and of Champion Ruler of Blaircourt (Reserve Best in Show at Crufts). Ruler sired probably the most outstanding show and stud dog of the decade in England in Champion Sandylands Tweed of Blaircourt.

PREPOTENCY

I have decided to concentrate on famous bitches of the past for the reason that the value of a brood bitch does not assert itself for many generations. It is through the progeny of a bitch bred to

DUAL CH. STAINDROP SAIGHDEAR AD 1944 By Glenhead Jimmy ex Out Lil. Bred by J. Murray Dewar, owned by E. Winter. A great stud dog who gave impetus to the yellow color.

different stud dogs that one finds an outstanding producer of quality and typical Labradors. Of course this is true of dogs as well; but, as already mentioned, it is through important bitches that the breed progresses. It is not only the first generation, but the second and third and more, that are often required to prove what we call a prepotent animal. It is the prepotent Labradors that we search for in pedigrees since they are the ones that have the rare ability to pass on to future generations a majority of desirable characteristics and few poor ones no matter to what dog such bitches are bred. A prepotent bitch has a great many dominant genes for wanted and desirable inherited characteristics that she by herself can pass on to her puppies as against a bitch that is not prepotent and needs the combination of her genes of inheritance with those of the dog she is bred to in order to produce superior puppies. In other words, a prepotent animal can be counted on to produce a higher than average number of exceptionally fine progeny because she has more than the average number of desirable genes to pass on to them.

108

With a prepotent bitch, it might be possible to take for granted that these desirable characteristics will be present in future puppies, and concentrate on eliminating faults. In this way you quickly get rid of bad points and hold onto good ones. In choosing the dog to mate with her, care must be taken to choose from among descendants of her important ancestors and not dilute what she has by too much outcrossing to unrelated lines.

NICKING LITTERS

Another rare occurrence comes with what we call "nicking" litters. In this case, it is the combination of the genes of both parents that produces more than the usual number of outstanding typical puppies in a litter. Since most desirable genes are dominant in inheritance, this means that what is lacking in one parent in this case is present in the other so that the combination of wanted genes from both occur in the majority of the puppies. It is through

CH. KINLEY SPRUCE 1966 By Kinley Sandylands Kricketer (By Ch. Kinley Skipper) ex Kinley Fantasy (pedigree contains Ch. Kinley Yorkshireman, Ch. Kinley Skipper, Ch. Kinley Comet). Bred and owned by Fred Wrigley. CC Crufts.

"nicking" litters that we often find the prepotent offspring. Consider three great bitches, the litter sisters Birkhill Juliet, Stewardess, and Souvenir. Without these bitches, we might never have had such noted stud dogs as Field Trial Champion Peter of Faskally and Dual Champion Banchory Bolo. And through these bitches came probably the greatest bitches of all time, the sisters Kirkmahoe Dinah and Brocklehirst Nell, that were evidently prepotent since they produced notable progeny when bred to different studs. It was fortunate that these bitches lived at the same time as Dual Champion Banchory Bob and were bred to him. Champion Ingleston Ben, Dual Champion Bramshaw Bob, Dual Champion Titus of Whitmore, and the yellow Dual Champion Staindrop Saighdear descended from these matings. The results from this line can be seen today. All four of the Labradors that have broken the Best In Show record in this country go back to the combination of Dual Champion Banchory Bolo and one of these sisters, as well as through Field Trial Champion Tar of Arden, the bitch that is responsible for such present day important field trial winners as the four generations through Dual Champion Shed of Arden, National Champion Cork of Oakwood Lane, and National and Amateur National Champion Super Chief. There have been other lines that have influenced today's Labradors, but this bitch line has had the greatest influence in this country. The great stud dogs Dual Champion Shed of Arden and Field Trial Champion Timber Town Clansman are the predominant stud dogs behind American bred Labradors.

The British founders of our breed were wise in concentrating on a few outstanding animals, bitches in particular. The early Labradors were pretty much held within a group of friends who were intelligent breeders and were interested solely in producing superior retrievers, principally Labradors. Puppies were not sold, as far as we know, but rather the good ones were traded among friends.

You may ask what can we do today even with a superior brood bitch to hold the best qualities of the Labrador for the future. The most important thing is the choice of what we hope will be the right stud dog for our bitch in hopes of producing that "nicking" litter. It is easy to breed her to the latest winner and the puppies will be easy to sell on his reputation but this may be entirely the wrong dog for her as would be revealed if the pedigrees are studied by a

CH. RUPERT MARLEIGH BINGHAM 1962. By Rupert Comet ex Ch. Rupert Foster of Spruce Brook. Bred, owned and handled by Dorothy Howe.

person who understands their meaning. Meaningful matings are based on a study of pedigrees, and every breeder should have a large collection available for study. American pedigrees can be traced through the 1961–1966 Labrador Club book and interesting ones could be rewritten in a form wherein comparisons could be made with other pedigrees. Photographs should be collected of both good and bad representatives of the breed. Look for old copies of the *British Dog World* and *Our Dogs*. The Christmas Annuals of these magazines were full of famous old timers. The March issue (Sporting Dog number) of *Popular Dogs* often has photographs of famous Labradors. Incidentally, collecting photographs is a good way to learn how and how not to position a Labrador in the show ring. However the most important thing to collect is every available bit of information, along with pictures, relating to your bitch. The puppies she produces to various sires indicates to you the genes she herself possesses; thus all available information about the sires of these puppies should be recorded along with photograph and pedigree of each stud. Breeding two of your own bitches with similar pedigrees to the same stud dog and observing and recording the differences between the puppies of each litter is an excellent way of reaching a better understanding of what genes of inheritance each of these bitches has in her make-up. Photographs and pedigrees of puppies a stud has sired from other bitches could also teach you about your own bitch.

Going to dog shows and concentrating on looking at the dogs and their progeny and making notes in the catalog for later reference regarding stud use is important. Make notes of both good and bad specimens as you can learn from both when checking pedigrees. Before and after judging, talk with knowledgeable Labrador people, not just one but as many as you can find. Keep your ears open and let other people do the talking. Forget that you have that wonderful bitch at home and all the plans you have for her and the divine puppies you have for sale, far better to listen and to ask intelligent questions about other people's dogs.

With the intelligent selection of a bitch puppy as your future brood bitch and a constant study of available stud dogs and their pedigrees to be compared with that of your bitch, the thrill of anticipating results to be compared later with what actually happens makes for continual interest and a dedicated Labrador breeder.

According to the AKC, the owner of the dam of a litter is the breeder of that litter. The breeder I write about is not just raising puppies but aims at raising the quality of the average for the Labrador. One litter does not make a breeder but the success or failure of a breeder depends on the results of several generations tracing from a bitch line that consistently produces puppies that develop into typical specimens of the best type of Labrador both mentally and physically.

11. BEGINNING AS A BREEDER

Luck is not really an element in breeding dogs, but various things that developed when I started with Labradors certainly happened without much thought on my part. I could have landed in another breed after deciding I wanted to raise puppies. There are other breeds that are good with children, which I determined was the best market for the sale of puppies. After trying about ten different breeds and still not finding satisfaction with any of them, I was given co-ownership of a Labrador. The other half-owner knew far more about Labradors than I and believed that our bitch, Lena, with her superb pedigree deserved more than the life of a stable dog.

My partner was supposed to plan the matings for Lena. But when she came in heat, the right stud dog was not available so it was decided to breed her to a local dog, and that the entire litter would be mine. I did not know it at the time, but fortunately the pedigree of this stud dog showed that his grandam was the sister of Lena's famous sire, Field Trial Champion Timber Town Clansman. I made a great mistake in not keeping one particular puppy from this litter to produce more than a couple of litters before selling her.

Subsequently my partner asked me if I wanted to co-own a second brood bitch on the same terms, stating that she would be delivered to me already bred. Before I saw the bitch, she had been sold for a huge price, half of which was offered to me. Since I had not even seen the bitch, I told my partner that I would not take the money but would be more than happy if she would let me have the other half of Lena.

Then I was on my own, but still ignorant about Labradors. I had learned however about a famous dog, Dual Champion Shed of Arden, and found a son of his in Vermont for breeding Lena the next time she came in heat. A beautiful litter of seven black puppies arrived and I realized that such puppies must go to persons who would appreciate them. Two bitches went on to a show career after being sold; Desdemona became a champion and Dusky

CH. LADY OF TRING By Ch. Ballyduff Orangemen ex Queenie of Battle-green. Bred by A. Hill, owned by F. Marland. CC Crufts.

missed the title by only one point. I retained Daphne as a future brood bitch and went to my first dog show with Dahomey as a puppy. At our first show I did not realize how important it was for Dahomey to place fourth in the Sporting Group under the Labrador breeder and judge, the late Jean Hinkle. Whether you choose to call it luck or a miracle, everything certainly worked out to my advantage in the beginning.

PREPARATIONS FOR BREEDING

Perhaps you too have the bitch that you want as the foundation of your strain. Perhaps you bought her already bred to the dog suggested by the breeder, but chances are that you got her over a year of age but not bred. In such case, she should have been x-rayed for hip dysplasia and the film should be examined by the veter-inarian you intend to handle all future problems that may arise among your dogs. This should be done before buying the bitch, or you should have some sort of guarantee on the subject from the seller. Write down when the bitch was last in heat (she should not be bred before the second heat), what type of inoculations she has had, and when they were given. A permanent record should be kept for each bitch, to include dates of inoculations, when in heat, when she was ready to breed, name of stud dog, and color of puppies. When there are several bitches, these records should be kept under the subject as well, so you can see at a glance when things should be taken care of. The American Kennel Club sells loose leaf books which are very convenient for keeping information in relation to brood bitches and puppies.

You probably bought your bitch as a puppy, and now she has reached the age when you can think about breeding her. She is due for her second heat; the stud dog has been chosen, and his owner notified as to the approximate time she is due in heat. A copy of her pedigree and a photostatic copy of the x-ray report should be sent to the owner of the stud dog. Her stool should be checked for worms and the right type of medicine given if necessary. Do not plan to worm her after breeding, as this may be dangerous. Remember that some worms may pass into the puppies before birth. You should already have a copy of the x-ray report of the stud dog as well as his pedigree. The stud fee and when it is to be paid should be arranged and other details written down to save possible misunderstanding later on. Such problems as when to ship the bitch (the bitch always goes to the dog to be mated), who pays possible veterinary expenses, and other details should be agreed upon in advance. You should have an understanding about the number of times the bitch is to be mated, and when the stud fee is to be paid. It is the custom for the stud fee to be paid at the time of requesting signature on the AKC litter registration blank. However, some owners of stud dogs demand that the fee be paid at the time of mating. There should be a definite understanding of what happens if there is no litter or only one puppy. This is entirely up to the owner of the stud dog, who has the privilege of refusing a return service at a future estrus. The owner of a well-known stud dog rarely takes a puppy instead of a fee, and only a novice breeder would even suggest that he might be interested in a puppy. The owner of the bitch should take it for granted that a fee is to be paid. However in some cases, when there is a particularly outstanding bitch, the owner of the stud dog may suggest that he would like a puppy and in some cases two puppies. In the case of choosing two puppies, second choice goes to the breeder with first and third to the owner of the stud dog unless other arrangements are made. Sometimes the stud owner will stipulate in advance the sex and color of puppies to be selected. A written agreement is the only certain guarantee against misunderstanding. It should be decided at what age the puppy is to be taken as well as the type of inoculations to be given and at what age. It should also be understood that until the puppy has been chosen by the stud owner the breeder cannot definitely sell any puppy in the litter. Orders may be taken on the condition that prospective buyers are informed that the owner of the stud dog has the agreed upon option. Occasionally the owner of a stud dog chooses to take his puppy at a very young age rather than trust the ability of the breeder to raise the litter.

To prevent all sorts of future misunderstandings, as many details as possible should be arranged in advance and be put in writing to cover all possible problems that may arise wherein a puppy is to be taken instead of a cash fee or as part of the fee for stud service.

The breeder should have the litter registration blanks on hand. As soon as possible after the puppies are whelped, one should be filled out and sent to the owner of the stud dog for his signature and annotation of other required information. AKC officials may require considerable time to check and recheck all information, and it often takes two months for them to get the necessary puppy registration papers back to the breeder.

START WITH THE SECOND HEAT

So now you wait for your bitch to come in heat for the second time so that you can breed her and start raising puppies. When that time draws near she should be watched carefully. A swelling of the vulva is usually the first indication and often associated with a possible change in temperament, as may be indicated by nervousness and disobedience. It is important to notice the first signs of a discharge as this indicates the approach of time for her to be mated. However, since Labradors are such clean animals, a bitch will often keep herself cleaned and there will be no drops to be seen on the floor until the flow of blood is copious. It is a good idea to wipe her with a piece of cotton every day if you are at all expectant that she may be

CH. RUPERT JURISPRUDENCE a daughter of Ch. Glenarvey Barrister, a typical female head.

CH. GLENARVEY BARRISTER a typical masculine head.

coming in heat. Here again you may have the rare but frustrating experience of having a bitch that never shows any signs of blood but has a clear discharge and the only indication of being in heat is the swelling. Other signs to look for are urinating more often than usual and bitches mounting one another. However they often mount each other at other times too, especially very young puppies.

The owner of the stud dog should be notified immediately when you believe your bitch to be in heat. He should have been told in advance whether your bitch is a house pet or not, so that a house pet is not put out in a cold kennel in winter.

An experienced owner of a stud dog can usually tell by the actions of his stud dog whether or not the bitch is ready for mating. However, he often takes the bitch to a veterinarian for precise determination of readiness. There is a vaginal smear test that can be given, but only in rare cases is this necessary. There are usually definite signs that will indicate the willingness of the bitch to be bred. Throwing her tail to one side (flagging) when touched on her rear and keeping it there, being very playful with the dog, and not sitting down to prevent mounting are such signs. However, it is very frustrating to realize that sometimes a mating takes place with practically no definite signs of the bitch having been ready and then, more often than not, a forced mating with a selected stud on a day that the owner of the bitch is sure is the right one results in no puppies. A bitch is supposedly in heat for three weeks or longer, but as a general rule there are only a few days (about the ninth to the fourteenth day) when the bitch will accept the dog. The number of puppies developed from a mating depends on the number of ripe eggs (ova) available to be fertilized within the bitch. If she is bred too early, there may be very few ova and the same is true if she is bred too late. The fact that some people believe the sex of puppies is determined by the day a bitch is bred has absolutely no basis in fact. There are several other beliefs often circulated that have proved to be "old wives' tales."

It is risky trying to mate two inexperienced Labradors. At least one of them should have been bred before in order to be sure of getting a successful mating.

If the stud dog of your choice lives at a distance that involves shipping by air, arrangements should be made well in advance of the shipping date. A crate is required and this can often be purchased at cost from the carrier. Solid crates are best for shipping and wire cages are no longer allowed by many airlines. Your bitch will be happier if you see that she is accustomed to the crate before shipping her off. Your bitch is required to be at the freight office at least an hour in advance (find out the time from your particular office). A health certificate with rabies number and date of inoculations is required For return shipping from Canada to the United States, a signed rabies certificate indicating that inoculation has been given not less than thirty days and not more than one year before is demanded. Make sure that you ship by air freight and not by express unless schedules have been very carefully checked. Recently a bred bitch was returned to me in frightful condition as a result of being shipped on a Friday with all express offices closed until Monday noon and I was unable to find out by telephone where the bitch was during this time. Air freight offices are open almost all the time; however, it is best not to ship a dog near the end of the week. When notifying the owner of the stud that your bitch has come in heat, you should find out where to ship her and when he prefers for her to arrive. You pay the charges of shipping both ways, and accurate information should be known about flight numbers, times of arrival at different airports, and any changes in flight numbers. In case of trouble, the bitch can then be traced. Without flight numbers, it is practically impossible to find your bitch if she happens not to arrive on time. On the crate should be a printed notice such as "hold until called for at .... airport." The name and address of sender and receiver and the telephone numbers of both should also be noted on the crate. When the bitch is being returned to you, make sure that you know the flight number and the scheduled time of arrival. It is also a good idea to know the name of a veterinarian who would be willing to pick up your bitch at any time of day or night in case something went wrong and you did not meet her. When she arrives, take her out on a leash to relieve herself and then into the car to travel home.

When possible, the bitch should be taken to the dog by car; and, unless circumstances preclude it, should be taken home again rather than being left to be called for another day. If you are in doubt about the correct time to breed her, let your veterinarian decide. All during the time she is in heat, make sure that there is no way for her to escape or otherwise become exposed to a male.

In my experience there was an instance of a bitch having been bred to my stud dog and either before or after that she was mated to another dog; since the resulting puppies could be from either or both stud dogs, I signed no registration paper in spite of the fact that I was convinced that both stud dogs were purebred Labradors. It is important that every Labrador should have the correct pedigree and in this circumstance there was no means of determining which stud sired which of the puppies.

Before delivery to the kennel of the stud dog, the bitch should be taken out and allowed to relieve herself but kept on leash and guarded from attentions of strange dogs during her exercise period. On arriving at the kennel of the stud dog, do not park near the house or kennel, and never under any circumstances take your bitch out of the car until asked to do so. I have had the experience of answering the door bell with the wrong stud dog by my side only to open the door and find the bitch on the door step. It was days before the odor left that area and stopped attracting dogs from near and far. If the stud dog owner sees that your bitch is not in good condition, it is his privilege to refuse to allow mating with his dog to take place. This is also true of a bitch that may not be typical of the breed.

Most owners of stud dogs prefer that the owners of bitches stay away during the process of mating but it is advisable to remain within calling distance in case assistance is needed to help in calming a bitch that is apprehensive in the strange environment.

TYING TOGETHER

Since this book is aimed primarily at new breeders, whom I do not believe should keep a stud dog, I am leaving out the part played by the dog during the mating. The new breeder should rely on the experienced owner of a stud dog to take charge. It is difficult to explain that after the dog's penis has penetrated the vagina of the bitch and ejaculation is accomplished, he puts one of his rear legs over the back of the bitch so they stand back to back for the duration of the tie. This tying together of the dog and bitch usually takes approximately fifteen minutes, and the bitch should not be allowed to sit down during this time. Nor should dog or bitch try to pull away while the tie continues. Usually the owner of the stud dog will tell the owner of the bitch what should be done after the tie is finished and the dog and bitch seem to be about ready to separate.

Place the leash on the bitch if she does not have it on already, and when told to do so, take her straight to your car and leave her there. At this time, the owner of the stud dog will probably tell you whether or not he considers it a satisfactory mating and what the next procedure should be if there is any uncertainty.

As a general rule, one mating is enough to produce a litter of puppies, but sometimes a second mating is requested. A day should be passed between matings as a dog's sperm stays active for at least twenty-four hours.

When you are sure that your bitch is no longer in heat, she may be washed with a quality soap or pet shampoo. In winter, risk no chance of chilling; it is better to skip the washing if she is to be in an unheated building. Any bitch that has to go into an unheated kennel when in heat should be left in this cold building as winter approaches and until after her heat is finished. Actually, no dog should be in a warm house and then put out in an unheated building for any length of time during cold weather.

Under no circumstances should you experiment with a product that prevents a bitch from coming in heat. Great damage has been done to valuable bitches in the past with one product that was on the market for a short time before being withdrawn.

If by some unfortunate circumstance your bitch was mated to the wrong dog, it is better for her to go through with having the puppies than taking a chance by aborting the puppies with an injection given by a veterinarian.

David Elliot, a great human being, with a good-looking Labrador.

12. BREEDING PRACTICES

Breeding dogs is called an art and rightly so for the reason that the breeder strives to produce in puppies what is intellectually believed will be true representatives of a particular breed. Art is not an emotional, superficially attractive object but must be the expression of some fundamental truth related to the particular material to be formulated. When used in connection with Labradors it means a living being with particular functions to which its body relates to its being a dog and a certain kind of dog. Mentally, a true breeder understands the original purpose of a Labrador and realizes why the breed has withstood the competition of other breeds with somewhat similar functions. He will not tolerate extremes, either mental or physical, but strives to produce the dog which he understands and believes will best function as a retriever for the hunter of both land and water fowl. The sports of shows and field trials are side issues of the original purpose and should not be the primary interest of those going into the art of breeding Labradors or any breed of dog.

A hunting dog should happily retrieve what and when he is asked to by the human being he loves and trusts. Since retrieving birds takes place relatively seldom, the rest of the time his purpose, as with all domesticated dogs, is to be a member of the family. Retriever trials, shows, and obedience trials are specialized events and the Labrador as a particular type of dog should never be lost sight of, with the human pride in winning in competition confusing the true reason for a dog such as the Labrador.

Success in the art of breeding Labradors entails many years of effort. One outstanding litter may give a person great impetus and satisfaction, but what follows in succeeding litters is the important function of a breeder.

TYPE

The aim of every person mating a Labrador bitch should be that the resulting puppies be of good type both mentally and physically. The experienced breeder of show Labradors understands a certain meaning of the word while a person interested in field trial Labradors has another meaning for the word *type*. This is unfortunate, but understandable in this age of specialization. To the beginner, a Labrador looks like a Labrador whether it is a good, bad, or indifferent example of the breed because he has no basis on which to form opinions.

Almost everyone knows a black Labrador when he sees one but many of us have been asked what kind of dog we have when possessing a yellow Labrador, and now it is the turn of the chocolate Labrador to be the unknown dog. General classifications, such as the difference between a Terrier and a Labrador, can be recognized much easier than that between a Labrador and a Golden Retriever. But when it comes to individuals within a breed, all look very much alike until the eye has been trained. No amount of reading of the Labrador Standard does much good until the novice has learned to visually compare one animal with another. In fact, comparing anything with another continually trains the eye to distinguish more and more subtle differences between ordinary objects whether it be through the ear, eye, or by touch. Developing one's senses makes for greater enjoyment of life and is essential when it comes to specializing in any field.

Once the novice has developed his powers of observation and comparison the desire to breed better Labradors often follows. After a few litters have been raised, he begins to prefer certain of his puppies to others. If an intelligent reason for his preference can be found, the novice is well on his way to becoming a real breeder. The experienced breeder aims for uniformity in his stock and hopes that all puppies rather than just occasional ones appear close to the ideal he has in his mind. This ideal has become fixed for him as a result of studying the Labrador Standard and comparing many good, bad, and indifferent types observed. Since it is almost impossible to describe a visual object in words, there is within the Standard much opportunity for choice of certain characteristics. In this way particular strains within a breed have been developed over the years. Some may hold up with time and others fall by the wayside, but all can be described as coming within the written wording of the Standard for the breed. In spite of numerous variations from the ideal as set down by those who made the Standard, there is still the general structure and character that distinguishes a Labrador from any other breed.

The beginner is totally confused when it comes to understanding how anyone can control the appearance of Labradors as regards particular characteristics. Control develops mainly through planning and in continually selecting for future breeding stock the puppy of each litter that appears closest to our ideal or to correct some fault in the line.

Development by selecting visually is a slow process involving many failures, often whole litters will be whelped with not a single superior puppy. Perhaps in such case the parents were visually close to the ideal but their genes of inheritance as shown in their pedigrees reveal great divergence. The more ancestors the sire and dam of a litter have in common, the more uniform the litter tends

Litter of puppies bred by Judith Wadson in Bermuda.

to become. Also in breeding there are certain qualities that go together, probably the most consistent being associated with the bones of the spine. If the backbone is long, it is usually true that the neck and tail are also long; thus it is difficult to develop a short "otter" tail with a long neck, which is desirable, and still keep the body short. Luckily the Standard accepts certain results of change by stating that a Labrador must be in balance all over.

With Labradors, the tendency of breeders to go in many directions is not as drastic as in other breeds, and is often limited to the difference between the show type with a possible soft temperament and the field trial dog with possibly a highstrung temperament and indifferent conformation.

It is true that some persons have bred outstanding Labradors without any knowledge of the workings of hereditary factors. We have what we call "in and out" breeders, such persons who raise a few litters, have a fair amount of success and then fade out of the picture and are no longer heard from. We also have breeders raising puppies from a huge breeding stock, possibly placing bitches with friends around the neighborhood. The truly dedicated breeder interested in breeding to type needs only a few bitches along with some understanding of heredity and genetics.

Today, with most of us having to do our own work, there is a need for keeping the fewest possible dogs in our kennels if we are to enjoy our chosen way of life. The fewer dogs kept, the more important it is that each should be retained for a definite reason. Therefore a breeder should make sure he is looking into the future of his breeding plans and not become tangled in sentiment and keep in his kennels a dog that does not fit into his "over all" general program. Each dog kept by a breeder does not necessarily have to be a perfect example of the breed, but each should have a definite quality which it is hoped in combination with another will produce many typical Labradors of highest quality.

Breeding to type is successful only in relation to the genetic composition of the sire and dam of a litter of puppies. It is a mistaken idea of novices that by breeding a mediocre bitch to an outstanding stud dog the puppies will resemble only the famous sire. Another misconception is that physical characteristics of the sire and dam are passed on to their puppies and that each puppy will be of perfect type if either parent is perfect. Experienced breeders know that like does not necessarily produce like.

Some knowledge of genetics takes the guesswork out of breeding and often fewer brood bitches are needed to obtain the desired results. One thing is certainly a mistake and that is to breed two

Labradors having the same serious fault, as it is reasonably certain that every puppy will carry it. It should also be remembered that once a recessive gene becomes established in a line it becomes very difficult to get rid of it. To produce top quality stock, a breeder should understand that what a dog appears to be is in direct relation to the combination of genes within him. These genes can often be recognized through a study of his pedigree and his progeny. A superior dog of bad pedigree is just as wrong to use as breeding stock as an untypical specimen of the breed with a good pedigree.

INBREEDING

There are various methods of trying to obtain desirable results in breeding Labradors. The most drastic is inbreeding, the closest forms of which are the mating of brother to sister, mother to son and daughter to father. We find a wide separation between geneticists, who in theory believe inbreeding should be done, and the public which has a great prejudice against inbreeding and has invented a new term, "highly bred" and blames all bad dogs on inbreeding. This "highly bred" means nothing, but is understood through constant use to mean a high-strung, nervous outlaw and a disgrace to have around. Since laws were passed to protect the human race against inbreeding, the average person believes that inbreeding induces some form of insanity or at least deterioration. We must learn to disassociate ourselves from the uncontrolled factors involved in human reproduction when we think about propagating dogs because it is possible to control results in close interbreeding of dogs by making certain that specimens sharing genes for faults are not mated.

In the breeding of animals, it should be understood and always kept in mind that inbreeding reduces the number of differing genes of inheritance going into the makeup of a puppy. Stray genes for undesirable characteristics are not often introduced and those for desirable traits are more frequently paired.

This results in less variation in type and establishes results that are very difficult to change. Thus if mediocre stock or worse is used for inbreeding, there will be a seemingly endless line of undesirable Labradors. Restricting of breeding stock to individuals of superior quality will, of course, lead to production of superior progeny.

CH. KINLEY SKIPPER, KINLEY AMIGO (to Australia), AMERICAN CH. KINLEY YORKSHIREMAN (before going to the USA).

It is important to realize that the genes of a dog are such as were inherited from the parents and nothing else can be passed on to its progeny. A tremendous amount of knowledge should be acquired before inbreeding is attempted. Poor judgment or unenlightened people producing inbred stock are the cause for prejudice in the minds of the public against inbreeding, and damage is done to the system of inbreeding. We all know the publicity that follows anything unsuccessful, so inbreeding acquires a bad name.

In reality the same practice of inbreeding that causes horrible mistakes to appear is also the means by which very superior Labradors are developed. The wrong use of inbreeding gets most of the publicity and the good gets very little attention. Great breeds of animals and strains within these breeds have been developed through inbreeding, and Labradors are no exception. However, inbreeding is something for the experienced breeder. Few beginners are capable of inbreeding with an understanding of what is involved. They have not produced enough litters from their bitch line to know what recessive genes (usually the unwanted ones) lay hidden within their stock. Neither are novices willing to admit

128

their mistakes, even to themselves, and efforts are made to cover up rather than to admit error and to take corrective measures. With our American trait of wanting results in a hurry, we find breeders who are inbreeding without understanding enough about their own stock.

A person with the experience and understanding gained through production of many generations of puppies decides to inbreed for a definite purpose. This type of person understands the dangers as well as the good results possible and realizes that he may have to destroy whole litters of resulting puppies.

The principal reason for starting a course of inbreeding is possession of a line of bitches that has been producing well (not only single litters but several, and from different dogs) and that he can now intensify effects of the genes in this line, and the quickest way to do this is through inbreeding. He will probably get a few shocks with revelation of a fault or two that he never

AMERICAN CH. KINLEY YORKSHIREMAN 1960 AV By Ch. Kinley Matador AL ex Kinley Mantilla AS. Bred by G. W. Stevenson, owned by Fred Wrigley. Imported to USA by Mr. Propst. Sire of Flax (frontispiece).

suspected present in the genes of his breeding stock. The reason for this is that the undesirable genes were carried in his own bitch line and not in those of the stud dogs used; thus they did not appear in earlier litters of puppies because they were recessive gene characteristics and only appeared when paired through inbreeding within his own line. From now on, he knows this gene is present in his line; depending on the seriousness of the fault and how widespread it is in Labradors, rests his decision about what to do next. In the future, he knows that a certain proportion of his puppies will be "carriers" of the gene for the undesirable trait but he does not know from appearance which are the "carriers" and which are the clear puppies; he can be sure only of those wherein the responsible recessive genes are paired and manifest their presence.

TEST-MATING

If the fault is one detrimental to the physical well-being of the breed, the logical thing to do is to test-mate. This is a system of breeding wherein the genetic make-up of the parents is discovered through the puppies produced. A normal appearing animal is bred back to an affected one; if the puppies in the resulting litter are all normal, the Labrador being tested is not a carrier. If even one puppy with the fault appears, the reverse is true and the test-mating proves that the tested animal is a carrier of the undesirable gene. In either case, all puppies in the litter are carriers (inevitable if either parent is a carrier) and must not be allowed to reproduce or the bad trait will have a chance of becoming thoroughly established in the breed. Of course, the ethical breeder never allows the known "carrier" of a serious fault to be used for breeding either by himself or anyone else. The next step for the breeder is to outcross and hope that in the future the dog he mates his bitches to will not have the identical gene he is trying to get rid of. It is well to remember that a recessive gene can lie hidden for many, many generations and rarely disappears entirely from the breed.

LINE BREEDING

A safer but slower approach to the problem of getting what is wanted in future puppies is line breeding. This goes rather on the same principle as inbreeding but is much safer and not so drastic.

IRISH CH. CASTLEMORE CLODAGH 1953 AP By Ch. Strokestown Duke of Blaircourt ex English, Irish Ch. Hilldown Sylver. Bred by Mrs. Eustace Duckett, owned by Miss Dowling. A great producing bitch. Dam of two Dual Champions.

In this case you have discovered which outstanding Labrador in the pedigree of your bitch is responsible for the excellent qualities that she is able to pass on to her puppies. From now on you search for stud dogs that will increase the number of times this name appears in the pedigree of the next generation. The closer this name appears in the pedigree, the more influence the genes have (the chances are there are more of them) and as generations progress, influence can be continued through closely related descendants. Through the keeping of a bitch puppy from every successful litter, you are slowly but surely developing a strain of Labradors.

In line breeding as well as inbreeding, the time may come when an outcross is needed in order to add some different trait to your line. It should be understood that an outcross only adds something but does not change what is already there. Since inbreeding and line breeding reduce the number of different types of genes, the

131

CH. POOLSTEAD PRESIDENT AZ 1964. By Ch. Hollybunch of Keithray AW ex Braeduke Julia of Poolstead. Breeder-owner Mrs. Hepworth. CC Crufts.

CH. HOLTON BARON 1951 AK By Sandylands Bob ex Holton Whimbrel. Breeder owner Mr. Gilliat.

AMERICAN CH. SANDYLANDS SPUNGOLD OF PENYFAN 1962 By Ch. Sandylands Sam ex Pentowan Sandylands Tiptoes. Bred by Mrs. K. B. Jackson, owned in USA by Dorothy Francke.

CH. SANDYLANDS TRUTH 1960 AU By Australian Ch. Sandylands Tan ex Sandylands Shadow. Bred and owned by Mrs. G. Broadley. CC Crufts.

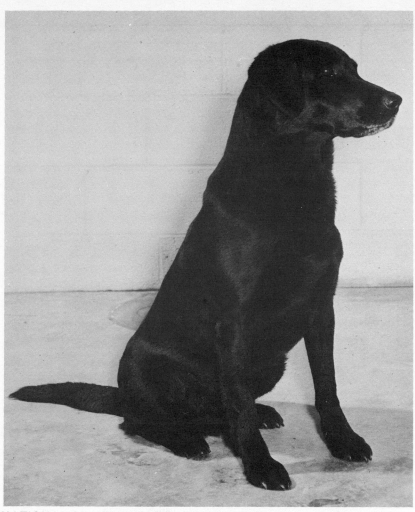

NATIONAL CHAMPION KING BUCK 1948 By Timothy of Arden ex Alta Banchory. Owned by John Olin.

principle behind an outcross is to add other genes. If you believe that your bitch line is what you want except for a few details, go back into that line again in the next generation. In choosing the stud dog for an outcross, care should be taken (through study of his pedigree) that he is not proved to be inbred or closely line bred to a different line or you may have trouble getting rid of unwanted genes in his line. His line may dominate that of your bitch.

134

The success or failure of line breeding depends primarily on the quality of the line of ancestors to which you breed and the amount of patience you use in the solving of the problems involved. If you are unwilling to study, do not have the necessary painstaking patience, and cannot survive the mistakes that are bound to occur, you had better go buy your winner and be done with it all, but you will miss the satisfaction that comes with producing or at least trying to produce that winner.

LAB + LAB = LABS

The important thing to remember is that the person who mates a Labrador to another Labrador just gets more Labradors. This person floods the market with mediocre puppies and downgrades the whole breed. Mediocrity produces more mediocrity or worse, rarely anything better than either parent. And general mediocrity is more difficult to breed out than any single fault. The true breeder goes to endless trouble to find the correct stud dog for his bitch. Through continual study of the progeny resulting from his own planned matings, as well as from other breeders'

TIBSHELF COFFEE 1967 Chocolate bitch By Ch. Sandylands Tweed of Blaircourt ex Tibshelf Tip Toe. Bred and owned by Tibshelf Kennels. This bitch produced all three colors in one litter.

(Left to Right) ROOKWOOD GOLD CREST By Dobrudden Tank Commander ex Rookwood Honeygold; MANDY OF BREAKNECK FARM By Camlark Sam ex Jane of Highleigh; ROOKWOOD HONEYGOLD AS By Ch. Diant Swandyke Cream Cracker AJ ex Mandy of Breakneck Farm and CH. ROOKWOOD PETERGOLD AU By Nokeener Newcracker AS ex Rookwood Honeygold AS. All at Rookwood Kennels.

bitches to various stud dogs, he continuously increases his knowledge of potentials. It is through much study and work, and particularly by the observation of as many Labradors as possible, that satisfactory results are obtainable.

What a breeder should aim for is not just one outstanding Labrador in a litter, or even one whole litter of uniform puppies that develop into truly typical representatives of the breed; the test of a successful breeder is the continual production of conspicuously superior Labradors over many years of endeavor. Typical representatives in England are Mrs. Broadley of Sandylands Kennels and Mrs. Wormald of Knaith Kennels; in this country, Paul Bakewell of Deer Creek Kennels and Thomas Merritt of Grangemead Kennels merit designation as successful breeders.

13. LABRADOR COLORATION

Let me try to make my position clear. I am against those so-called breeders who begin operations with no experience and have no interest in learning anything about genetics. Breeders are guiding production of living things, and just because some person mates a dog and a bitch and happens by chance to get a winner, does not indicate that others should proceed in such haphazard way.

We all know that there is no such thing as perfection, but the constant struggle to approach it in mating purebred dogs should be the aim of every breeder. My own interest is concerned with a Labrador that is not only beautiful and approaches the Standard for the breed, but must be a devoted companion and have the natural ability to retrieve as well. I am against the idea of mating ANY bitch to ANY dog for the sole purpose of producing puppies for marketing.

GENETICS

Genetics is a very complicated subject. Some persons have spent years studying various aspects of the science. It does not come within the scope of a book such as this to do more than skim the surface of the subject. However, since all living things carry genes of inheritance, whether they be human, lower animal, or plant, a few fundamentals should be understood.

Genes function in pairs, one inherited from the mother and the other from the father; they operate as a team, either alone or in combination with other pairs of genes, to determine the characteristics of each individual. They are characteristically of two kinds, dominant and recessive. A dominant gene is strong enough to influence a characteristic alone, whereas a recessive gene manifests perceptible influence only when coupled with another recessive gene. Put in another way, pairing two dominant genes or a dominant with a recessive gene will produce the same visible characteristic; whereas pairing of two recessive genes is required to cause visible manifestation of the recessive variation of the given characteristic.

BLACKS AND YELLOWS

For example, black coat in Labradors is a dominant character and yellow is a recessive one. Black Labradors carry two dominant genes for black or the black dominant black gene in tandem with a recessive one for yellow; unless one parent is known to be yellow, the genetic pattern can be guessed only by tracing heredity lines or by the sudden appearance of yellow offspring. Such an occurrence can result only when both parental and maternal lines carry the hidden (recessive) gene for yellow and these by chance become paired in particular puppies. These puppies, having the paired genes for this recessive characteristic are pure in this respect and matings between such animals will produce nothing but yellow progeny.

Matings between blacks produce progeny of a different sort, depending upon their genetic background. If both parents carry paired genes for black, are pure for that color, all puppies will also be pure for black. If one of the parents carries a recessive gene for yellow, the puppies will all be black but half of them will have the genetic makeup of one parent and be pure for black; half will have the genetic structure of the other parent, appearing black but carrying one dominant and one recessive gene. It is to be understood that fractions used in discussions of genetic probabilities apply on the average, in the long run, and are only approximate, of course, regarding a particular mating.

Should both parents bring a dominant and a recessive gene to the mating, three-fourths of the young will be black and one-fourth will be yellow and pure for that trait. A third of the blacks will also be pure; the others will be of mixed (hybrid) strain. Disregarding appearance, the result can be expressed genetically as one fourth pure black, one fourth pure yellow, and one half hybrid.

To return to the consideration of the pure recessive yellow, two further mating results can be expected by breeding such an individual to a black. If the black is also pure, all puppies will be black but they will be hybrids and carry a gene for black and one for yellow. However, if the black mate is a hybrid, half of the pups will also be black and hybrid but the rest will be yellow and pure for that color.

All other characteristics of simple recessive inheritance as influenced by combination of dominant and recessive genes may be

138

INHERITANCE OF YELLOW COLOR IN LABRADORS

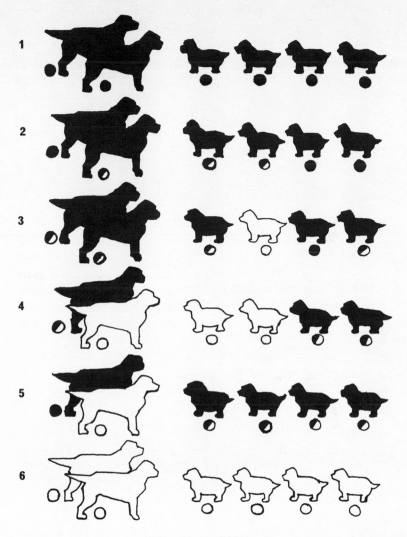

Litter 1, solid black, no yellow genes; Litter 2, one parent carries yellow genes, all puppies black but half carry yellow genes; Litter 3, both parents carry yellow genes, one puppy all black, two puppies black but carrying yellow genes, one puppy yellow; Litter 4, one parent yellow, other parent carrying yellow genes, two puppies black but carrying yellow genes, two puppies yellow; Litter 5, one parent yellow, other parent black, four puppies black but carrying yellow genes; Litter 6, both parents yellow, all puppies yellow (two yellows bred together cannot produce a black).

TIBSHELF OCHRE 1962 Chocolate dog sired by Tibshelf Sultan ex Ullingswick Amber. Bred by Mrs. Lewis, owned by Mr. Severn.

NORWEGIAN CH. AND SWEDISH DUAL CH. KAMRATE CAREENA 1964 By Finnish and Norwegian Ch. Diant Dobrudden Braydon ex Int. Swedish Ch. Cookridge Cola. Bred by Inge & Inge and Marie Eson Theor. Owned and handled by Fru Brit-Marie Brulin. Dam of two chocolate champions in Sweden. (Pedigree 22.)

plotted in the same manner, and may perhaps be more clearly visualized by reference to the chart. Three factors must also be kept in mind by the breeder. Some characteristics are not controlled by a single pair of genes, and the more pairs that are interrelated for action, the more complicated become the problems of control. Secondly, it must be remembered that recessive genes manifest their presence only when brought together and paired in one

140

individual and may be carried in a heredity line for many generations before chance brings such a pairing. Finally, both hybrids and animals that are pure for a dominant characteristic appear to be alike; the breeder cannot distinguish between them, and can do no more than rely upon future litters to establish probability of a pure strain of dominance.

I traced the pedigree of an American-bred yellow Labrador back through most of 500 names and could not find even one yellow ancestor of this dog. However the name of that great black bitch F.T. Champion Tar of Arden known to have produced a yellow ran all through the pedigree and I suspect it was through her that finally a black dog and bitch both with yellow genes were mated to produce this yellow dog.

Grace Lambert's famous black import the English, American, and Canadian Champion Sam of Blaircourt does not have genes for the yellow color. His first litter in this country was out of my yellow bitch Champion Rupert Aurora Borealis and when the litter of nine puppies arrived there were no yellows. This was the proof that this famous Labrador stud was genetically pure for black. Subsequently every one of these black puppies produced yellow offspring. The only way to have a litter with no black puppies is to breed yellow to yellow, and the only way to have all black puppies with no yellow genes is to test-mate both parents and so make sure neither has hidden genes for the yellow color.

Let me emphasize again that this chart is for the simple recessive found in the color yellow in Labradors (not necessarily true of any other breed) and should not be used for the inheritance pattern of other genes unless they are known to be of exactly the same type, which much genetic inheritance is not.

CHOCOLATE

According to correspondence with breeders interested in chocolate Labradors, the color is not inherited as a simple recessive. The proof was provided by a litter of ten whelped in Minnesota; both parents were chocolate, but the pups were five yellow and five chocolate. If this had been a simple recessive inheritance, all of the puppies would have been chocolate. Incidentally, all the yellows in this litter had light eyes but apparently none of the chocolates had them. Whether or not this indicates a way of telling whether or not a yellow has the ability to produce chocolates has yet to be proved. Mrs. Hall, who has taken over the Tibshelf Kennels in England since the death of Mr. Servern, writes that she has seldom produced yellows from chocolate parents but when she has done this "they often have failed to get the attractive black points." Furthermore, when a chocolate puppy is produced from one chocolcate and one yellow parent, a rarity, she does find that "the chocolate color is slightly lighter than when both parents are chocolate, or one parent is chocolate and one black." From Kentucky comes a letter telling me of nine puppies from a chocolate bitch bred to a yellow dog. There were no yellow puppies, but five chocolates and four blacks.

The chocolate Labrador has been known in the breed practically from its beginnings. The Duke of Buccleuch mentions in his stud book that there were a few chocolates in his time. Some kennels have specialized in the color, and for twenty-five years or so Tibshelf Kennels have been producing chocolates. At first Mr. Servern had trouble producing chocolate bitches with which to carry on his line. Light eyes were also a problem. In a chocolate individual of any breed, it is not possible for there to be black anywhere on the body, and some geneticists believe that the color is produced by the action of modifying genes which dilute other colors. Since dark eyes are inherited as a dominant in most breeds, it may only be possible to darken the eyes of chocolates through the use of chocolates having black parents breeding to blacks with the ability to produce chocolates.

There is some indication that there may be different genetic patterns depending on bloodlines. Mrs. Hall tells me that some lines produce all chocolate progeny from chocolate parents but that another line from chocolate parents will produce chocolates and blacks but hardly ever any yellows. Litters have been produced with all three colors in the puppies. At Metesford Kennels, it was the bitch Coffee Bean of Metesford bred to Tibshelf Choc that produced a litter with puppies of all three colors.

I have found through tracing pedigrees of chocolates in this country that many go back to Metesford breeding and also through Cookridge and Ide. Coming up to the present, the great stud dog Ch. Sandylands Tweed of Blaircourt is responsible for quite a few chocolates. Tweed produced in England the first champion

CH. COOKRIDGE TANGO 1961 AW Chocolate bitch By Ch. Sandylands Tweed of Blaircourt AS ex Cookridge Gay Princess. Bred and owned by Mrs. M. Y. Pauling. The first chocolate champion in England.

chocolate, a bitch Ch. Cookridge Tango. With a great number of Tweed-bred progeny being imported, we may see an increase in the occurrence of the color. It must be remembered that the inheritance for chocolate is genetically different from that for both yellows and blacks and has not as yet been definitely established.

Mrs. Pauling (Cookridge Labradors) tells me she finds that chocolates seem slower in maturing and consequently "the eye continues to darken up to a period of twelve months or so." However, she thinks that better eye color can be produced by breeding chocolate and black. When her Tango was mated to a black, the result was all black puppies. She later bred one of these blacks to a chocolate bitch and produced chocolates of very good quality.

Kennels in Britain which have produced chocolates are Chiltonfoliat, Braeroy, Logan, and Lochar. Chocolate producing kennels in Canada and the United States include Arden, Chevrier, and Invail; Deer Creek (with Dual Champion Bengal of Arden and his litter-mates) is credited with several.

In Sweden there is a locally-bred chocolate bitch produced through the line developed by way of Tweed and Cookridge Cola. This bitch has not only become a dual champion herself, handled by her breeder-owner Frau Brit-Marie Brulin, but has whelped puppies which have become champions.

AND OTHER KINDS

As in many fields of endeavor, every once in a while the best laid plans go wrong; this is true with genetics, and various characteristics from the past show up in the present day Labradors. We may think that black spots on a yellow Labrador occurred haphazardly, but we should realize that black spots on a dog that is supposed to be spotted follow a definite and inherited pattern. Black spots on yellow Labradors are rare indeed; but when they do appear, a definite genetic pattern is indicated and a possible Foxhound cross in the past can be suspected.

To an American, this means an indication of a mongrel; however, most breeds of dogs, and especially Labradors, were developed by way of many planned crosses, and to the British, who developed our breed, various off-colors are not too important unless they become established in a breed.

In her book on the Labrador, Lady Howe mentions stripes of black on a yellow Labrador, and I have seen a puppy marked in this way except that it was grey with black stripes running around the body. She also mentions white toes and was convinced that any Labrador showing this must come down through her Dual Champion Banchory Bolo. White toes are fairly common on Labradors today, but are possible to breed out. In both the past and present, there have been grey puppies of a lovely silvery color at whelping, but they very soon start to darken.

In many breeds, puppies that are supposed to be solid black suddenly develop white hairs, giving them a pepper-and-salt appearance. At one time it was suspected that this might be caused by a reaction of some types of worm medicine. However, pepper-and-salt and grey puppies keep darkening and by six months of age have become completely black and never go off color again. I do not know what happens to the black stripes on yellow puppies. As for white toes, depending on the amount of white, they sometimes retain this feature.

Willingness to enter water and retrieve is among the Labrador's standard requirements. This is Michael II of FAYERWEATHER 1965 By Ch. Scawfell Seekon ex Ch. Rupert Marleigh Bingham. Bred by D. Howe, owned by Peter Rice.

14. CULLING AND SELECTING

No matter how many litters of puppies a breeder has produced, the most thrilling part is that first cry of life of the newborn. When this excitement is over, the time has come to start observing what the puppies as a whole look like. From now on the breeder's wisdom in the choice of a sire for those puppies will be tested. Even the most experienced breeder will make frustrating mistakes, but this is no excuse for not trying to avoid them. Sometimes it is easier to learn through mistakes than successes, and both should be used to advance one's understanding of the responsibility for producing living things of quality.

The irresponsibility of those human beings who mate a dog and a bitch as the result of some whim is inexcusable and shows a lack of sensitivity to life in general. The breeding of Labradors should be given careful thought and should not be attempted unless the resulting puppies are to be a credit to the breed. A true breeder plans to keep a bitch puppy as future breeding stock, therefore the effort to discover which is the best one in each litter becomes the continual problem. When a breeder has had the experience of many litters from a closely related, consistent line of bitches, he has a certain amount of knowledge and understanding concerning the faults and good points which are apt to appear in puppies from these bitches. It is possible to anticipate certain qualities either desirable or unwanted, though depending on hidden recessive genes that may appear when an ancestor of the bitch and dog are characteristically identical in certain respects. With some luck and much study and a belief that the right genes will combine, each litter may turn out to be better than the last. The experienced breeder will often base his selection of future breeding stock on the correction of a particular fault in his bitch line, in spite of the loss of a good point which he understands will probably come back in a future litter.

SELECTING PARTNERS

In order to select partners for purposeful matings, one must be able to compare two or more objects or qualities. At first, all black Labradors look alike, but gradually in the process of training the eye, the heads start to look wider or narrower, legs become longer or shorter, with tails varying in length, and the thickness of a bone is seen in relation to thin ones. Expression on a Labrador is very important too. We have all seen the dog that looks up with adoring large dark eyes waiting to be told what to do. This is the essence of Labrador expression and what every breeder should strive for in his line.

THE STANDARD

Never having heard of the standard for a Labrador, how would anyone know whether the tail should be long or short, both of which are often seen in the show ring at the same time and at times both types winning. The reason a standard is set up for any breed is to select those characteristics that would distinguish one breed from another breed and to try and keep a certain amount of uniformity within the breed in the future. Therefore it becomes important that everyone becomes familiar with the standard. Later the trained eye and mind will come to see first the Labrador as a whole (which includes the way it moves) before looking for and evaluating virtues and faults. The untrained eye can usually recognize an outstanding dog or a horrible example of the breed, but the majority of the Labradors that lie between these extremes seem

At nine months of age, this puppy's conformation is excellent. He's BAROKE DO-DAD, By Ch. Harrowby Baron ex Ch. Harrowby Storm. Bred by Dr. Keith S. Grimson, owned by Larry Donnigan.

to look alike. People with imagination have an easier time visualizing in their minds the type of Labrador that they believe is perfect and well-balanced all over, but others should be able to acquire the art with some practice.

The novice breeder when faced with his first litter sees them all

147

CH. KINLEY SKIPPER 1959 AP By Ch. Kinley Matador AL ex Kinley Mantilla AS. Bred by G. W. Stevenson. Owned by Fred Wrigley.

CH. KINGSBURY NOKEENER MOONSTAR 1968 By Ch. Nokeener Moonrocket ex Nokeener Nightlight. Bred by Mrs. R. Willliams, owned by Mrs. Preston. CC Crufts at ten months of age.

as future champions. It takes an educated eye to see differences, particularly if one is faced with an all-black litter. When a litter is first whelped, and again at eight weeks of age, puppies seem to be more in proportion than at other times. Puppies seem to grow various parts of their bodies at different rates of speed and to go through stages when their legs seem too long or they are in general all out of proportion. Usually they can be counted on to have feet that outgrow the legs, and tails that we despair of ever looking like what the standard calls for as being short and thick at the base. What seem to be the last parts to develop are width of body, and the head and the nose tend to lengthen and the eye to darken more slowly than other parts.

FIRST DAYS

During the first days of life, puppies give you a chance to observe them as a whole and not as individuals. Perhaps they vary in size and you think that you have a runt that should be destroyed. Do not be too quick about this, as he may turn out to be the best of the lot. And you may have chosen a stud dog with genes for smallness, which in some cases is desirable. At a very young age, good "otter" tails can be seen as they have a tendency to hang down, whereas a longer, thinner tail will curl up.

By watching the litter as it develops, it is noted that puppies gradually become individuals, and certain ones seem to stand out from the others. It is only by watching the group as a whole that some puppies become noted as different from others. Temperaments soon start to develop as the puppies move about and become familiar with your voice. Teach them to listen by talking very quietly and you will notice that by four weeks of age they will come running when you call them. Watch to see if the same one is the first to learn everything, the first to eat, and probably the one that gets all four feet in the dish reaching for food in all directions. Perhaps one barks at you with impatience when it is hungry. Another puppy may hang back as if a bit anti-social, and will probably need special attention. A mildly timid one often makes an excellent pet as it becomes dependent on the family and will not be readily tempted to wander off in search of excitement. If the trait is inherited and not acquired, the timid individual should not be used for breeding, so watch to see if there is some reason for the puppy having become anti-social. Sometimes through the study of previous litters, either from the same bitch or another one bred to the same stud dog, you might find timid puppies that have not appeared from matings with other stud dogs. Another possibility would be the duplication of a certain ancestor on each side of the pedigree of the puppies as a reason for shyness coming through.

SIX-WEEK CHECK-UP

When the puppies are about six weeks old, start setting each puppy on a table to look it over. Make sure that the table is a steady one and not slippery. A rug or bath mat makes a good surface. The puppies will be nervous at first since it seems to be the nature of an intelligent puppy to be a bit cautious of new situations. In fact, one test for a timid puppy (perhaps at eight weeks) is to set it down in new surroundings such as a room in the house. At first it will shiver and shake in one spot. Soon the timid one will get under the sofa and stay there, whereas a normal Labrador puppy will soon start investigating his surroundings and finally wag his tail with joy. In trying to evaluate puppies in a litter at this time, take all the bitches first (since there is one you plan to keep for the future of your kennel) and look at them one at a time.

You might as well start putting them in the show stance from the beginning. The right hand with one finger under the chin is used to give your puppy the idea of keeping its head high. With your other hand, stroke the under side of the tail and eventually the puppy will learn to hold it up. At first, a puppy will not let you move its feet into position, but eventually you can place the rear legs with the hock perpendicular. It is enough at this point just to move the legs about. The front legs should go straight down to the ground, turning neither in nor out. Toeing out is less of a fault than toeing in because the widening chest tends to push the elbows out and so straighten the legs. A puppy will pull back and you will have difficulty getting it to stand straight up on the front legs at first, but eventually it will learn to hold a posed position. We have all seen nervous dogs in the show ring that refuse to stand up straight on their front legs. Poor early training is the cause of this. Your puppy may look long in the body, especially

Rupert Counsellor at eight weeks.

if its head is not held high. A breast bone that sticks out in front is an indication of fine shoulder placement in the mature dog. Thick thighs, a bend at the stifle, and width across the rear are good points, and the thicker-looking the bone the better. Length of tail is measured by following the curve of the body and it should not extend below the hock joint, and the shorter the better. The head should show width between the eyes with a drop between the forehead and the start of the nose (the stop) so that the forehead and nose are not in a straight line. The nose should not be longer than the distance from the stop to the occiput. Do not worry if the top of the skull protrudes; it will flatten later and add to the width of the head. Depth of lip should be less in bitches than in dogs and should not give the appearance of a Setter jaw. The eyes should be wide apart, which makes for that delightful, friendly

Labrador expression; however, the true color will not show up by eight weeks. An experienced person can, by looking carefully, see any indication of a light eye coloration, which is not attractive on a Labrador of any color.

EIGHT WEEKS AND DECISIONS

Since you have been going over your puppies often, you are by eight weeks ready to make decisions. The yellows will have their black noses, foot pads, and eye rims at a very young age, and will vary in depth of coat color, which makes them so much easier to identify individuals than the black ones. Their color will deepen as they get their final coat, which may not happen until they are almost two years old. They will also look darker in winter than in summer, as their final topcoat is dark and the undercoat much lighter in color. The color of a yellow puppy's ears indicates the final color of the top coat along the back.

Work out a system for identifying the individual blacks and keep notes on them as you look them over. By clipping hair of black ones in various places, this will be made easier, but you will be surprised at how quickly this clip grows out. I reserve a clip of hair from the end of the tail of the one I like best. However, make sure you hold the end of the bone on the tail to assure that you do not clip too closely.

At this age, undershot or overshot jaws can be spotted; if the condition is not too bad, it will adjust when the puppy gets older. This is an inherited fault, so it bears watching and evaluating in relation to other good points or faults in the litter. The feet should be compact like those of a cat, especially on the front legs. The rear feet may look as though the toes are too long, thus giving the appearance of flat feet, but do not worry about this as it has a great deal to do with the way a puppy stands and moves when young.

Viewed from the front, the sturdy little puppy with front legs that go straight to the ground from the shoulders is a delight to see, but more often it will toe in or out. If it toes in, the puppy is out at the elbow. This may improve with age but rarely becomes straight. It is difficult to get a long neck with a short body and tail, and yellow Labradors tend to have better tails than the blacks, whereas the blacks have longer necks. The yellows often have too much skin on the under side of the neck, which does not give the clean appearance possessed by the blacks. I think this is a minor fault, although it is becoming widespread within the breed and tends to appear even worse with a very heavy coat on a short neck. The very dark colored yellows seem to have less-heavy coats and cleaner necks, but often not as good tails as the cream colored ones. These darker ones sometimes do not have as good dark pigmentation around the eyes and I would not be surprised if it were found someday that the dark yellows and the pale ones come through definitely different lines. The chocolate puppies will have no black anywhere on their bodies but should otherwise look like a yellow or black in conformation. Many of the imported Labradors of all colors have curly hair on the back over the rump; more yellows than blacks have this, whereas the American-bred dogs tend to have a smoother if thinner coat. The heavier coats on the yellows grow faster at first, with the blacks catching up later on.

Puppies enjoy the snow. This one is an eight-week-old daughter of Rupert Pamela of Tedco. Bred and owned by Chris Woelfel.

Coats that will mature into the correct double coat are often fluffy on young puppies before the coarse hairs of the outer coat grow through. If you plan to breed yellows, it is very important that the one you keep has good black pigmentation as this is one of the characteristics which is fairly easy to lose and hard to get back again. This is also true of a good "otter" tail, and beware of breeding to a long tail that curls over the back. Anyone owning a black and wishing to improve the tails on future puppies might breed to a yellow with a really good tail. However, remember that when you do this you may get an all-black litter and also have great trouble getting rid of yellow genes in future generations, supposing that you do not want any yellow puppies.

After going over each puppy separately and picking out which you think are the two best of each sex, you had better forget it all until the next day; then with a fresh eye and perhaps a better understanding of what you want in the bitch, you can plan definitely which you desire to keep.

Remember what I am writing is relative and you may end up with nothing important if the sire and dam of your puppies are not of top quality in both looks and breeding. The better the quality of the parents of a litter, the harder it is to evaluate the puppies as they tend to have only slight differences between them. As you gain experience, you may choose for future breeding a bitch puppy that may not appear to be the best of the litter. You may pick this one because, despite her faults, she does not have others that you have been trying to breed out in previous matings. This becomes entirely your decision in relation to your future as a breeder and to the seriousness of the various faults and the difficulty you have discovered in attempting to breed each fault out. For instance, a light eye is unattractive and inherited as a recessive which means your bitch carries the genes for it if one appears in a litter from her. In the future you must remember always to breed her and her offspring (which may be carriers for the gene) to dark-eyed stud dogs. This will tend to reduce and perhaps eventually eliminate the genes for light eyes from your stock.

SHYNESS

An experienced breeder can tell the difference between inherited shyness and that which may be acquired and to a certain extent

154

At six weeks, CH. RUPERT JURISPRUDENCE enjoyed something soft and light in weight, such as a glove, to retrieve.

counteract this in a puppy, but for the novice it is much more difficult. This depends a great deal on how much handling a puppy gets, whether or not its dam is highstrung and may have injured it, as well as various other things which may have happened to it in growing up. For older puppies, "kennel shyness" is a problem which will be discussed later.

You will be lucky if you ever find a puppy that always looks right no matter in what stage of development. It is a rare individual that stays in proportion, has a perfect temperament, and moves to perfection every time you look at it. You never have trouble identifying this one as it stands out from the group on every occasion. Even a person who has never seen a Labrador puppy will choose it as the one he wants to take home. Do not be tempted at any price to let this one go if it is a bitch puppy. On the other hand, there is sometimes a tendency to want only perfection, with the result that excellent puppies are sold when at least one should have been kept. I made the mistake when I chose a lovely bitch from my first litter and sold her after she had produced only one litter, and no "super puppy" appeared. Sheba was a lovely bitch and one litter sired by a mediocre stud dog was not a fair test of what she might produce if bred to a good one. I wanted every puppy to be perfect and I learned the hard way that perfection seldom appears. A beautiful specimen is a rarity, and many litters must be produced before, perhaps once in a lifetime of breeding, one special puppy will appear. Always hope for it to happen and that it will be a bitch.

BREEDER QUALITIES

The most important quality a breeder must have is an educated mind and eye with which to compare and evaluate puppies and dogs observed. Without this trained eye, a breeder is lost in the confusion of meaningless words found in the Standard, written in books, and heard in conversations with other dog people. Words cannot describe with complete accuracy what anything looks like, and a breeder must therefore acquire the habit of comparing related characteristics and balancing them against the Labrador Standard, and what he knows of the background of his stock. A breeder must also learn to evaluate contemporaries; the less a person knows, the more vocal he is in giving out inaccurate information while using scientific terms in the wrong way. Keep in mind that a knowledgeable person usually translates technical words into ordinary language which the layman can understand, whereas the one with only a smattering of information tries to cover up lack of knowledge through the use of verbal gymnastics.

15. RAISING AND TRAINING PUPPIES

Some persons believe it necessary for the health of the bitch for her to have puppies. Others find their bitch in heat and suddenly decide they will breed her and let the children have fun with the puppies. Then again a family has a much-adored pet which is getting along in years, and the desire for another like her becomes the propelling force for breeding her. These reasons lay a foundation for yet another litter of unwanted puppies thrown out on the world when they become a nuisance. Types of people breeding for the above reasons never think about planning for the future of the puppies. They raise the litter to the age at which the puppies become unattractive and suddenly they are unwanted and off they go to any persons who want them. In raising puppies it should be the desire of the person owning a fine, well-bred bitch to produce puppies that will be a credit to the breed and to avoid degeneration through ill-planned or haphazard matings.

This approach involves thinking ahead and consulting with knowledgeable persons about the ideal mate for the particular bitch. The breeder of a fine bitch should have more interest than most other people in the problem and should be consulted. A good breeder usually has a program thought out in advance and often stud dogs have been chosen for future generations of his stock. Such a person is always glad to make suggestions to owners of Labradors he has bred.

THE BEST SEASON FOR PUPS

The time of year to produce puppies for sale depends to a certain extent on various situations. However, there is almost always a demand for puppies in early spring and again in late summer. Christmas produces a big demand for puppies, but care should be taken in planning to deliver them during that busy season when shipping may be hazardous. It might be well to hold the puppy until after Christmas; children have enough excitement at that

157

time without a puppy to add to the confusion and will likely create a situation to the detriment of the puppy. During the summer, families are generally moving about too much to want to give a puppy the needed attention. The market is also usually flooded with puppies at this time of year because raising puppies in the spring is a convenient time for many breeders. Having a litter in winter is a good practice if you have a place where the puppies can be kept warm and dry. By seven weeks of age, a properly brought up Labrador puppy is active enough to be permitted to go out and play for short periods even in the snow on sunny days and a litter need not be confined to the house all winter.

PRENATAL PREPARATIONS

In preparation for the birth of puppies, a room should be chosen that can be set aside for their exclusive use and the bitch should become familiar with it before the time for whelping arrives. A box with dimensions of about thirty by forty inches with sides twelve to fourteen inches high should be provided. One end should be made in two sections and be hinged so that the upper half can be lowered when the bitch is heavy with puppies and raised later when there is no danger of her hurting herself. This also allows for the open end to be pushed against a radiator to allow more heat in the box when the bitch is not in with the puppies. Later the hinged end can be raised at night to confine the puppies and lowered during the day when they can be out around the room. They soon learn to sleep in the box and to do their "chores" outside of it. For a whelping box, a friend of mine has successfully used a children's old plastic pool lined with a piece of old rug.

Plenty of old newspapers should have been collected well in advance and stored to become very dry. Fresh newspapers are less absorbent than old ones and the ink comes off and begrimes the puppies. Odd pieces of old rugs or other heavy material are good for the bottom of the box. These should be of a type that prevents puppies getting underneath, and non-slippery so they can get a purchase with their rear legs when crawling about.

The bitch will tear up the papers before whelping and they should be allowed to reach quite a depth so that soiled ones can be replaced with fresh torn strips to keep the box as dry as possible despite dampening by the pups. During whelping, leave the bitch alone as much as possible as she usually knows instinctively what to do. But be near and keep watch ready to assist in the event something goes wrong. It is occasionally necessary to help the bitch expel a puppy that is part way out and she is not having much success in pushing it further. In such case, it may be possible to hold the slippery legs of the puppy with a piece of cotton or soft cloth and withdraw it by pulling gently as the bitch pushes. However, the danger here is that the difficulty may be caused by the head being too large, or the front legs may be in the wrong position to permit birth of the puppy.

WHELPING

Normally a Labrador bitch has no trouble with whelping, and it should be remembered that she is guided by instincts which

CH. SHAMROCK ACRES COTTON CANDY 1960 By Ch. Shamrock Acres Light Brigade ex Whygin Dawn of Shamrock Acres. Five-day-old puppies bred by Sally McCarthy, owned by Mrs. James R. Getz.

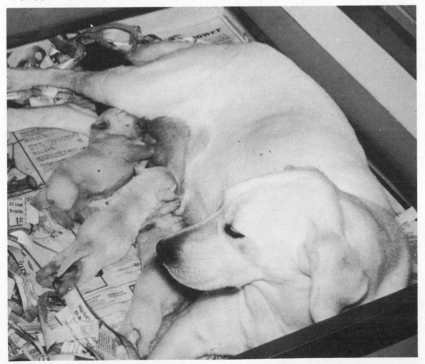

direct actions that are best in normal circumstances. With her teeth, she will cut the cord which separates her from the after-birth, then clean and dry the puppy by licking it, knowing instinctively that this stimulates the puppy and starts it moving about in search of warmth and nourishment. The real help she will need from you is to keep the box clean and dry, and if she is a house pet she might like her favorite person near by.

Since whelping will be easier for the bitch if the puppies are relatively small, care should be taken not to overfeed her during pregnancy. This becomes a matter of judgment respecting each bitch. Some bitches will stay very thin with all their food going to the puppies within them. Another will keep both herself and the puppies in top condition with proper feeding. Usually you will not notice any difference in a bitch's size until about three weeks before she is ready to whelp and at this time her intake of food might be increased. When she really seems to be swelling, divide her food in two parts and feed her one meal in the morning and the other at night. Theories about feeding vitamins have changed and supplementing of diets must be done with care.

It is cruel to send a bitch away to a strange place such as another kennel or the veterinarian for whelping. She needs to be in familiar surroundings with people she loves and trusts. She depends on you to understand what is happening to her and you will probably be conscious of when she is about to produce her puppies. There are stages a bitch usually goes through such as tearing up papers and general restlessness a few days in advance of whelping and increasing nervous excitement as the time draws near. If in doubt about when the time is due (nine weeks is the average gestation period), take her temperature for several days before she is due. When there is a sudden drop in temperature, you may expect labor to begin within twenty-four to forty-eight hours. The normal temperature of a healthy, grown dog is about 101.5°F. Puppies born more than three days before or more than three days after the anticipated time may mean trouble and you should notify your veterinarian.

Normally, when the time approaches for the puppies to be born, the bitch, besides being restless, will breathe heavily and keep looking at her rear and possibly push it against the box. The vulva will be swollen and soft and often a clear mucus can be seen coming out of it (this often happens several days in advance as well as at this time). With a Labrador, a sure sign that the puppies will arrive within twenty-four hours is refusal of food by the bitch, although some will eat every meal. If she is not hungry, watch for signs of heaving and straining and make a note of the time labor contractions actually start. The time from the start of labor until the first puppy arrives varies also and it is sometimes difficult to tell with a nervous bitch when labor actually does begin.

WATER BAG, UMBILICAL CORD, AND AFTERBIRTH

Each puppy is encased within a "water bag" which bursts before the puppy descends the birth canal. Whether the puppy emerges head first or feet first makes no difference as either way is normal for Labradors. The puppy up to this time is attached by the umbilical cord to the "afterbirth" which covers the puppy and appears to be a tight-fitting plastic bag. Normally the first thing the bitch does is to take this covering off the nose of the puppy so it can breathe. Then she will try to sever the cord by chewing it about six inches from the puppy, which is no longer entirely dependent on her but must breathe and find nourishment for itself. Allow the bitch to eat the "afterbirth"; it is reputed to stimulate the milk flow within her. She seems rather rough on the puppy as she rolls it around in attempting to dry it off with her tongue but this stimulates the puppy and you will soon hear that first cry of life and the puppy will start moving towards the warmth of its dam and begin the search for milk.

If more than three hours go by before the next arrival, you may anticipate trouble, but Labradors are usually "easy whelpers" if in good condition. It is hard to tell whether or not all the puppies have arrived and it is well to write down the time of each arrival so that your veterinarian will have some idea of what has happened in case of trouble. A bitch will usually not eat or drink anything during whelping but appreciates liquid in the form of warm broth or milk later. The chances are she will not be hungry, but you might offer her a bit of her regular food in a very liquid form. Do not worry if she refuses it.

Any time you are worried about the bitch, take her temperature

161

(you already know what her normal temperature is if you have taken it before the puppies are due). If her temperature suddenly goes up, call your veterinarian immediately as there may be infection which should be taken care of as soon as possible. Remember that the role of the breeder in relation to whelping is observation and diagnosis of possible trouble, and that it is important to call the veterinarian at once if difficulties arise.

Normal temperature of a bitch by rectal thermometer—101.5°F.

Slight temperature—102.5°F. (often after whelping)

High temperature—104°F.

Dangerous—105°F.

Over 102.5°F—call your veterinarian

POSTNATAL CARE

When things finally settle down and you and the bitch are convinced that there are no more puppies coming, clean up the whole box; put down a fresh, warm, dry piece of rug; cover it with more torn paper, and take care that the bitch does not get a puppy behind her and lie on it. With a large litter, one puppy may get

Puppies are weaned at 6 to 8 weeks and need supplementary feeding before that time. Rack over feeding dishes is convenient for carrying, and also keeps puppies from climbing into bowls.

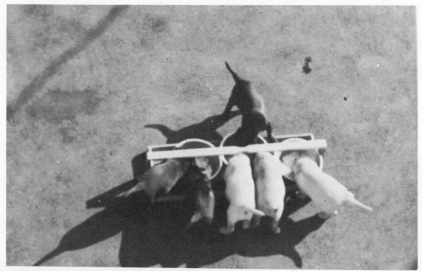

behind her and there is not much she can do about it without disturbing all the others quietly nursing in front of her. Many whelping boxes are fitted with an inside rail to prevent smothering of a puppy that may get behind its dam.

It is a mistake to handle the puppies any more than necessary at this stage; however, with a large litter (seven puppies is average for Labradors) and a nervous bitch, it may be important to move the puppies to one corner of the whelping box while another is in the process of being born, but do not remove them from the box. Some persons weigh puppies as they arrive, but I think it better to wait a day or so. Leave even counting the sexes until the next day; you will be so excited that you will probably miscount anyway as it is easy to mistake the stump of the cord as indicating a dog puppy.

NURSING

Puppies find the nipples of their dam by moving toward the warmth of her body, so do not keep the room too warm. If by any chance you think the puppies are not warm enough (such as when you need to move them to a corner of the whelping box), the old-fashioned idea of a jar of very hot water wrapped in a flannel cloth will keep the puppies from becoming chilled until their dam settles down again.

The bitch will not leave the box if there is any question of the puppies needing her, but she should be given a chance to go out and relieve herself is she desires to do so. It is well to offer her food and liquid in the box for the first day or so, after which time a dish of food may be left near the box so she can help herself when convenient, and of course plenty of fresh water should always be available.

Until two and a half weeks of age, the puppies will be well taken care of by their dam, except for cutting their nails. When cutting the nails (about the twelfth day), use cuticle scissors and cut only those on the front feet. The puppies need the nails on the back feet for crawling about.

FIRST FEEDING

Depending on the size of the litter, at about two and a half to three weeks of age, start supplementing the milk of the bitch with

Litter from which CH. RUPERT SEARCHON came,
shown at five weeks.

SEARCHON at eight weeks.

Growing fast at three months.

(Above) First snowfall for SEARCHON, at 4½ months.

(Below) SEARCHON at 6 months.

Beginning to look like show material.

Approaching adulthood at 10 months.

CH. RUPERT SEARCHON at 10½ months.

solid food for the puppies. The best way to start is by offering them bits of raw hamburger in your fingers. It is surprising how quickly a puppy will learn to eat with enthusiasm. The next step is a shallow dish of high protein Pablum type baby food mixed as directed on the package but be careful not to get it too liquid. To this add a little hamburger. After about a week of Pablum feeding, a small amount of their future adult food should be added gradually so that by four weeks of age they are off Pablum entirely and onto adult food. The sooner they are on the adult food the better off the puppies will be. By timing the feeding to periods when the puppies have not been nursing, you can change them to solid food and gradually keep the bitch away from them for longer and longer periods and by eight weeks of age they are completely weaned from their dam and she has no more milk. Be careful though not to take the bitch away too suddenly or she may get caked breasts from their filling with milk while no puppies are sucking it out. Do not worry if the bitch regurgitates her food in front of her puppies as she is helping them by partly digesting their food while teaching them to eat. The yolk of eggs is good for dogs, but do not give them the raw white as this is apt to cause diarrhea and robs the system of certain nutrients.

BREAKING APRON STRINGS

Puppies develop very rapidly both mentally and physically. Their eyes start to open at about ten days, and soon they are getting up on their feet, at which time the hinged end of the box should be locked up if it is not against a radiator (incidentally the radiator should have a cover on it so the puppies cannot touch the hot coils). As soon as the puppies start moving about in the box and their dam begins to stay away more and more, the puppies will start going out of the box to do their defecating on newspaper you have spread around the room and as a result the sleeping box will be kept clean and dry. Before the time comes for taking the bitch away from her puppies, you can help by giving her a place where she can get away from them. A board can be placed across the door over which she can jump but the puppies cannot, or the whelping box can be turned upside down and the puppies given a rug in a corner for them to sleep on out of a draft while the bitch sleeps on top of the box. The puppies cannot reach her while she is on top of the box, but she will be available and near when they need her.

About this time, the puppies will be producing many stools, particularly after eating, and dry newspapers should be placed continually on top of the dirty ones and the whole lot cleaned out at least once a day.

THREE AND A HALF WEEKS

By three and a half to four weeks of age, the puppies can be petted and cuddled resulting in development of that divine temperament and wagging tail so typical of a Labrador which has complete trust in and love for human beings. This mutual love and affection is needed, especially for those puppies leaving for new homes at nine weeks of age, as their future response to training endeavors depends considerably upon their love for human beings.

FOUR WEEKS

At four weeks of age, the puppies become quite active and this is the time to start training them to come when called, which, as with most training of Labradors, is connected with food. As you put the dishes of food in front of the puppies, call them and repeat the same words every time you feed them. Later, individual puppies can be taught their names in the same manner. Let the puppies out of their pen to run around and investigate while you are mixing their food. NO can be taught at this time as they will probably try to jump up on you. Bump them with your knee (don't kick) to knock them off balance, and at the same time say NO. When their food is ready, repeat KENNEL and go towards their enclosure with their food dishes in your hands. They will soon connect going into the kennel with the word and something pleasant, such as eating. Later this same word can be used for going ahead into the house, automobile, or anywhere else. The main thing in all training of Labradors is repetition of the same word or phrase. NO can also be taught by remote control. Chewing a rug is one of the first things a puppy will start to do, so resist the impulse to rush up and stop him. Say NO and repeat this word until the puppy looks up at you to find out what is wrong. At this moment tell him in a singing voice how wonderful he is to stop that chewing. The contrast in tone of voice between the sharp NO and the soft, singing words of praise are very important in training. STOP THAT are harsh words and are quite effective to use for curbing unnecessary barking.

PROPER PICK UP

It is important that children, as well as adults, understand how to pick up and carry a puppy. It should never be lifted by the front and a carried puppy's weight should be evenly distributed. The best way to do this is brace the puppy before the front legs with one hand and behind the rear ones with the other. An adult then transfers the puppy to the length of his forearm with the puppy's chest resting on the palm of his hand as the three middle fingers are placed between the puppy's front legs to steady him.

The rear of the puppy is resting on the hip and held close to the body by the elbow. Children should be handed the puppy and instructed to carry it by using both arms, or let them sit on the floor with the puppy where it will not stand a chance of being dropped.

DIARRHEA

Diarrhea is often a serious result of something wrong with a puppy and the cause should be discovered as soon as possible. If only one or two of the puppies have diarrhea for a short while, it probably just indicates over-eating, but notice if the same ones seem to have it while the others do not. Also at times there will be one puppy that seems small and rather thin. This one should be fed separately to make sure that he gets his share of the food.

WORMS

The time to check up on the health of puppies is when their stomachs are relatively empty before feeding in the morning. If their stomachs stick out, the chances are they have round worms, as most puppies do. There is a non-toxic powder that can be mixed with their food as soon as they are eating well; it requires no fasting, and the puppies like it. This is called Piperazine and dosage is regulated by the weight of the puppies, which at this stage are eating out of the same dish. Some breeders prefer to administer Piperazine tablets, as in this way a puppy will still get its medicine even if it does not eat a full meal. If you see worms the next day in

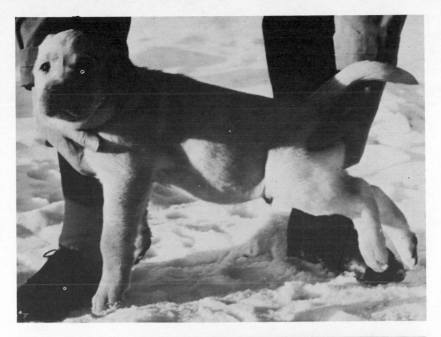

Young puppy should be picked up by placing hands before the front legs and behind the rear ones.

He should be carried braced on person's hip and held with fingers encircling front paws and chest so he does not suddenly wriggle free and fall.

the feces, you can be sure the puppies had too many and should be wormed again in perhaps ten days. If you see no worms at all, this does not mean there were none, only that they were dissolved by the medicine. Always remember that medicines are made for definite types of worms, and many of them are strongly poisonous. It is important to watch the feces of puppies (and older dogs) as an indication of their health.

SHOTS

All puppies should be immunized against distemper, hepatitis, and leptospirosis before going to their new homes. So should the one you plan to keep yourself. There are various ways of doing this. The most recent was discovered at Cornell Virus Research Laboratory and is an administration of a human measles vaccine (people are not affected by it). When measles vaccine is given to puppies as young as two weeks, they will develop immunity to distemper. Puppies that have received their dam's first thick yellowish milk (colostrum) are protected against most infections as well as immunized against distemper. The length of time the dam's immunity protects her puppies varies with the amount of immunity the dam herself has. There is a test that gives the amount of immunity each dam possesses and is able to pass on to her puppies for them to develop their own immunity. The majority of puppies have lost their dam's immunity by eight weeks of age and at this time should have a shot of modified live virus, which immunizes against distemper, hepatitis, and two forms of leptospirosis. To be on the safe side, repeat the shot of modified live virus at sixteen weeks of age in case of the bitch having a stronger than average immunity. Another system that has been used for many years in immunizing puppies involves giving three shots, not of the modified live virus. This type is usually started when a puppy is fairly young and continued after it has gone to its new home. The measles vaccine is the only type of protection wherein the dam's immunity does not interfere with developing that of the puppies. The measles vaccine is expensive and generally has to be ordered in advance as many veterinarians do not keep it on hand. It is wonderful for use if there is any chance of puppies having been exposed to distemper. With other types of vaccines, puppies MUST be susceptible to distemper in order to develop their own immunity.

This means that it is important that a puppy does not leave the kennel until at least three days after inoculation, and it is also important that the inoculation be given at the correct time. For the benefit of the future health of puppies leaving the kennel, the breeder should write down what inoculations have been given, with dates and trade name of type, as well as the serial number and expiration date noted on the bottle. The date of the next inoculation (booster shot at sixteen weeks) and a reminder that this booster should be given at least once a year throughout the dog's life should be recorded. This information, as well as worming record and type of medicine given, should go with each puppy for the use of the new owner's veterinarian. Since puppies must be susceptible to distemper if the inoculation is to be effective, it is advisable to have the veterinarian come to your house to give the shots or ask him to do it in your car rather than to take the puppies to his office. Another thing to be careful about is getting the puppies mixed up so that one gets two shots and another none at all. Especially with a litter that is all of one color, a method should be devised to prevent confusing the treated and untreated. Transporting the puppies in an egg-crate (of the type divided to hold fifteen dozen eggs in each half) solves this problem handily as pups can be moved from one end to the other as they are inoculated.

TATTOO

It is becoming customary to tattoo puppies and dogs for permanent identification. In some communities, the SPCA will do it, and perhaps more veterinarians will begin doing this as a convenience for their customers. Have your puppies tattooed if possible, as we will probably always have with us unethical persons who will steal dogs and falsify papers.

REGISTRATION

Everything to do with the American Kennel Club takes time, so the registration blank for registering your litter should have been sent off to the AKC a few days after the puppies are whelped; the individual registration application will then be back from the AKC and ready to give to each owner of a puppy when it is delivered. There is a registration application (blue slip) for each puppy, and it is against the AKC rules to give one of these slips out without its being filled in with the name, address, and other data concerning each new owner of a puppy. In this country, it is just about impossible to sell a dog without a registration certificate. Unless a puppy has been paid for in full, you should, as your protection, keep the blue slip until full payment is made. The AKC *Dog Ownership and Breeding Record* is an excellent record book and every breeder should have one. It is surprising the number of persons who lose their registration papers and write back to the breeder for another, which the breeder does not of course have. A breeder should keep the records of all transactions, as well as registered names and numbers of all puppies, as it is just about impossible for the AKC to trace names without the correct numbers.

NAMES

In naming a puppy, try to find a dignified one that does not sound silly, suitable only for a mongrel, or not typical of a Labrador. Personally, I like to name my puppies giving an indication of which sire I used for that litter. Others might like the sound of certain names already in the pedigree of the puppy. However, do not take a kennel name (prefix or affix) even if it is a foreign one. As a pet name, anything may be used.

CLAP AND COME

Teaching a litter of puppies as a group to come when you clap your hands works well, and even children of a new owner can clap their hands and their puppy will come running. When group training is over, with most or all the puppies having gone to their new homes, you can concentrate on the one you will keep to be your next brood bitch.

Part of raising a litter of Labrador puppies is making an effort to give the puppies the typical Labrador temperament. By four weeks of age each puppy should be picked up, cuddled, and talked to quietly for a few minutes each day. A low pitched very quiet calm normal voice should always be used. This makes the Labrador more attentive. It also makes a sharp command more effective. As the puppies become active, a board or fence of some sort is put across their doorway so that they cannot rush out when the door is opened and you can step over it when leaving the pen.

HISTORY OF LITTER OF JONTY AND CHARM

Charm (yellow) in heat August 12.

5th day shipped by air freight to Washington.

12th day bred to Jonty (black).

Puppies due 9 weeks, October 25.

October 25 Charm would not eat her supper.

October 27 at 7.30 AM first puppy arrived.

9.30 AM last puppy arrived. 3 black dogs, 1 yellow dog, 2 yellow bitches (two puppies a bit small).

7 days weighed $1\frac{3}{4}$ pounds.

14 days weighed $2\frac{1}{2}$ to $2\frac{3}{4}$ pounds.

13 days cut nails on front feet.

13 days started opening their eyes; noses turning black.

15 days started walking.

18 days started to play.

18 days started eating Pablum and horse meat, milk after eating.

21 days weighed 3 to 4 pounds.

21 days cut nails on front feet.

23 days fed them outside of their box.

26 days Charm not with them except after the noon meal and at night.

27 days started on Ken-L-Biscuit (small size) and horse meat.

28 days turned whelping box upside down for Charm; puppies on blanket out of draft on the floor; newspapers all over the floor.

28 days weighed $4\frac{1}{2}$ to $5\frac{1}{2}$ pounds.

28 days wormed with Piperazine for round worms.

30 days moved from whelping room to the big kennel.

31 days Charm in the next pen except at night when she is with her puppies.

32 days Charm only with puppies at night.

35 days weighed 6–$6\frac{1}{2}$ pounds.

35 days on full-size Ken-L-Biscuit and raw hamburger four times daily.

37 days eating well (two puppies to a dish) (drinking water from a pail), to each puppy four times daily, $\frac{1}{2}$ cup of kibbles soaked five minutes in very hot water plus 1 tablespoon of hamburger.

42 days weighed $7\frac{1}{2}$ to 8 pounds.

45 days drinking milk after each meal.

45 days Charm nurses puppies only every other night, at 9 P.M.

At eight weeks, RUPERT OLIVIA by Jonty of Keithray ex Rupert Charm.

47 days reduced feedings to three daily, with milk substituted for
9 P.M. meal.

47 days Charm nursed puppies, 48 hours since last nursing.

48 days weighed $9\frac{1}{2}$ to 10 pounds.

49 days Charm out two days and nights.

51 days puppies out (10 minutes) for a short run in the snow, freezing
temperature but sun was out.

53 days dosed with Piperazine for roundworms.

55 days weighed 10 to $11\frac{1}{2}$ pounds.

58 days inoculated with modified live virus.

9 weeks of age weighed 12 pounds.

Three days later all puppies went to new homes except one yellow
bitch to be kept and one black dog not yet sold.

Eating $\frac{3}{4}$ cup of kibbles 3 times daily plus 3 tablespoons of raw
hamburger to each puppy and milk at 9 P.M.

16 weeks weighed 31 pounds; booster of modified live virus given
for distemper, hepatitis, and two forms of leptospirosis.

MORE ON FEEDING

I do not believe that weak Labrador puppies should be saved; however, there is a difference between a weak one and the so-called "runt." The small pup in a litter is very likely produced because one or both of the parents carry genes for inheritance of smallness. This small one may turn out to be the best of the lot for a breeder who may be hoping to reduce the over-all size in his line of Labradors. A small one among others of average size may possibly indicate a temporary set-back of some sort and he will eventually catch up with his litter-mates. However, it may be well in the process of weaning to feed it separately as there is a chance that a small puppy is not getting its share of food. At any rate, the runt should be observed to make certain that smallness does not result from a physical cause.

There is a difference of opinion as to the number of puppies a bitch should be allowed to raise. My personal opinion is that this decision depends on the willingness and ability of the owner to understand and help out with the problem. A bitch has ten teats and if there are more than ten puppies they cannot all nurse at the same time and some may not get enough milk. The first milk (colostrum) of the dam is the most important factor in the health of the puppies because it is through antibodies in the colostrum that the puppies are protected against most infections. Thus it is very important to make sure that each puppy nurses its dam during its first days. Then starts the marathon of medicine-dropper feeding by taking the spare puppies and feeding them by hand. At the same time it should be remembered that there is great strain on the bitch and that she needs plenty of the right kind of food and liquid. Her regular diet could be left with her continually under these circumstances and as soon as one dish is finished, leave another. As soon as the puppies begin partaking of other foods, the bitch's intake should be returned to normal. The sooner puppies start eating solid food, the better, and they can often be started on such fare as soon as they can stand up, possibly at fourteen days of age.

Puppies should receive some nourishment within three hours of the time they are whelped; and, since bitch's milk is very different from cow's milk, a special formula should be given them if the dam does not have enough or the puppies are orphaned. There are canned formulas produced by the big milk companies especially for puppies. (The best bet is to use evaporated canned milk, five parts to one of boiling water, if such a formula is not at hand.) You may add one teaspoonful of dicalcium phosphate (obtainable at drug stores) to each quart of the formula. This formula supplies 30 calories per ounce, and for the first week a puppy should have 60 to 70 calories per pound of body weight each day. Feedings need be only three times a day if the correct amount of a proper formula is taken. Do not feed it immediately after mixing as it will probably be too hot. Each week the daily intake should be increased about 10 calories per pound of body weight. In hand feeding, it is a good idea to underfeed slightly in the beginning until you are quite sure the puppy's digestive system is adjusted to the formula, then increase to the regular schedule—

1st week: 60–70 calories per pound of body weight per day,
2nd week: 80–90 calories per pound of body weight per day,
4th week: 90 plus calories per pound of body weight per day.

If your newly whelped puppy weighs 10 ounces, 40 calories would be needed daily during the first week. Feedings should be made using a measuring cup marked off in ounces to assure that each puppy gets 1.5 ounces of formula (30 calories per ounce of formula) each day. With a formula such as this, the amount given can be divided into three feedings a day, each of 0.5 ounces fed at eight hours interval.

Dipping a small piece of rubber about the size of a nipple in the formula and drawing this back and forward over the tongue will stimulate a puppy's sucking reaction. When the puppy shows signs of attempting to suck, change to a formula-filled medicine dropper, the bulb of which has been pierced several times with a large, hot needle. (The milk or formula should be warmed to blood temperature, about 100 degrees.) Hold your finger over the tip of the glass end and hope that the puppy starts sucking. If this does not work, place the liquid drop by drop on the back of the tongue. If all else fails, try dipping a paint brush in the formula and feeding with it by spreading formula on the tongue gradually. If the puppy develops diarrhea, reduce the amount fed and then gradually increase it as the condition improves. Keep the formula refrigerated and do not prepare more than is needed for forty-eight hours. Remember in feeding to keep the dropper and eventually the bottled tipped up so that the puppy is not sucking air.

As soon as the puppies are eating from a pan, at least by two and a half weeks of age, they can be fed as any normal puppy using the formula until five weeks of age when it can be replaced with the evaporated milk reduced to a mixture of half water in place of the stronger mixture that has been used up to this time. All changes both in feeding and timing should be made gradually.

During the first five to seven days, defecation and urination of puppies must be stimulated after each feeding; if their dam does not do this, it is up to whoever is taking care of the puppies. This can be accomplished by stroking the anal region with absorbent cotton or a piece of flannel dipped in warm water. Watch the puppies' daily habits and stimulate only as necessary. Small puppies should be sleeping when not eating and should not be handled except by the person or persons responsible for their care.

The temperature of the room for the puppies for the first five days should be between 85 and 90 degrees and everything possible done to prevent chilling as this is usually fatal to a newborn puppy. If puppies are with their dam or there are several together, they are kept warm by contact with each other and the room can be a normal temperature after the puppies are dried off. Otherwise this higher temperature is needed but can be reduced gradually to normal room temperature as the puppies start moving about, which with Labradors normally comes at about the 17th to 21st day.

Sometimes a young bitch with her first litter of puppies will not have enough milk to feed a large litter and supplementing with a formula helps. Usually this bitch will increase her milk production if fed properly so there is no more need to help her. However, remember that very little milk is needed at first for an average (seven Labrador puppies is average) or below average number of puppies.

TRAINING PUPPIES

It is fascinating to observe how a bitch protects, disciplines, and instructs her puppies when they are left with their dam beyond the infant stage. Introduction to water is one of the most interesting. I was fascinated in watching Flax as she took her puppies into shallow water, placing herself between them and deep water until she knew that they were ready to swim. She then led them and they followed her without fear of this new experience. They went in again and again and obviously enjoyed their swimming. The next step was leading them into an area with a gentle current, but Flax realized that the puppies were not strong enough for fast waters and protected them from going into the "white" water.

We can learn a great deal by observing bitches like Flax. Persons who acquire a nine-week-old puppy fresh from its nest must first of all develop mutual love, understanding, and trust before any training is attempted. Without this basis, very little if anything can be accomplished in a puppy's education. It is easy to love a Labrador puppy, but love is not enough if it is to mature as an ideal Labrador, whether a pet, hunting companion, or show prospect. Labradors are bred for intelligence but if they are allowed to develop physically without mental training in the form of definite "do" and "don't" restraints and directions, they will not adjust to the world as it is and no amount of future obedience training by professionals will be able to solve the problems that arise.

First of all it should be understood that timing and patience are prerequisites for handling a puppy; an animal acts by instinct, and the trainer must think and observe and never go ahead of the puppy's physical and mental capabilities. Exercising a puppy to exhaustion or requiring it to sit over-long on command is too much for a young one. The young of any species cannot accept complete discipline, and accepting any must be taught gradually by giving praise for accomplishment no matter how minor the action performed through a desire to please. The rewards for achievement are words of praise, bits of food, and manifestations of love expressed in petting. Most important is that the puppy be made via your responses to understand what is desired and to learn that compliance is rewarding.

START AT NINE WEEKS

Puppies removed from their dam and litter-mates at nine weeks of age are physically ready to go to new homes, and at this age are ready to adapt to new surroundings if members of their next family understand certain basic requirements of all young things and of puppies in particular. The bitch has already started their education by allowing them to eat and not be dependent on her for nourishment; she has settled disputes among them as they arose, and taught them the elements of self defense, and instilled some

RUPERT SEASHELL 1969 at three months of age. By Ch. Nokeener Pinchbeck Seafarer ex Rupert Piccadilly Dame. Bred by William and Jean Bischoff. Owned by Mrs. James Getz.

discipline in her way of telling them NO or "out of bounds."

Anyone having a well-bred Labrador should understand that the puppy will do what is expected of him if the human being is capable of making him understand. The problem is not with the puppy but with the human being, whose first approach should be to develop mutual affection. However, we must take care that whatever we want to teach our Labrador is not beyond its capacity to learn. There is a temptation to show off an intelligent Labrador, and sometimes to go a step beyond what the animal is capable of understanding.

It is the duty of the breeder of a litter to set the stage for the future of each puppy in the group. Among other things, this involves bringing out the correct, loving Labrador personality. Through talking quietly while cuddling a puppy, training can be started at a very early age. Always remember that a Labrador puppy is a special kind of puppy (no baby talk, please) and it thrives on trying to understand everything going on. It is unhappy when separated from persons of the family but can gradually be made to understand that there are times for being quietly alone.

COME! STAY! AND OTHER COMMANDS

With a litter, certain types of training, such as coming when called, can be accomplished, as is most training with Labradors, through food. Have a definite phrase to use when calling the puppies. The tone should be gentle and convey a hint of excitement, never sound as if scolding or demanding. The greatest mistake a person can make is to call a puppy or dog and scold or chastise it when it responds. This is a certain way to teaching a dog NOT to come. Calling the puppies to come and eat, in spite of the fact that they are right at your feet, is the quickest way for them to learn to come, but the important objective is always to make coming attractive to them. It is well to have a definite phrase or word that is used every time, as they will become confused with a continual change of words. When whistling, it is well to use a group of three sounds as such a signal is used for the "Come Back" call in field trials, whereas a single blast means to sit and look back. A single puppy will learn his name quickly when it is used in calling as his pan of food is set down in front of him. After a group of puppies have learned to respond to voice or whistle, they can be taught to come running when you clap your hands. This accustoms the pups to sounds of percussion (of value if later to be used in hunting), and as the puppies are taken to new homes, anyone can clap hands and the puppy will come. The only trouble with this is that children will often be delighted and clap their hands all the time to the utter confusion of the puppy. This early and pleasant introduction to percussion effects can later be advanced by banging on the food dish and making other noises while a puppy is eating.

As soon as the puppies are old enough to want to play and have learned to defecate in one area of their yard or kennel, clean tin cans can be given them to play with. Observe which puppy investigates this strange object first, and which one picks it up before the others; this is your extrovert and probably your best prospect for future hunting and retrieving. Before giving them anything to play with, make sure that the whole area is as clean as possible. Take away cans as they get dirty and substitute fresh ones.

A Labrador should have self-confidence and a calm temperament, which can be developed or destroyed through upbringing. Self-confidence is not shown by dashing into everything and getting into trouble. A stable but self-confident personality looks over a new situation before going into action. Self-control instruction should be an early lesson for a Labrador puppy, but always remember that you are dealing with a young thing and that you should not expect perfection until later. A show dog should not be made to sit, but control can be taught in such other ways as not being allowed to eat until given permission even though the dish has been placed before him. Teaching a puppy that is moving away from you to turn and come back can be fun if plenty of praise and a biscuit is found on the return to you. OUT or BACK is a good word to direct leaving, with STAY used when desired distance has been covered. Since all Labradors get to be a nuisance with their continual demand for being petted, such a command as ENOUGH! might be used. Like children, Labradors know when company is present and they try to get away with things that at other times they may not attempt. Don't spoil your pet any more than you would a child under the same circumstances.

RUPERT DUSTY AND RUPERT DESDEMONA 1947 as puppies. By Dauntless of Deer Creek ex Lena. Bred by Dorothy Howe, Dusty owned by Frances Herrick, Desdemona owned by Mrs. Johnson Smith.

Many things can be taught by signal after a dog has learned to follow sound directions. Remember that a Labrador is intelligent and thrives on the attention involved in repeating known things and learning new ones. House pets can be allowed to rush out the door or made to stay back and wait until told to go out. A Labrador sensitive to its owner can be taught to stay back and not go out the door until after looking back and receiving a nod or other signal which has been taught as permissive, but this is rather sophisticated training and depends a great deal on mutual understanding. An easier way to teach without words is the transfer of the word NO, learned early in a puppy's life, to pointing a finger to mean the same thing. This is very convenient when in the middle of a fascinating conversation which you do not want to interrupt by speaking to your dog. Dogs do not like to be pointed at any more than people do, and they quickly learn its meaning. Of course, all transferring from sound to visual training should in the beginning be switched back and forth until thoroughly understood. Subsequently, all this can be developed into hand signals for use around the house and later be transferred to field training with no trouble at all. For instance, the word OUT or BACK can be learned along with the overhead hand signals used later in the field, as can right and left signals and the word OVER.

To teach one dog to come out of the kennel and the rest to stay back is not difficult if you are consistent about it and understand a bit of dog psychology. A dog naturally wants to come out of the pen and be with you, and the training is done by rewarding all those that do NOT come out, using plenty of praise and bits of food. In this training, ONLY the name of the dog to come out should be spoken, and the gate should be held open only wide enough for one dog to come through. If another starts through, which happens in the beginning, shut the gate; you will be surprised to note how quickly the called dog will manage to get into position to come through while the rest stay back and wait for the food or the praise to be given in reward for remaining until called.

CAGED PRIVACY

A dog in the house, especially when there are children, should have a place which is "out of bounds" for everyone but him. A cage is good for this, as you can move it from place to place and take it with you in the car when you go on vacations. Labradors love these cages and, if fed in them, will consider them their home no matter where they are. These cages fold into a small space and are easy to carry. A cage is particularly useful in summer; all the windows in the car can be left open in hot weather or the cage can be placed in the shade if you wish to leave your dog somewhere temporarily. Training a dog to enter a cage is easily done by throwing a biscuit in first. However, feeding puppies individually in cages, starting at about ten weeks of age, makes them love their cages throughout life. In fact, they will run into their cages, turn about, and look up at you to let you know that it is time for feeding.

DON'T GRAB

One bad habit to avoid with a Labrador is allowing him to grab something in your hand. Owners should learn to hold a bit of food in their fingers and let the dog take it away without moving the hand. Many persons tend to pull the hand away just as the dog tries to take the food. This teaches the dog to grab, and frightens persons who think the dog is biting. Never let anyone pull anything out of the mouth of a Labrador. This is the surest way of making the future hunting dog become "hard mouthed." If the dog has something in his mouth you do not want him to have, put the fingers of one hand back of the big teeth at each side of the mouth and speak a command such as GIVE. A Labrador you intend to use as a retriever should never be trained to drop anything; teach that the object should always be placed in your hand. Also, to prevent forming bad habits, anything that is thrown should be required to be brought directly back to you and not allowed to be used for a plaything. A retriever must be taught to understand that whatever is thrown is to be brought to you and is never chewed or played with. Objects which are handed to a puppy are different, and the puppy can do as desired with such things.

POISE, PLEASE

Vision in puppies is slow in developing and it stands to reason that a person working around puppies should move slowly, and, on entering the presence of a dog, should speak to afford recognition. Somewhat later, the puppy will recognize the way you turn the door knob, or walk, but it is well also to speak. This tends to keep a Labrador calm and friendly. The same quiet approach is used when you intend to catch a puppy; it should never be suddenly grabbed. Call the puppy; if it does not come, trot away from him and he will follow. You can then catch him as he goes by, and praise him for following you.

HEAR ALL, SEE ALL

A dog's hearing and sense of smell are superior to ours and a Labrador can distinguish between the motor of your car and that of any other. He can be confused, however, when you step out of a strange car. A dog can identify something under four or five feet of snow. You will notice that your dog will want to sniff you when you come home; this is to see where you have been and whom you have been with. A Labrador should be taught, or rather encouraged, to trust his nose through finding what he is looking for. This can be done early in life and can be made a game in the house by playing hide-and-go-seek, with the use of hand signals later on when you assist in finding another person or a hidden object.

UPSTAIRS, DOWNSTAIRS

Self-confidence is developed as a puppy learns to investigate and to trust his senses in new experiences, which should be many and varied. Such experiences as climbing stairs, if not taught while a puppy is young, may always frustrate certain individuals. The best way to teach going up and down stairs is to sit just out of reach with food in your hand. If there is a platform part way up, so much the better; by placing the puppy there, it has to go either up or down, and after a bit of howling will try to come to you. Puppies think it much riskier to go down than up, and you may have to conduct separate courses of training. Traversing stairs, once learned, is never forgotten.

ANTIJUMP TACTICS

Try to teach a puppy while very young not to jump on people by anticipating when it is going to jump up and putting your knee out at the right instant to knock him off balance, and perhaps over backwards. Another action that often helps is putting both your hands in front of you with fingers spread wide, again anticipating

186

the jump. When puppies are grouped behind you as you are mixing their food, some will jump about; but, if you keep your feet moving while repeating NO, they soon learn that in jumping they will bump into your heels.

TIMING AND APTITUDE

Timing is an important factor in all training. There are rules according to books on the subject, but none of them take the place of observation and learning through understanding the nature of your own dog. What factors bring failure and success in training a Labrador are the most important things a person can learn in rearing a dog, and teaching is not difficult when successful factors are combined with patience. Not all persons are capable of training a dog, and the dog should not be blamed for failing to learn under an impatient or incompetent instructor.

REINFORCING OBEDIENCE

A Labrador rarely needs chastising. Tone of voice in a good verbal scolding is usually enough to communicate your displeasure. But when a dog does something that could be dangerous to itself or to a person, it must be taught in no uncertain terms never to do that again. A slap on the side of the muzzle along with the scolding should do it, if not used too often, or a rolled up piece of newspaper hitting your hand and making a noise could be effective. However, remember regarding a future hunting dog that this is a form of percussion and all such sounds should denote pleasant things to a retriever. Labradors have remarkable memories and, once anything is learned, they never forget. The contrast between sharp words such as NO or STOP THAT and the singing words of praise should be the principal way of training. It is the words of praise which are the most often left out in training; and as a result, the puppy does not understand when it has done right.

PUPPY EXERCISE

Up to the age of about six months, a puppy should not have too much exercise. In the process of fast growing typical of a Labrador puppy, bones and muscles should be given a chance to develop before being subjected to heavy strain. Puppies may be allowed to run around a bit, but not to the point of becoming exhausted.

Young puppies should not be taken on long walks for the same reason.

CARS

Staying quietly in a car can be a problem, and carsickness usually results on the first ride. Never feed a dog during a period of at least four hours before taking it anywhere by car; it is far better to let a puppy go hungry than for it to become carsick. Even a drink of water before a first ride should be avoided. If a puppy is carsick on a first ride, it may never want to ride again. Most Labradors like to go places, and the usual problem is keeping them out of any car with a door left open. The person who allows a dog to chase a car should not have one. An owner is not only responsible for the safety of the dog, but also regarding injury to those in an automobile trying to avoid a dog. Owners should anticipate that their dog will run after anything that moves, especially if it is the family car going away, so preventing that first dash is the only solution. Once the habit of chasing cars is formed, it is nearly impossible to correct.

LEASH AND COLLAR

A leash is a terrifying thing to a puppy and it must be introduced to the idea of restraint carefully. If there is only one dog in the family, let it first become accustomed to wearing a collar, but make sure that it is not so loose that it can catch on something and cause injury to the dog. If there is more than one dog in the house, the collar will be chewed off in no time. Since my dogs are never out of my sight and not allowed to run free unless I am with them, there is no need for a collar. The best way to start a puppy on a leash is to use a very light nylon lead. Pull the clasp end through the handle and you will have a collar and leash all in one piece and one that can be slipped over the head of the puppy. At first, be prepared to go everywhere the puppy goes. The idea here is that the puppy should not suddenly find itself jerked into control. You will get plenty of exercise and, if you have any breath left, keep talking to the puppy with a calm voice of reassurance. When you think it is no longer worried by the idea of a leash, give the leash a little tug as you call the puppy and walk away. It is best to walk past the puppy so that the jerk of the leash merely attracts attention

Get him used to a leash at eight weeks. Here's how to slip leather lead through handle for first leash training.

and is not mistaken as a dragging attempt. Step out; call and praise; you can make it fun for the pupil with plenty of patting and bits of food. The hardest part of leash training seems to be teaching the owner to keep the leash loose at all times. If the leash is not loose, the jerk of attention cannot be effective, and mere tugging will be resisted. Unless properly trained, the puppy, when larger, will drag the owner all over the place and be completely out of control. In fact, the dog will be in control of the person. When the puppy seems no longer afraid of the leash, a collar can be added for use with a long leash. There is a right and wrong way to put on a collar so that it loosens after that jerk for attention; and, if kept up behind the dog's ears, control is more effective than if it is allowed to fall lower down where it tends to choke the dog. The best collar, I think, is one that is double and loosens the quickest. The training is next turned to teaching the puppy to move at your left and not in front or in back of you. If the puppy tends to go in front, turn, give the jerk, and step out in the opposite direction. This should be done in a continuous operation without waiting for the puppy. If the puppy drags behind, try going faster and calling him, or you can turn and try to get him to catch up with you. Making the training exciting and fun is important when working with a young animal. If the puppy moves too far away from your side, go around in a circle and with little jerks bring him back into position. If he moves too close, go in a circle towards him bumping his nose with your knee as you go around. Proper leash training is based on the principle that you are protecting the dog from future dangers until such mutual confidence is established that you can trust him to stay

How to Make and Put on a Collar

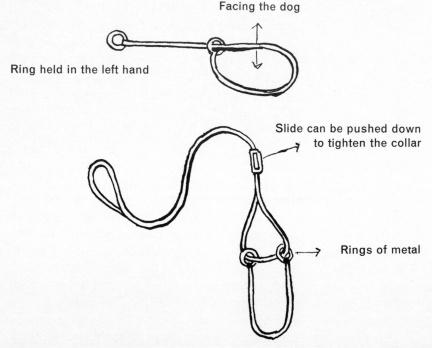

Facing the dog

Ring held in the left hand

Slide can be pushed down
to tighten the collar

Rings of metal

with you when the dog is older no matter what provocation, and includes staying in a designated place indefinitely on command. It is well to teach him to defecate while on a leash; there will probably be times when this will be necessary, and it is best to teach this as a first routine of the morning. The most important thing to remember in leash training is that it is not a test of strength, as the dog will always win. With a light leash continually kept loose and ready to give the slight snap for gaining attention, the puppy is soon taught what is expected of him. The way to teach a young dog not to drag you around is to have the long, light leash attached to a collar. Since the word NO is already understood, the game is to anticipate just before the puppy reaches the end of the leash as it rushes away and to utter a sharp NO as you give a jerk on the lead and turn away calling to follow. When he does so, praise him. The tendency in all leash training is for the trainer to slow down and wait for the puppy; whereas the system works better if you snap, turn and step right out, without giving the puppy time to rebel. Any time he becomes frightened, stop, pet him and go back to some part of the routine that is understood. Of course, all these training sessions should be very short, perhaps five minutes at a time at first. Continually changing pace keeps a puppy alert, and changing direction has the same effect. Once he has become used to the leash, take him out into the wide wide world of a city street with its confusion of automobiles and strange noises. At this point, take a pocketful of dog biscuits, giving them to persons you meet and asking each to give one to the puppy. This is not recommended if you intend later to teach your dog not to take food from strangers.

MEETING OF THE MINDS

Some persons have the knack of very quickly developing that perfect understanding between man and dog, and anyone who can do this need not be told how to train a puppy. My suggestions here are for those who do not have this natural instinct for establishing rapport with a dog. However, the sort of person who believes in forcing his will on a Labrador should not be allowed to have one, as a Labrador is bred for the give and take type of relationship. Once this has been established, fabulous things can be taught, and it is usually the human being that is at fault when things go wrong. A person should learn how to communicate with a puppy through

GRAEME OF GARSHANGAN 1963 at ten months of age. By Coulter-craigs Simon ex Ch. Gussie of Garshangan. Bred by Lt. Col. and Mrs. Hill.

becoming constantly alert and trying to understand the reason for various reactions in the puppy. Such a person understands that puppies, like all young things, have to go through various stages of development and that some habits (such as chewing on things) can be very annoying. One of the reasons for such destructive actions is that he may be changing to adult teeth. But a Labrador dislikes being left alone and usually reacts to being separated from persons by barking, scratching on doors, and chewing. This chewing can be controlled to a certain extent by catching him in the act, giving him a definite NO, and substituting a nylon bone for the article being chewed. However, beware of giving dogs balls or whistle toys that are small enough to swallow.

HOUSEBREAKING

Housebreaking a Labrador puppy should be easy as they are instinctively clean and are bred to please people. Some persons can take a nine-week-old puppy home from a kennel and see that it never makes a mistake but others seem to have trouble with the problem of housebreaking. I think it a mistake to allow a dog to scratch the door or bark to be let in or out. The best procedure is to be alert and let the dog indicate to you that it would like to go out into the yard. Of course if he is loose you will be with him and can let him in again when he is finished. A person should understand the needs of a dog, such as going out after eating, the first thing in the morning, and the last thing at night. Of course a puppy will need to go out in the morning, and the last thing at night, and rather often during the day. If you are observant, you will find that your dog soon gets on a regular schedule for going out and you should try to conform to it. If kept in a cage at night, a puppy will not mess unless absolutely necessary and will become housebroken very quickly. It takes patience and willingness to stay with your puppy almost continually at first, but this will be worth it in the end. The idea is to prevent that first mistake and then he will quickly catch on to the idea of going outside to "do his chores." A dog usually has definite mannerisms and once you have learned them, the battle is won. You must adjust to a puppy, but an older dog should learn to adjust to your routine and not make you get up early in the morning when you would rather sleep. A puppy will usually pick one outside spot for use as a toilet and it is well to help in choosing the spot by taking him there and waiting a seemingly endless time for accomplishment of mission. If you must leave a young puppy in the house before it is housebroken, confine him to a small area and the chances are that the newspapers you have put down will be used as a result of early paper training.

In all training, it is well to remember that repetition is important and also to consider the puppy's ability to learn and to avoid progressing too fast.

KENNEL SHYNESS

The problem of kennel shyness comes up when a single puppy is left in a kennel to grow up by itself without human contacts except for feeding. Such a puppy becomes so used to living behind wire that it knows nothing of the outside world. It will whine or bark from loneliness even when kenneled in the same area with other Labradors and should learn to be by itself gradually. It is easy to put this one in with an older puppy so they can play together. In such circumstances, however, it will learn to get along with other dogs but not with human beings.

The mental development of a puppy should be continually developing. When a dog is left in a kennel it is forced to depend on other dogs and picks up what it can of good and bad habits from them instead of learning about life from human contacts. Being neglected by the human being soon starts leaving its mark on such a puppy and the effects may well prove permanent.

Suddenly at six months of age just when you think you have the most beautiful puppy in the world, you enter him in a show only to discover he is afraid of people. This in spite of the fact that you have taken him out for many runs with the other dogs and he seemed adjusted to everything around home. When taken to new surroundings, he runs behind you and is timid among strangers and in new situations. This phase seems to have come on suddenly but has in reality been developing slowly without your realizing what has been happening. Instead of expanding his knowledge through human companionship at a crucial time in his life, he has picked up bits from other dogs and in reality remained relatively static all this time. In order for a puppy to develop normally, it must learn to love and trust people and share in their lives. The ideal Labrador temperament grows steadily by way of association with people. There is more to raising puppies than seeing that they have the correct food.

Puppies, particularly those raised in the country, should become accustomed to different noises. A radio could supply some of this but if left on continually day and night it is not as effective as leaving it turned off for a day or so. All Labradors appreciate being spoken to even if you are just passing through a kennel, and this should be in a relatively quiet tone of voice reserving a harsh or sharp pitch for the scolding they sometimes need.

Puppies should want to ride with you wherever you go, but take care that they do not become carsick by being taken in the car too soon after eating. Walking a puppy around town is a good way for him to learn about traffic and strangers. In winter, when the ground is hard, perhaps he could be turned loose in some enclosed area to run around and investigate his surroundings. In fact, the more places he can be taken, the better off he will be. There is a barrier

CH. RUPERT DAHOMEY 1947 By Dauntless of Deer Creek ex Lena. Bred, owned and handled by Dorothy Howe.

that can be purchased to confine dogs to the rear of a station wagon and prevent them from jumping into the front seat. Since the floor of a station wagon is slippery, it should be covered with an old rug or heavy canvas so the dog will not slide about.

At the kennel, it is a good idea to have a yard going out from the runs. This not only makes the safe double-door arrangement which prevents the dogs getting out by mistake when a door is left un-latched, but makes a good exercise area also. Any time that you are in a hurry or when the weather is bad, some dogs can stay outside

195

the fence and others inside, in this way they chase each other up and down the fence while you stand and watch. This area could also be used to advantage by having various obstacles the dogs will have to go through, over, and under when called in for their dinner. These should be changed from time to time to other varieties.

Early lessons in retrieving light-weight objects that are not too hard make for interest; but, if you plan to use your Labrador for hunting, there are right and wrong ways of teaching to retrieve. For instance, a puppy will often want to play with the object thrown for retrieving and not want to bring it directly back to you. This can be a very bad habit and one way to control it is to run away from the puppy; when he chases after you, you can catch him on the way and get him to give you the dummy. Maybe I break all the rules, but in the beginning, I sometimes take the dummy and give the puppy a biscuit instead. Be careful in such teaching that the dummy is given to you and not dropped on the ground.

In a kennel it is a good idea to keep moving the dogs about so they do not become used to only one area. The same is true in keeping dogs together. They should become accustomed to being with various members of the group, and exercising the whole group is a good experience for them and good training in controlling them for the owner. It sometimes works to put a dog that has become kennel shy with one that loves people and wiggles all over with joy when a person comes near. The shy one may get the idea and want to be patted and loved too. Neglect can easily cause kennel shyness as the temperament of a Labrador is such that human companionship is a real need.

16. HOW TO READ A PEDIGREE

IN GENERAL

One of the most confusing things the novice runs into is a pedigree. The serious beginner realizes that this list of names is more than a status symbol and even the pet owner now knows that "the pedigree a mile long" no longer means anything and neither does adding up the number of Champions named on it.

The beginner does not even know how to find the males and females in the pedigree. Here the upper line indicates the male with the sire at the left of the sheet and the dam also on the left but below with her pedigree. The further to the right the names extend the farther back in generations behind the Labrador in question. Champion is abbreviated to Ch. and Field Trial Champion to F.T.Ch. with Amateur Field Trial Champion and Dual Champion (meaning that a Labrador is both a show and field trial champion).

A name that is repeated as a prefix or suffix in a pedigree usually means that the Labrador comes from a kennel of that name. A kennel name is supposed to designate a dog produced by a breeder who owns that name, but the idea has been misused and we find dogs imported from England into this country with the addition of an American prefix. In England, owners have been allowed to add their own kennel name to a registered dog but our AKC states that once a dog is registered the name can never be changed. The British are now in the process of accepting that "a person may not register a dog with his or her prefix unless they have bred it or unless the sire or dam holds the said prefix."

The novice interested in breeding typical Labradors should start immediately becoming familiar with the names of important Labradors through the history of the breed. In this way he not only learns of famous dogs but arrives at some understanding of how our present day Labradors were developed by former breeders. Where we find close relatives bred together they should be remembered, and in line breeding, the name that is repeated becomes

CH. REANACRE MALLARDHURN THUNDER 1960 AB By Sandylands Tweed of Blaircourt AS ex Mallardhurn Pat. Bred by D. N. Robinson, owned by Mrs. J. Johnson. CC Crufts.

important. When looking at photographs of different generations from a particular dog, the repetition of certain traits makes for a better understanding of that animal. Just looking at one generation gives no indication of his make-up. It is not enough to become familiar with individual names, but each name must represent definite visual characteristics and some knowledge of which of them they are able to pass on to future generations. The problem of how to go about making names in a pedigree become something with distinctive features is a frustrating experience at first. One way to learn is to search for common ancestors behind a line of Labradors with the problem in mind. This tends to develop interest and knowledge along the way. Take a Labrador that has ears that are too large and heavy and has been used extensively at stud or one who throws consistently beautiful tight, cat feet. Trace his pedigree back at least five generations, keeping in mind everything possible to do with his pedigree, in particular in regard to duplication of names on one side and a possible outcross on the other.

Note any close inbreeding such as a brother and sister. Look at the dog and at as many of his progeny and ancestors (through photographs if not in the flesh) as possible. Make notes on various qualities you find repeating themselves quite often. In this way you may be able to notice where the untypical ears and beautiful feet come from. When you come across an exceptionally good or bad offspring, trace the pedigree of the dam of this one as well as seeing as many of its brothers and sisters as possible. It will not be long before names in a pedigree, which at first were just groups of letters, will develop into personalities with certain traits and when the name appears in another pedigree it is like coming across an old friend and the progeny can almost be visualized in the mind before being seen.

Collecting photographs is an excellent way to check up on what you discover. However, remember that a photograph does not tell everything since it may have been taken when the Labrador was too young or out of coat. Also look at the angle at which the picture was taken as a good rear on a dog can look weak if the picture is taken from too far in front. Also a nose may look very long in a head portrait unless a telephoto lense is used. Again a young Labrador may look weedy but later develop into a typical

AMERICAN CH. KINLEY COMET 1953 AM By Ch. Kinley Matador ex Ch. Kinley Charm. Bred by Fred Wrigley, owned in USA by Harold Florsheim. This dog had great influence on the color in the USA. He sired CC winners at Crufts and BOB winners at Westminster, the Chicago International. (Pedigree 16).

specimen. A bitch in particular seems to improve after a litter of puppies. It is well to remember though that the genetic make-up of the dog and whether or not he is capable of passing on his traits cannot be told from a photograph. It is the combination of his pedigree plus what his progeny are like (the more offspring examined the better) that indicate the genetic make-up for certain traits you may like or dislike. This investigation may become complicated when it is discovered that the particular stud dog you are interested in has sired hundreds of puppies out of any bitch that came along with perhaps only a small proportion of these being superior and a very large percentage being extremely poor representatives of the breed. Here it might very possibly be the influence of an outstanding bitch that has made the difference between the quality of the progeny from this dog. At this point, trace the pedigree of the particular bitch which produced the good ones and look for common ancestors and in this way yet another name in a pedigree

CH. BRITISH JUSTICE 1948 AG By Banchory Jack ex Pont-Du-Fahs. Bred by A. C. Higgs, owned by Lorna, Countess Howe. Twice CC winner at Crufts. This dog with his brother Druidstone are found in many of today's pedigrees.

CH. POOLSTEAD POWDER PUFF 1964 AY By Ch. Reanacre Mallard-hurn Thunder AV ex Braeduke Julia of Poolstead AU. Bred and owned by Mr. and Mrs. R. V. Hepworth. CC Crufts.

becomes important. The same system can be used for tracing derivation of unwanted characteristics as well as for desirable ones.

When a famous stud dog has been bred to a bitch with a rather unkncwn pedigree, you ask yourself whether the progeny will show the influence of the sire or dam. In breeding your own bitch, would it be better to breed to a famous son or to his sire in order to stand a better chance of getting the desirable characteristics? If you cannot have everything at once, are you willing to sacrifice some working ability for a better looking Labrador or vice versa? Would you be happy with a Labrador of less typical appearance if he was an outstanding worker?

It should be understood that one pedigree is not enough. It is through comparison of one with another, also true of one Labrador with another, that any sort of results can be anticipated in future progeny. The true breeder judges the past and the future of the Labrador he sees before him. When it comes to compromising on faults as against good qualities in an individual and his pedigree, it should be done from knowledge and not guess work.

FOXHANGER MASCOT P.D. ex (police dog), T.D. ex, W.D. ex, U.D. ex, AQ 1957. By Copperhill Cheerful AP × Foxhanger Lass AQ. Bred, trained and owned by Lady Simpson. Won 33 awards at field trials and many awards at shows.

AMERICAN CH. STROKESTOWN TRAVELLER 1949 By Dual Ch. Staindrop Saighdear ex Ch. Strokestown Sulia. Bred by Major Pakenham-Mahon, owned in USA by Mrs. Austin. Shown at Labrador Specialty show.

A famous breeding line can go wrong through the mistaken choice of an individual dog within that line and here again pedigrees show the main line along the way that has survived mistakes of breeding. In the present we are too close to the important dogs and bitches to know which ones will outlive the tests of time through their progeny. History is made in the present but not understood until it becomes the past. With dogs, this is very unfortunate since they are so short-lived that most of the important ones are gone before they become great. Of course by "great" in this case is meant the ability to influence the breed as a whole in the direction of the ideal Labrador. Perhaps great bitches have been wasted because their owners through ignorance did not breed them, preferring a show career. Also the better the bitch the more important it becomes to search for the right stud dog to mate her to. The same could hold true but to a lesser degree with a dog, in this case being bred to inferior bitches and his potential not being realized until late in life. Of course with a stud dog, the owner must rather prove to the public that he is a great one either in the show ring or the field before breeders bother to investigate his pedigree and progeny since it is the owner of a bitch that chooses the dog to which she is to be mated.

MATCHING PEDIGREES

Matching pedigrees is as important and perhaps more important than matching the visual qualities of a dog and bitch. It should be remembered that the further back in a pedigree an important Labrador appears the less influence is felt in the present. However the power of the genes may increase as the individual's name appears repeatedly, especially when it appears on all four sides of the ancestry. By the same token, the more often an ancestor appears in a pedigree the more important it becomes that he be of exceedingly fine type both mentally and physically. It is well to remember that you are establishing a bitch line and through the use of a stud dog with one ancestor appearing several times in his pedigree the direction of your bitch line may change if he is a drastic outcross. For instance, if you have been linebreeding and consistently intensifying the breeding to a certain dog only to discover that your puppies are all developing unwanted characteristics in many litters, you decide it is time to change. It is not necessarily important that you change to another line; in fact, it might be a great mistake to start all over again if for a few generations your original line proved to be all right. What can be done is to find a stud dog with a pedigree strongly linebred (with possibly the name of the desirable dog appearing several times in five generations) in the same direction as your bitch line a few generations back. In other words, what you are telling yourself is that the puppies in the last few litters have gone wrong, whereas the one previously whelped had been all right. In circumstances herein you believe that your bitch line has been successful, care should be taken not to breed to a stud dog which is strongly linebred to animals not related to your line or you may loosen or weaken the line you have been working toward.

AKC SYSTEM

The American Kennel Club has a complete file of every registered dog back to the original ones imported into this country, and anyone can trace through their stud books all pedigrees with the exception of foreign ones where they publish only one generation indicated by a star in the stud books. Some people write up pedigrees for a price and in this case the number of the sire and dam of the dog in question should be given. On the registration paper from the AKC every dog has a number and after the number is printed an entry such as –10–70, indicating the pedigree will be found in the October issue of the stud book of 1970. Only within the last few years has it been possible for us to trace pedigrees through the British records, for which reason I started collecting their monthly Gazettes wherein all registered dogs are listed. Their system made it possible to trace pedigrees only of certain Labradors that qualified for entry in their annual stud book, which of course left out a great many dogs and in particular bitches. I was lucky enough to obtain back issues (to 1925, although not complete) through an old Scottish friend. From these I developed a system of listing litters in loose-leaf books by kennels and am now able to trace pedigrees through many generations, often all the way back to the original Labradors from Newfoundland.

Because British pedigrees are so difficult to trace, compared with ours, I have included some of those that will be found behind current American-bred Labradors. As far as possible I have tried not to duplicate so that stud dogs which appear as sires, such as Ch. Sandylands Tweed of Blaircourt. I have not given him a separate pedigree although he is prominent as a stud force in the breed. The same is true of bitches; I have left out a separate pedigree of Lena (my foundation bitch) as she is recorded as the dam of a famous litter. I have tried as far as possible to include

ENGLISH, CANADIAN, AMERICAN CH. SAM OF BLAIRCOURT 1957 AR By Hawk of Luscander ex Olivia of Blaircourt AP. Bred by Mr. and Mrs. Grant Cairns, owned in USA by Grace Lambert. This well known dog sired many champions in this country and beat the existing record with nine Bests In Show as well as winning the Labrador Specialty three times. In England, he was the sire of the bitch Sandylands Shadow. Pedigree 19.

pedigrees of bitches that have been outstanding producers through the history of the breed, as they have been slighted in favor of dogs. I have included few Labradors that are still alive for the reason that not enough generations have been produced to prove their value as breeding stock. Several generations bred to various stud dogs, not just one, are necessary to establish a reputation as a prepotent bitch or dog. Also, the more generations in a direct line from a particular source, the more chance there will be for future outstanding individuals to appear through thoughtful and understanding breeding. Consider for example, the line backward and forward through F.T.Champion Tar of Arden, the great

TIBSHELF SULTAN 1960 AW Chocolate dog sired by Tibshelf Achievement ex Tibshelf Excelsior. Bred and owned by Mr. Servern.(Pedigree 21.)

producing bitch that is behind practically all of our important American-bred show and field trial Labradors.

It should be realized that extensive campaigning of certain Labradors may give a false impression of their breeding worth since there is a tendency to believe that all Champions are of equal value in a breeding program. Therefore it is important not to be satisfied with just one pedigree, or seeing one Labrador, but to investigate as many as possible through many generations.

Probably the most famous line of bitches comes through the sisters Brocklehirst Nell and Kirkmahoe Dinah (possibly the third sister Kinmount Pax should be added). These bitches trace back to Birkhill Juliet (dam of F.T.Champion Peter of Faskally), and Juliet's sisters Souvenir and Stewardess also appear to have been prepotent. It would be hard to find a pedigree of an important Labrador in this country today that does not include at least one of these bitches. It is remarkable they were able to pass on so many of their great qualities to future generations. Unfortunately there are no records regarding the physical appearance of these bitches.

17. HOW TO USE A PEDIGREE

By looking at the pedigree of BUCCLEUCH SAILOR whelped in 1892, there can be seen the close breeding behind his sire and dam which was probably responsible for the strength of establishing this prepotent line of bitches that has come through so many generations of Labradors, yellows and chocolates as well as blacks.

With the famous line of Dual Champions through Shed of Arden in this country I have printed the pedigree of the fourth generation rather than that of Shed himself. I have done this also with Champion KINLEY COMET, having had such an influence on outstanding show dogs, in particular the yellows. In this case, I have given his pedigree in the record of one of his famous American-bred offspring.

Probably the most famous and prepotent stud dog of the past was Dual Champion BANCHORY BOLO; when this dog was bred to either of the litter sisters BROCKLEHIRST NELL or KIRKMAHOE DINAH, the progeny had tremendous influence for good in the breed. Bolo's pedigree goes back to the original Labradors through his sire, but his dam's ancestry does not have much meaning. Here is obviously a case of the result of close breeding behind the sire of Bolo, dominating the genes that gives Bolo his place in the history of Labradors.

Working strains in this country have also come through these same lines with NATIONAL CHAMPION CORK OF OAKWOOD LANE going back to Bolo as well as AMATEUR NATIONAL and NATIONAL CHAMPION SUPER CHIEF doubling such lineal descent through DUAL CHAMPION GRANGEMEAD PRECOCIOUS and F.T. CHAMPION TAR OF ARDEN. An outstanding Champion and in 1968 the first yellow to beat the all-time record with twelve Bests in Show wins is CHAMPION SHAMROCK ACRES LIGHT BRIGADE going back through Whygin and Rupert breeding again to the same lines as have all Labradors beating the records.

DUAL CH. BRAMSHAW BOB AND DUAL CH. BANCHORY PAINTER
1936. Painting owned by Mrs. Robert Clark Jr.; painted by Ward Binks.

In England, the same line is behind that great stud dog CHAM-
PION SANDYLANDS TWEED OF BLAIRCOURT. This
present-day stud dog has been used so extensively and been such
a great producer that it is difficult to find in many countries an
outstanding show dog that does not include his name.

Through the history of the breed there have been other lines
developed from time to time, but through the generations this one
has endured and dominated the others. What impetus will be given
in the present or future towards the production of a larger than
normal percentage of excellent and uniform type Labradors has
yet to be demonstrated. This lies with the dedicated breeders who
take their work seriously and have the courage to survive and the
ability to learn from inevitable mistakes and continue to aim for
the ideal type of Labrador. Which particular dogs and bitches will
influence the future of the breed is thrilling to contemplate but
has yet to be proved. All true breeders should believe that success
is just around the corner and must never be satisfied with the
present.

18. THE LABRADOR STANDARD

INTRODUCTION TO STANDARDS

The purpose of setting a Standard for any animal is an attempt to set down in words a description of the visual appearance of an ideal animal, and especially what makes the particular breed different from any other. There is not, and never will be, a perfect Labrador. During development of the breed, persons in England who realized the importance of various characteristics, both mental and physical, set up a Standard for Labradors as guidance for future breeders and judges.

Those who wrote the original Standard probably had no particular Labrador on which to base criteria and described a composite Labrador, using what they considered the important and distinguishing features as their ideal of the breed. Luckily for our breed, very few changes have been made through the years in this Standard. When members of the Labrador Club in this country wrote our Standard of Perfection, they accepted the English version with the chief difference being to allow an inch more in height for both dogs and bitches.

It is difficult to visualize from the written word, and it is only through constant comparison of one Labrador with another that people are able to develop in their own minds a mental image of what a good-looking Labrador should be like. The fact that within the Standard for the breed, various written descriptions can be interpreted in different ways makes it possible for breeders and judges to prefer certain dogs to others. Without these differences there would be no dog shows and the life of a breeder would be very frustrating.

Since there has never been any question but that the Labrador was developed primarily as hunting dog (called shooting dog in Britain) this fact should be taken into consideration by both the show and field trial group as the physical features of a dog should denote the work it is bred for, and its mental characteristics should be equally important. The way a Labrador moves is in direct relationship to how it is put together. A dog intended for speed is made differently from one whose function is dependent on strength and endurance. Along with love and willingness to please his master, a Labrador should have courage, independence, and persistence that keep him hunting out cripples.

The demand was for a retriever in the early days of the development of the breed and speed was not considered as being important. Speed in general denotes a stream-lined build with light bone and a narrow, less wind-resistant body with a curve in the spine. Retrievers must have the endurance to work all day in all types of weather, on land or in the water, searching for and carrying in their mouths any and all game shot down. The Labrador was designed in particular for retrieving ducks and geese, which requires the development of a powerful body, with a strong neck and a tail that makes a good rudder. He must have a coat that prevents the cold from reaching his skin and a mentality that will induce him to stick to the job at hand until he finds the downed bird, whether dead or wounded and still mobile.

There are many intangibles that make up a Labrador and it is impossible to be specific about these and other qualities in a written Standard that is based on appearance. Through the history of the breed, all writers have agreed that very light eyes are not attractive and preference is for quite dark eyes. Lady Howe once described the color of eye she preferred as "burnt sugar." Such characteristics are immaterial to function. It has been proved in our breed that color has nothing to do with the ability of a Labrador to do his job.

The double coat of a Labrador is very important; without it, his short straight hair could not stand the cold water. He must also have various parts of his anatomy in correct correlation. For instance, there may be a good rear with a powerful thrust from the hocks; however, if his front is faulty and cannot take the pounding that results from this thrust, the dog is not capable of doing a day's work and will tend to tire and break down.

Balance is a subtle thing and difficult to describe. When we see a Labrador covering the ground with seemingly no effort, even the inexperienced person realizes how beautiful it is to watch and the

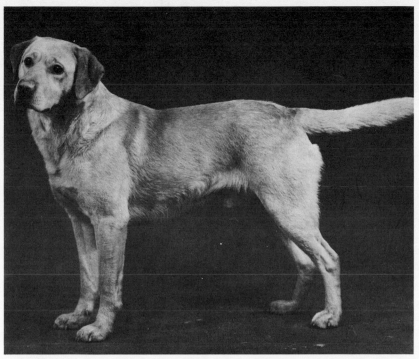

DUAL CH. KNAITH BANJO 1919 AE By Poppleton Golden Russet AE ex Knaith Brilliantine AD. Bred and owned by Mrs. A. Wormald. This pedigree shows chocolate breeding and other early breeding.

more experienced one understands that here is a dog in balance. What is meant is that all parts to the whole are in perfect relationship. It should be understood that the feet tend toward single tracking as an animal increases its speed. This is shown on the ground by footprints in a straight line, each behind another. The Labrador Standard designates that legs should be perpendicular to the ground, but it should be mentioned that this would obtain only when the dog is standing still or moving very slowly.

Breeders and judges should never lose sight of particular characteristics that differentiate one breed from another and a Labrador should look like a Labrador with no question of its being related to any other breed. A head with the forehead and nose seeming to continue in straight line with no indentation (stop) between the two is reverting to the Flatcoat breed and this often goes along also with lack of width of head and body in a mature Labrador.

Small eyes set close together can be seen in some Labradors and are as unattractive in a dog as in a person. When the lower lid is a bit loose, red shows below the eye (haw eye) and goes back to a Bloodhound. This is not a serious fault but does not belong on a Labrador. Another trait that cannot be designated in words is a feminine look in a bitch or dog. This is an asset in the one but a fault in the other.

In considering color, it should be understood that when the Standard specifies a body color, the designation includes variations in the shades of yellow and chocolate, even on the same dog, but does not include various color patterns belonging to other breeds. Spotting occurs in definite patterns in some dog breeds, as black-and-tan coloring is typical of the Gordon Setter, but such coloration patterns do not belong on Labradors.

Splay feet may be either of genetic origin or acquired. When a dog's nails have been allowed to grow too long, the feet go out of shape. There will always be enough leeway within the Standard for breeders and judges to have their own preferences on certain characteristics, such as dark- or light-colored yellow. All persons will never agree as to what makes the perfect Labrador, and no definite rules can be made for perfection. The Standard is presented in the hope of preventing the ugly and raising the quality of the mediocre while trying to keep a Labrador distinct from any other breed. At the same time, it should always be acknowledged that what is visual must be related to that which is functional.

Labrador coats vary among dogs at various times of year. It stands to reason that in cold climates the coats will be thicker than where it is warm or the dogs are kept in heated houses. One must judge whether a particular dog lacks a good double coat because he does not have the genes for it or because of the weather and time of year. A judge should realize that a double coat takes longer to grow in than a single short coat and that the tail on a Labrador is about the last to get its full amount of hair. A good "otter" tail tends to tip up at the end when not in full coat, and will have a decided bump, and often fringe beyond that bump, because it has not yet settled down to the bone. The future of such a tail can be determined by feel, starting at the body and running the hand down the tail. The more pronounced the bump, the better will be the future tail. The tail may even look as though it were broken;

CH. SPRINGFIELD MISS WILLING By Harris Tweed of Ide ex Ch. Kimvalley Cinderella. Bred and owned by Mrs. Robert Clark Jr. (Ped. 36.)

when the hair has grown out to a certain length, it seems to irritate the rear of the dog and the tail is held away from the body. That part beyond the bump will hang straight down and give the appearance of being broken at that point. The good "otter" tail usually has a good thick covering of hair, whereas the longer one often curls up at the end, sometimes even over the body. It seems to be easier to get a good tail on a yellow than on a black; and, other points being equal, the black with a good tail should be judged over the yellow in competition.

Noses on yellow Labradors turn pinkish in winter but will be black again in summer. Coats too change color on the yellows because the undercoat is what shows in summer and it is lighter in color. When the top coat comes through to its full length, the coat appears dark again. In the Standard there is mention of a "Dudley" nose, which practically nobody has seen on a Labrador. It is described as pink without pigmentation; since noses get such coloration in winter on the yellows, and it is not penalized, I cannot see the point of putting it in the Standard. There is no mention of this in the British Standard. Breeders and judges should observe general trends in Labradors whether it be towards narrower heads, too much "tuck up," or splay feet. When only a few individuals are seen with a fault, it may not be too important, but when it becomes rare to see the compact feet similar to those of a cat, it is time to do something about it. In fact much of breeding and judging might have more relationship to faults becoming too common in a breed than to an isolated fault.

What we hope for in a Labrador is not some flashy, high-strung dog but one with the type of self-confidence that takes the world in its stride and is so perfectly in proportion that it indicates strength and endurance and above all expresses intelligence and a love of people.

LABRADOR STANDARD

GENERAL APPEARANCE: The general appearance of the Labrador should be that of a strongly-built, short-coupled, very active dog. He should be fairly wide over the loins and strong and muscular in the hindquarters. The coat should be close, short, dense, and free from feather.

HEAD: The skull should be wide, providing ample brain-room; there should be a slight stop, with the brow slightly pronounced so that the skull is not absolutely in a straight line with the nose. The head should be clean-cut and free from fleshy cheeks. The jaws should be long and powerful and free from snipiness; the nose should be wide and the nostrils well-developed. Teeth should be strong and regular, with a level mouth. Ears should hang moderately close to the head, rather far back and set somewhat low and not be large and heavy. The eyes should be of a medium size expressing great intelligence and good temper and may be brown, yellow, or black, but brown or black is preferred.

NECK AND CHEST: The neck should be medium length, powerful and not throaty. The shoulders should be long and

214

sloping. The chest must be of good width and depth, the ribs well-sprung and the loins wide and strong, with stifles well-turned and the hindquarters well-developed and powerful.

LEGS AND FEET: The legs must be straight from the shoulder to the ground with the feet compact, toes well-arched, and pads well-developed; the hocks should be well-bent and the dog must neither be cowhocked nor too wide behind. He must stand and move conventionally. Legs should be of medium length, showing good bone and muscle, but not so short as to be out of balance with the rest of the body. In fact, a dog well-balanced in all points is preferable to one with outstanding good qualities and defects.

TAIL: The tail is a distinctive feature of the breed; it should be very thick toward the base, gradually tapering towards the tip, of medium length, should be free from any feathering, and should be clothed thickly all around with the Labrador's short, thick, dense coat, thus giving that peculiar "rounded" appearance which has been described as the "otter" tail. The tail may be carried gaily but should not curl over the back.

COAT: The coat is another very distinctive feature; it should be short, very dense and without wave, and should give a fairly hard feeling to the hand.

COLOR: The colors are black, yellow, or chocolate and are evaluated as follows:

(a) BLACKS: All black, with a small white spot on chest permissible. Eyes to be of medium size, expressing intelligence and good temper, preferably brown or hazel although black or yellow is permissible.

(b) YELLOWS: Yellows may vary in color from fox-red to light cream with variations in the shading of the coat on ears, the underparts of the dog or beneath the tail. A small white spot on chest is permissible. Eye coloring and expression should be the same as that of the blacks, with black or dark brown eye rims. The nose should also be black or dark brown, although fading to pink in winter weather is not serious. A "Dudley" nose (pink without pigmentation) should be penalized.

(c) CHOCOLATES: Shades ranging from light sedge to chocolate. A small white spot on chest is permissible. Eyes to be light brown to clear yellow. Nose and eye rim pigmentation dark brown or

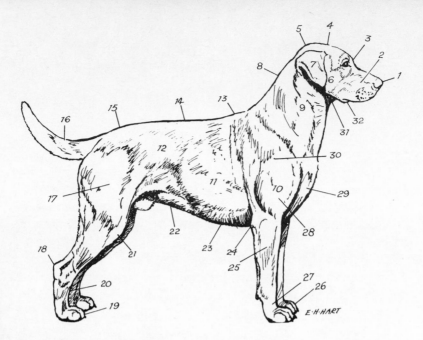

EXTERNAL ANATOMY OF THE LABRADOR

1. Nose. 2. Muzzle. 3. Stop. 4. Skull. 5. Occiput. 6. Cheek. 7. Ear. 8. Crest of Neck. 9. Neck. 10. Shoulder. 11. Ribs. 12. Loin. 13. Withers. 14. Back. 15. Croup. 16. Tail or stern. 17. Thigh. 18. Hock Joint. 19. Rear Feet. 20. Metatarsus. 21. Stifle. 22. Abdomen. 23. Chest. 24. Elbow. 25. Foreleg. 26. Front Feet. 27. Pastern. 28. Upper Arm. 29. Forechest. 30. Shoulder Blade. 31. Throat Latch. 32. Lip Corner.

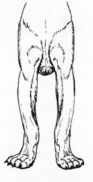

EXCELLENT LAB FRONT

FAULTY FRONT Too narrow. Toes out (east and west). Pinched in at elbows.

FAULTY FRONT Loaded in shoulders. Feet toe in. Too wide.

216

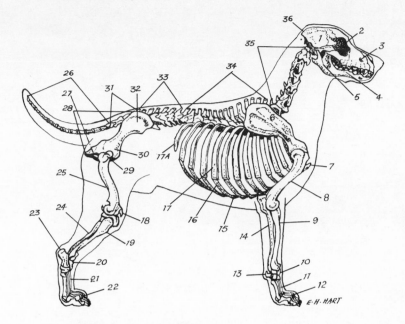

SKELETAL PARTS OF THE LABRADOR

1. Cranium (skull). 2. Orbital cavity. 3. Nasal bone. 4. Mandible (jaw bone). 5. Condyle. 6. Scapula (shoulder blade, including spine and acromion process of scapula). 7. Prosternum. 8. Humerus (upper arm). 9. Radius (front forearm bone—see Ulna). 10. Carpus (pastern joint. Comprising seven bones). 11. Metacarpus (pastern. Comprising five bones). 12. Phalanges (digits or toes). 13. Pisiform (accessory carpal bone). 14. Ulna. 15. Sternum. 16. Costal cartilage (lower, cartilaginous section of ribs). 17. Rib bones. 17a. Floating rib (not connected by costal cartilage to sternum). 18. Patella (knee joint). 19. Tibia (with fibula comprises shank bone). 20. Tarsus (comprising seven bones). 21. Metatarsus (comprising five bones). 22. Phalanges (toes or digits of hind foot). 23. Os calcis (point of hock). 24. Fibula. 25. Femur (thigh bone). 26. Coccygeal vertebra (bones of tail). 27. Pubis. 28. Pelvic bone entire (pubis, ilium, ischium). 29. Head of femur. 30. Ischium. 31. Sacral vertebra (comprising five fused vertebra). 32. Ilium. 33. Lumbar vertebra. 34. Thoracic vertebra (dorsal, with spinal process or withers). 36. Cervical vertebra (bones of the neck). 36. Occiput.

FAULTS OF

Too pronounced occiput. Not enough stop. Small, almond eye. Snipey muzzle. Ewe neck. Shoulders lack angulation. Lack of forechest. Weak (down) in pasterns. Thin, hare feet. Too long in legs. Lacking in bone. Lacking in depth of chest. Tuck-up too pronounced. Roach back.   Tail too long and thin. Lacking angulation in hindquarters. Too straight in stifle. Lacking strength throughout.

EXCELLENT HINDQUARTERS

POOR HINDQUARTERS

Cow-hocked.

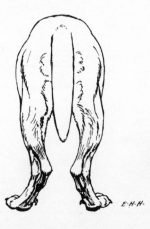

218

THE LABRADOR

Too pronounced stop. Head too thick and heavy. Ears too large and houndy. Muzzle too houndy and deep with loose lip flew. Neck too heavy and thick. Pronounced dewlap (throat latch). Body too long. Back weak. Overbuilt (over croup). Tail set on too low. Evident feathering on tail. Sickle hocked. Could have more elegance throughout.

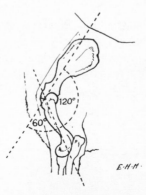

EXCELLENT SHOULDER

Showing desired 90 degree angulation in shoulder.

POOR SHOULDER

Angulation not sufficient and uneven. Dog lacks reach.

liver colored. "Fading" to pink in winter weather not serious. "Dudley" nose should be penalized.

MOVEMENT: Movement should be free and effortless. The forelegs should be strong, straight, and true, and be correctly placed. Watching a dog move towards one, there should be no sign of elbows being out in front, but neatly held to the body with legs not too close together, but moving straight forward without pacing or weaving. Upon viewing the dog from the rear, one should get the impression that the hind legs, which should be well-muscled and not cowhocked, move as nearly parallel as possible, with hocks doing their full share of work and flexing well, thus giving the appearance of power and strength.

APPROXIMATE HEIGHT AT SHOULDERS:

DOGS: $22\frac{1}{2}$ to $24\frac{1}{2}$ inches.

BITCHES: $21\frac{1}{2}$ to $23\frac{1}{2}$ inches.

WORKING CERTIFICATE: No member of the Club whose dog has won a bench championship shall use the title Ch. unless the dog has a working certificate from the club. To be eligible for a working certificate, a dog must satisfactorily complete under AKC rules both a land and a water series in the same trial. Requests for working certificates under this condition must be approved by an officiating judge or a club director. Or upon request and subject to approval, place, and convenience of the trial giving club, a dog not entered in a regular stake may be awarded a working certificate by any director of the Club or any AKC judge upon written certification to the Club secretary that the dog has met minimum Working Certificate requirements designed to prove that:

1. The dog is not gun shy.
2. The dog will retrieve a shot bird at approximately 50 yards on land.
3. The dog will retrieve two ducks from water, either as a double or in immediate succession, in order to prove willingness to re-enter.
4. Steadiness is not required, so a dog may be held on line.

At the Club's trials, dogs may be entered for the purpose of obtaining a working certificate and not in the regular stakes, and the fee for such test shall not be in excess of $5.00.

A working certificate will not be issued until the dog has won its bench championship.

19. SELLING

Some persons are salesmen by instinct. They need none of the advice given here. For others it should be remembered that the most important thing in selling is a satisfied customer. The right puppy sold to the right person at the right price builds the kind of reputation for a new breeder that makes it possible to sell future puppies to the right kind of people. Since the aim is for every puppy to sell another in the future, a few ideas may be of help to the beginner with his first few litters trying to establish himself as a Labrador breeder.

Since Labradors popularly considered are among the top ten breeds registered with the American Kennel Club, there is tremendous competition in selling puppies. Unfortunately, the majority of these puppies will have been produced by breeders totally ignorant of what they are doing; buyers of such puppies form the market that the new breeder should make an effort to break into. Take it for granted that there will be numerous dissatisfied persons in this group; the problem is how to find them, and then how to convince them that you have what they want.

Long before your puppies are ready to be sold, perhaps as soon as they are whelped, some means should be found of letting prospective purchasers know that you will have puppies for sale. One advertisement is practically useless. A series is much better. Unless you live near enough to a big city for people to come and see the puppies, there is not much point in advertising there. It is better at first to carry an ad in the most widely read local paper. Find out what might be the best advertising medium in your area.

Since you have started with a well-bred bitch and bred her to the best possible stud dog, you should notify both the breeder of your bitch and the owner of the stud dog that your puppies have arrived and what you have in the way of colors and sexes. At certain times of the year, most experienced breeders have many more requests for puppies than they can supply. Also an established breeder is not too interested in the pet market and aims at selling puppies as future breeding stock, in which case they gladly turn over pet orders to others carrying their stock. Also people often want a puppy at a definite time and here again the new breeder has a chance to get help from other breeders. However, he must not send out mimeographed sheets praising his puppies to the sky to everyone listed in dog publications.

When you have a telephone call referred to you by the breeder of your bitch, control your excitement and resist the temptation to do all the talking. Answer questions as best you can, admitting ignorance rather than trying to bluff your way through. Your objective is to get interested persons to see your puppies even if they are not old enough to be released to purchasers. Remember that good, well-bred puppies in clean surroundings will sell themselves if you have the right approach and the price is right.

The correct approach of course differs with different people and rarely are two situations alike. On the telephone, by letter, or face to face, the novice has to establish confidence through knowledge and belief in his breeding stock. There is a tendency among beginners in many fields to quote rather than to back up what is quoted with well-thought-out reasons.

Forced selling is employed to dispose of cheap, inferior puppies. (Do not offer faulty puppies for sale, and never employ high-pressure selling methods. Better to miss an occasional sale than to have a single dissatisfied buyer.) Inferior puppies by the dozens are sold to unsuspecting persons who take them home only to find there is something wrong and the puppy dies or is faulty in some respect. The market for the sale of good puppies to persons who have learned through past mistakes is very good. Your local veterinarian could be a great help with this market. In fact, persons looking for any breed of dog or puppy would do well to get on friendly relationships with the veterinarians and ask for names of dependable breeders in the area.

Since your aim is to establish yourself as a breeder of good stock and a person in whom a customer can have confidence, you must learn eventually to be an independent thinker, but at first what you learn is mostly theory. The intelligent person starting a new project realizes that he does not know all the answers.

When you are relatively sure of why your puppies are better than the average, and when the timing is right, go ahead and

EMMA HAMILTON 1968 By Foxhanger Puck ex Princess Vaughn bred by Lady Barlow in Newfoundland.

express your views. Then, if a person shows any preference among the puppies, pick it up and put it in his arms. In fact, it is effective for everyone present to hold a puppy including yourself, while you talk. Be careful about running down stock of other breeders; rather put emphasis on positive features of your own puppies, but be sure you know what you are talking about and do not give the impression of knowing everything.

When it comes to pricing a litter there are various methods for the beginner who has not yet learned to grade young puppies. The novice breeder is very likely unsure which, if any, of a litter

223

will become a near-perfect Labrador. One method is to price them all the same. Generally this is done in relation to the stud fee paid. Another way is to go over the litter with a customer standing each puppy he seems interested in on a table and going over each one point by point in relation to the Labrador Standard. Previous to this you have established your top price for the first choice of the puppies, with a graduating scale down to the least desirable of the lot. It is well to keep constantly in mind that you are building for the future and that you cannot expect to charge high prices such as you paid for your bitch. You are now looking for satisfied customers who will tell their friends that they can trust you and the quality of your puppies.

A satisfied customer gets his money's worth, whereas the bargain hunter generally does not. When customers ask the price of your puppies on the telephone, you can be quite sure above all else that they do not want to pay very much, but be polite and do not tell them to go to a pet shop. A rather better approach would be to give your price range, stating top and bottom prices, or the price if graduated prices are not used. Sometimes it might be a good idea to give a middle price, especially if you are reasonably sure that the caller will be coming to see them. However, in this case, you should have a particular puppy in mind that you think will probably be by-passed in favor of another of better quality and higher price. In such cases, a customer will very often not take the cheapest one.

There is a growing number of persons looking for pets, but who also desire dogs to be proud of and will pay a good price for a really beautiful one. These are the persons who realize that the original price of a puppy spread over the years of the dog's life does not amount to much. A bargain puppy may cost less in the beginning but more when veterinary bills and medicine are added up.

Low-priced puppies are those that are mass produced for sale at the wrong time of year or are a bad age to appeal to buyers. If you have not sold all your puppies by the time they are twelve weeks of age, it might be better to give them away; from that time on, they are practically unsalable. If by chance you have a puppy with a fault such as an undershot jaw, it should be sold cheaply and strictly as a pet without registration papers, as the fault is an inherited characteristic.

NOKEENER NEWSFLASH AY 1963. By Nokeener Newcracker AS ex Rookwood Black Diamond. Bred by Mrs. Rasbridge; owned by Mrs. R. Williams.

Many persons shop around for puppies, which is all right. You and I probably would too. However, do not believe a puppy is definitely sold until the money is in your hand, and never save a particular puppy for someone only to discover later there was no intention of buying. You can ask for a deposit on a given puppy, but never hold one back unless a deposit is paid. If you want to go into the part-payment idea, that is all right; but you should explain that the new owner can take the puppy but that the registration is in your name until full payment is made.

Remember that with livestock of all kinds there is no definite scale of prices as there are many intangibles, the most important of which is past performance. For a breeder of Labradors, the performance of the ancestors of a bitch puppy in relation to whether or not she can reproduce herself in her puppies determines her value since she is being chosen as a brood bitch because of her superior qualities. Behind her are probably other ancestors able to pass on a higher than average number of good qualities. Whether or

AMERICAN AND CANADIAN CH. GOLDEN CHANCE OF FRANKLIN 1958 By Ch. Troublemaker of Franklin ex Pretty Iris. Bred by Walter M. Swords, owned by Grace Lambert. Four times Best of Breed Labrador Specialty show, and many other wins.

not these are all champions or field trial champions is not necessarily important, but a very good thing to have in a pedigree. A champion or field champion sire or dam, depending on the buyer's area of interest denotes a certain standard of quality, but the farther back in the pedigree these titles appear the less value they have unless there is also prepotency.

When to talk about the pedigree, titles, and prepotent ancestors is important and depends on your sensitivity to the person you are talking with. If you have learned your lessons from the breeder of your bitch, you will know the important names and what they stand for, and the chances are that your customer will also know a few names. Let him show off what he knows, but be careful that you do not do so. Confidence can be established quite quickly if you let him do the names quoting, and you mention an important ancestor in the pedigree of your line and explain why this one is important to your puppy. In other words, do not call his bluff, and make quite sure you know more than names. Remember that the public is apt to know the name of the latest top-winning stud dog, and to your customer, this name indicates quality. If your puppy does not have this name behind him, you must give a valid reason why not without disparaging the publicized dog. However, if that famous dog is included in the pedigree of your puppy, it is advisable to mention some of the high points that have been responsible for his reputation. It is important though to keep coming back to your bitch and making sure that the customer understands her great qualities as a brood bitch and why the particular stud dog was chosen as a sire for the puppy. He should be made to understand that the puppy is a result of your particular bitch bred to a certain stud dog which makes a litter of puppies likely to be outstanding Labradors. It is the reputation of your bitch that you are making an effort to establish and it is important to put across the idea that your good name as a breeder will mean something in the future because of her qualities.

Self-confidence and a calm temperament are part of the Labrador's makeup. Instruction in self-control should come early. Here, Rupert puppy learns at eight weeks to stand for showing.

The professional breeder with his own kennel has a selling advantage over the "backyard breeder" and pet shop owner, who are generally not as well informed on the background and nature of the puppies they have for sale. Be sure you have pedigrees, AKC registration papers and immunization records ready to accompany each puppy. Have the bitch on hand and in good condition to show prospective owners how their puppies will look when grown. The more training you can give the puppies, the more impressive they will be, even at eight weeks of age. While pet shops must keep their stock moving, your aim should be to find owners who are interested in entering Labradors in shows and field trials and in breeding them properly. Make certain that puppies do not go to new homes until each one has had a shot of modified live virus on the appropriate date.

Have a written report prepared for the prospective owner's veterinarian, and feeding instructions for the buyer. Pedigrees should be ready for potential customers and it is often a good idea to hand them out rather freely as the chances are quite good that they will be shown around among persons who might become interested in owning a dog. A good pedigree can help advertise your kennel among knowledgeable people, so do not be stingy with your time in making them out.

A good salesman must believe in what he is selling and be able to understand what a potential customer would like. Sometimes a customer believes he wants a certain thing, such as a bitch puppy in preference to a dog; but since the reasons given for the preference have often been advanced by another person, you might tactfully change the viewpoint with convincing alternative statements. The same is true of color. Persons often express a preference for black, yellow, or chocolate, but unless they are really sure of what they want, you may be able to change their minds. But don't become "pushy." Your purpose is not to get rid of this puppy at all cost but to fit the puppy to the customer to produce a happy situation and sell your future puppies to the buyer's friends. In this way, your reputation as an ethical breeder of outstanding Labradors grows over the years to the point that all your puppies go to ideal homes with practically no effort on your part.

20. OBEDIENCE TRAINING

IN GENERAL

Formal obedience training classes are held in a great many towns and cities all over this country. For some, attendance is just for the fun of another field of interest for dog and master, but for others it is learning how to communicate with a dog.

There is usually confusion as to whether the Labrador or his owner is the one that needs obedience training. This confusion arises from the fact that some owners become desperate when their dog is out of control and believe obedience training is the answer to their prayers for having a good, well-behaved dog. The dog is sent away to be trained, with the owner not realizing that it is the human being in need of the training. Another misconception about obedience training is that a dog will be returned after a few days or perhaps a week as a perfectly obedient Labrador. The owner should remember that it takes time to break old bad habits and to instill new ones in both dog and master, and the master should listen carefully as to how to carry on the good work in training the dog.

For those who instinctively know how to train a dog and get that perfect cooperation between man and animal which becomes one of the most satisfactory relationships, formal obedience training has a different meaning. In such case, obedience classes are another chance to do things together and show off what a delightful companion you have. There are "drop outs" among those persons who have no ability to understand a dog and whose general attitude is to blame the dog for everything that goes wrong. The persons lasting the whole six weeks of the classes are the ones who enjoy doing anything with their dog.

A dog is desirous to learn everything as it comes along. A well-bred Labrador is intelligent, loving, and anxious to please. Such a dog will do anything within reason if it understands what is expected, and no forced training is needed or desirable for the ideal relationship between dog and owner.

The first meeting of an obedience training class is utter confusion with all shapes and sizes of dogs milling around, barking, and often trying to fight, and with nervous owners trying to control their animals. The teacher and his dog are the only calm and collected individuals in the whole room. That dog is usually seen sitting in the center of the room observing everything with a look of disdain at such bad behavior. The teacher and his dog demonstrate how easy everything is, and, it is not until the beginner tries the simplest thing with his own dog, that he realizes there is a right and wrong way of doing things even with a dog, and begins to understand a bit of dog psychology. Even putting a collar on a dog has to be done correctly in order to be effective, and one of the hardest things to learn is how to control a dog on a loose lead.

It is surprising how soon dogs and owners get the idea of what is expected; if the home work is done consistently and well, dogs are heeling off leash, sitting, staying, coming when called, and in general are well-behaved at the end of a six-week course. Dogs are also taught to sit automatically when the handler stops, and this creates a problem for some show dogs as they are not supposed to sit in the ring. If it is explained to the teacher at the first class that your dog is going to shows, he will probably allow you to have your dog stand rather than sit automatically at your left side. However, when it comes to the test in order to qualify for the C.D. (Companion Dog), there has to be uniformity.

COMPANION DOG (C.D.)

In order to qualify your Labrador for C.D. it must obtain a score of at least 170 out of a possible 200 points, and 50% of each test must be completed under three different judges. Most of the dog shows have obedience tests, and dogs need not be entered in conformation classes in order to compete in obedience. However, they must be registered with the AKC. The scoring system is based somewhat on how cooperative your dog is in such matters as the speed with which he sits at heel, whether or not he lags behind when moving off leash, and he is of course disqualified if he leaves the ring in search of you in the long sit and down tests. Anyway, it's all great fun.

CH. COPSCOURT CRACKERJACK By Ch. Onaway Monty ex Ch. Copscourt Regina CD. Bred and owned by Mrs. A. Courtenay-Beale. Best exhibit in show of 1,000 entries all breeds in 1963 in Australia.

COMPANION DOG EXCELLENT (C.D.X.)

The next degree is C.D.X. which among other things, involves jumping a barrier to retrieve a dummy thrown by the owner and coming back over the same way to deliver it. The tendency of the dog in such a situation is to go around the barrier rather than over it. The part of this test that is questionable for retrievers is the "drop on recall." In this test you call and your dog is to drop to the ground at a place designated by the judge. The objective is to be able to stop your dog when you see he is in danger such as in crossing a street. This test has a tendency to slow a dog down when he returns with the retrieve, since he anticipates being stopped on the way back to you.

UTILITY AND TRACKING

There are tests for dogs handled by both amateurs and professionals, and the most advanced are the Utility and the Tracking tests, which are not done at dog shows.

Line up of Labradors at Guidewell Kennels in England.

OBEDIENCE MISCELLANY

Obedience training is fun, but, as is true with most teaching, the system is tuned to the ability of least intelligent ones in the class and a Labrador often gets bored. One of my favorite Labradors, and the only one I ever did formal obedience training with, was my Champion Rupert Brookhavens Angell, C.D. This bitch would do everything to perfection when we did exhibition work in New York City, but it took a long time to qualify for her C.D. and I never could finish her at outdoor shows because she preferred to watch the birds instead of watching for my signals. She would sit there understanding perfectly well what was expected of her but teasing me like a naughty child to make her do it before the judge. Obedience training with Angell had marvelous side effects that I have never been able to get with any of my other Labradors. I could sit her in a designated corner of a huge shop, and then go off and leave her while I shopped other parts of the store and trust her never to move until I came back, perhaps an hour later. There she would be, surrounded by admirers telling her how wonderful she was. Another thing that Angell would do was to control other dogs of mine and I have no idea how she did it. I could trust her not to let other dogs jump out of the station wagon even with all the windows open and the tailgate down and while parked overnight at a motel. You can imagine the amazement of persons walking by the rear of the car and seeing this sort of control. Angell has now been dead about ten years and I am sure I will never have another pet I will love and could trust as I did her.

SCENTS

With more advanced obedience training comes scent discrimination, which can easily be taught at home. This involves picking out the one object among a group that carries the scent of the dog's owner. Some Labradors also learn to distinguish by sound direction, and will take the designated object from a group, even being able to distinguish between closely related sounds such as "stick" and "stone." This is not required in formal obedience testing, but is just part of the fun of working with a dog.

GROUP WORK

If you enjoy working with your Labrador in a group, you can keep going from training class to training class and more and more advanced tests. Some sections of the training are easier for one type of dog than others. For instance, in the tracking test, a dog such as a Bloodhound, (bred to trail by his highly developed sense of smell) shines in his glory while another type (bred to hold his head high and search by sight) has more difficulty. There are also endless possibilities for you and your dog to give public exhibitions.

COMMUNICATE

Communication between dog and master should be the basic idea, and I believe that it has been lost sight of in the present methods of testing. Situations wherein the judge is allowed to set up a test and each person is allowed to have his dog complete it any way he wishes could be of great interest and usefulness. Such a test might be getting your dog to come out of a large group while all the others stay back. This to be done by voice, hand signal, or other means. Holding your dog back in the group, also to be done in any way the owner wishes, could be another test. The human being should be tested at least once to see whether or not he understands how to communicate with his dog; this might be in the form of the word NO with the judge putting in the test at any time during the testing. Scoring of these tests should be based on reaction between the owner and his dog. Shouting commands should be stopped, as dogs have much better hearing than human beings and a dog answering to whispered commands or hand signals should score higher than one shouted at.

In fact, the use of hand signals should be mandatory at some stage of the training since to be able to control a dog beyond hearing distance or in the midst of surrounding noise is important, as well as being convenient when greeting and talking with guests at home. Of course, any of these and more can be taught at home by persons who are "half dog" themselves, but could be added to formal training and add interest to both trainer and spectator to say nothing of the judge at an obedience test.

21. SHOWS

IN GENERAL

Persons become involved in dog shows for many reasons, perhaps the chief one being the discovery that they have a beautiful puppy which everyone tells them to show. Since most of us have a bit of competitive spirit, it soon becomes obvious that the puppy must go to a dog show and bring home blue ribbons. Other individuals decide to enter their puppies at dog shows because they plan to breed Labradors and must talk with other breeders and learn more about the problems involved. This type of person has already bought a bitch puppy and joined a dog club in the area and is thinking of going to the next sanction match put on by this club. A sanction match is a friendly informal affair put on by a local club and sanctioned by the American Kennel Club. The purpose is to teach the club group how to run a regular point show and give beginners a chance to take puppies or dogs to a show where there will be other persons hoping to start a show career. Even the judges at such shows are amateurs, and everyone is friendly and desirous of helping one another with various problems that turn up.

The ribbons you bring home from a sanction match are not blue, red or purple such as are won at point shows, but they are still important and are the first step before going to a regular show and trying for points towards a Championship. Your puppy is still a baby; but with success at his first show, you are convinced that he will win every other show too. At sanction matches, puppies may be entered at three months, but the point show requires them to be at least six months of age. Realizing that it is important to present your puppy properly, you try to find out at sanction matches how they should stand and move on a leash.

The objective in showing your Labrador before a judge is to present it in the way it looks best. It should have been brushed and probably washed. The whiskers should be cut and the hair on the end of the tail shortened either by burning or clipping. This shortening of the hair on the end of the tail should have been done

CH. TUDOR LINCOLNSHIRE POACHER 1968 By Ch. Kimvalley Crispin ex Ch. Kirbyhall Gingham. Bred, owned and handled by Edward Squires. Best of Breed Westminster.

at least a week in advance of the show in order for it to look its best, and it should not be blunt-looking but slightly tapered.

STANCE

In showing, you hold your dog's head in your right hand with your fingers in the hollow under the jaw or in some other way so that your hand does not show on the side toward the judge. His front legs should go straight to the ground from the sides and the puppy should not pull back, which sometimes happens because of nervousness. If he stands straight up on his front legs, his cat feet will look well and hopefully he will not toe in or out. The back should be level and taper slightly towards the tail. In order to have the back appear straight, the rear legs should not be directly under the dog but placed back or to the sides. Some judges like to see the legs stretched back and others to the sides. You can tell which manner is preferred by watching other classes the judge is going over. At any rate the rear legs from the hock joint to the ground should be straight up and down. In my opinion, the tail should be wagging, and I do not agree with persons who think it should be held out like a Setter's, which is supposed to have feathering on its underside.

PRELIMINARY TRAINING

You should have already trained your dog to understand that the judge wants to look at his teeth to see if they touch with the lower incisors slightly behind the uppers. A puppy should show a

CH. DARK STAR OF FRANKLIN 1955 By Ch. Labcroft Mr. Chips ex Ch. Pitch of Franklin. Bred, owned and handled by Mrs. B. Ziessow. Eight times Best In Show and Best of Breed Labrador Specialty. (Pedigree 30.)

happy, carefree spirit when moving on a leash, but neither should he trip you up nor jump on the judge. He must move on your left side, not too fast and yet not at a crawl. The judge may tell you to go faster or slower; but, if you have watched other classes, perhaps you can tell the speed you should assume. If there is any question, it is better to go too slowly than too fast, unless there is something wrong with the way the dog moves and you hope to offset it in that speed tends to be a cover-up for some faults. All this is preliminary training.

POINT SHOW

Point shows are usually run by professional superintendents who send out premium lists to interested persons. The AKC or the various magazines will give you a list of these superintendents and you can write to one who covers your area and ask to have your name put on the list. It takes about two months before you start receiving these premium lists, so have patience.

BENCHED OR UNBENCHED

Shows are either benched or unbenched. A benched show will have numbered stalls for each dog. Dogs must be on them for most of the day. With the benched shows, all dogs must arrive by a definite stated time, usually 11:30, and any dog not arriving by that time is not allowed inside the building or show grounds. At unbenched shows, you can arrive any time before the judging starts and leave your dog in the car if you wish, or in a cage under a tent or any other place where there is shade on a hot day. Admission card for your dog usually arrives the Monday before the show, but all the information has to be given to the superintendent three weeks in advance and on official AKC forms they supply.

CLASSES

The class that is the correct one for your dog varies with the situation. Qualifications for the various classes are printed in the premium list. Classes are divided between the sexes with all dogs being shown before bitches until the Champions come into the ring. I believe that puppies should be entered in puppy classes as long as they are under a year of age on the day of the show. If a dog is over puppy age and still inexperienced or immature looking, it

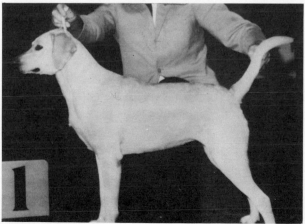

(Above) CH. WINROC'S NADA BEAR By Ch. Lewisfield Beret ex Sara's Dixiana California. Owned by Mr. and Mrs. A. L. Foote.

(At left) Showing the Labrador Retriever . . . badly held tail.

might go into novice class but in this class it may be the only one as this is not a popular class. Bred by exhibitor and open are the two classes for experienced dogs and handlers with American-Bred class customarily used for those not ready for keen competition. All imported dogs, whether foreign Champions or not, must go

CH. WHYGIN POPPITT 1951 By Ch. Rupert Dahomey × Cedarhill Whygin, bred and owned and handled by Helen Ginnel.

into open until they become American Champions. The dogs placing first in each class go into the ring again for Winners. Here they compete against the other blue ribbon winners and the dog or bitch selected from this class is called Winners Dog or Winners Bitch. There are also Reserve Winners (second best) in dogs and bitches; if for any reason Winners is disqualified, the reserve gets all the ribbons and any prizes awarded. The class called Best of Breed is for competition for classification of Champion of both sexes, with Winners Dog and Winners Bitch included. The final job of the judge at a regular show is to pick out the Labradors he considers the best of the lot for Best of Breed, Best of Winners, and Best of Opposite Sex. The Best of Opposite Sex depends on which sex was chosen as Best of Breed. Eventually Best in Show is chosen for the final event; but before this, the winning Labrador has to compete in the Sporting Group which is made up of the Bests of Breed from all sporting breeds. Dogs are divided into six groups for show purposes with the winner of each group competing for Best in Show. There is a Reserve Best in Show in England, but not in this country. In America, there is one supreme winner of a dog show, with no second best designated.

TO WIN

This may all sound very easy for a person convinced that he has the most beautiful puppy in the world; but no matter how outstanding a puppy may be, there are bound to be difficulties along the way and many disappointments. In the first place, judges vary in opinion as to what constitutes beauty, as do you and I; and, if your dog is not presented well, the judge may not be able to see its outstanding qualities. Signs of a beginner are having his hopes too high, and when the blue ribbon is given to another dog, he questions the judge about why the other dog won. We all like to win, but dog shows are not set up for every dog to go away a winner and the slow climb must be the usual pathway to success. Any dog that is to become an eventual Champion must be under judgment at a great many shows and be what is called *campaigned rather*

CHAMPION LEATTIE BICKERTON SALMON QUEEN 1960 By Dobrudden Buffer ex Bella Mischief. Bred in England by Mrs. Marsland. Owned in USA by Dr. Clifton P. Rose. The first Labrador bitch to go Best In Show in the USA. She also placed Best of Opposite Sex at Westminster. Dam of Ch. Black Jim of Rosecliffe BOB Westminster.

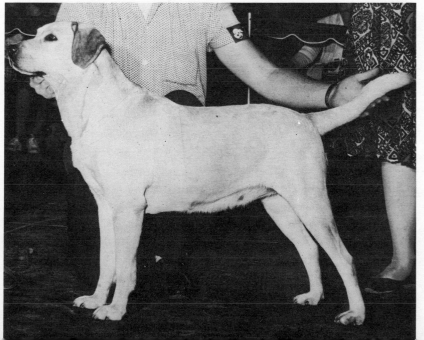

intensively while still young. It must acquire fifteen points, which are only awarded to Winners Dog and Winners Bitch and, of these fifteen points, it is required by the AKC that two major wins must be included. Major wins are those shows where enough Labradors are present to account for at least three points (maximum number of points allowed in any one show is five). These two majors must be won under two different judges; and of the balance of the points at least one must be won under a third judge.

The AKC decided on a system for designating various sections of the country as having more or less interest in showing Labradors (as well as other breeds); in those areas where few Labradors are shown, it is still possible to win classification as a champion although varying numbers of competing Labradors are needed for winning points. Acquiring the two majors is the most difficult part of becoming a Champion. This is where the biggest difference in competition is found. The scale of points varies according to what has happened during the year preceding, with the eastern division having the hottest competition and thus requiring more dogs and bitches present at a show for major points than is necessary in any other section of the country.

CIRCUITS

Anyone really interested in showing can go to two shows every weekend as well as on what we call "circuits." These circuits are a fairly recent development in this country and came about as a result of the great distances people have to travel with their dogs in order to attend some shows. In New England, we had one of the first circuits since being up in the northeastern corner of the country it seemed that the only way to induce people to bring their dogs to a show was to have a series of them scheduled on successive days and so make the trip worth while. So we put on three shows in Vermont and, with a free day between, New Hampshire has three more. In this way, people could plan a vacation in Vermont and New Hampshire, showing their dogs over the period of a week, and still stop on the way home for another weekend of shows. The circuits have been quite a success and now almost any section of the country has them during vacation time: in Texas and other southern areas during winter, and in summer farther north. It is customary for circuits to be unbenched and with Labradors usually judged early in the morning, so that the rest of the day is free for visiting or seeing the sights. The professional handlers liked these groups of shows as they did not have to do as much traveling and could often stay in one area and radiate out to shows from there. It was also a good place to try out new dogs; and, since the shows are often smaller than those more centrally located, the dogs trying for Group and Best In Show often made the grade.

Of course, no matter what enterprise is put forward, there are usually those who misuse it. In the case of circuits, stacking the entrees by some breeders is an effort to make up a Champion by entering a lot of inferior dogs for the number-of-competitors requirement necessary for the winner to gain enough points for a major, and there is not very much a judge can do about it. However, with all entries being listed with their owners in the official AKC magazine, the rest of us see what is happening.

DO-IT-YOURSELF HANDLING

Those of us who handle our own dogs in the show ring have an added sense of participation that no sitting on the sidelines can give. Ring manners, if not instinctive between you and your dog, can easily be acquired through observation and the routine of such things as always moving your dog counter-clockwise around the ring and keeping your dog between you and the judge. Many dogs going to their first shows are upset by the noise and confusion and part of their training should be walking them around town on a leash, weaving in and around cars and watching trucks go by. It is well to take along some biscuits to hand strangers, asking them to give one to your dog. In this way your show prospect gets used to strangers and new experiences and you, and not the puppy, will probably be the nervous one in the ring. However, judges are usually very understanding of a novice with a puppy and will help all they can. Even old-timers learn from judges. Not too long ago, I was told by a judge to take a longer stride as my dog was moving at a choppy gait.

One of the rules while in the ring is not to mention your dog's name, and you are not supposed to talk with people on the sidelines or to smoke. Incidentally, when the judge asks you to move your dog in the ring, you start in front of him and he tells you whether he would like you to go to the corner opposite him across the end of the ring and then back or whether he just wants you to take your dog straight down and back. It is a good idea, if you can do so, to train your dog so that when you stop back in front of the judge at the finish it remains very alert with ears up and head high, as if saying to the judge, "Look at me, I am a show dog!" This is one of the finer details of the show game and the beginner will not have developed his power of observation to notice such things. But, like everything else, the more one practices observing every detail and relating it to why it should be so, the more capable one becomes of seeing the future champion. Intelligent observation is perhaps the most important single item necessary for anyone hoping to succeed in the dog game and it is always a surprise that the novice who needs it the most is the one who rarely watches what is going on in the ring.

The beginner goes to dog shows to learn basic things in his breed, but an old-timer goes for other reasons. The breeder wants to see how his strain compares with others, both through his own observations and those of the judge. In this way, he is helped in deciding his future breeding program and choice of stud dogs. A competent, unbiased judge is a great help in this direction as the experienced breeder is apt to become "kennel blind." The ideal in all competition, no matter what the field of endeavor, would be a knowledgeable, honest, courageous judge and exhibitors willing to accept all placements as designated. Of course, this situation is impossible as no judge can know everything and every exhibitor wants to be on top.

A written description of what a Labrador should look and act like is stated by the Labrador Club but within this Standard there can be many variations. At a dog show, a great deal depends on the competition a dog is up against on a particular day. The ideal might be to judge a particular dog against this standard and any entries that did not qualify would not be given awards. But since this is not the custom, judges compare the merits of the Labradors before them and relate one to another, leaving Group and Best in Show wins for judging against the ideal for the various breeds. This creates misunderstandings at the ringside as owners of dogs that have been consistent winners at smaller shows, and even placed in Groups, sometimes cannot understand how it happens that their entries go unplaced at shows where the competition is really keen.

In the first place, at the big shows the judge is usually chosen from the ranks of those who have had great experience in the particular breed in contrast to smaller shows where a judge is often relatively new.

Some persons go through the process of studying how a judge has placed an individual animal and, on the basis of this, decide whether or not to enter their dog under him. Personally, when I wanted to know how one of my dogs moved, I would enter him under the late Dr. Mitten (an orthopedic surgeon) knowing he would never put up a bad mover. Very often a judge who is a breeder in a different breed makes an excellent judge. Such an individual is usually not prejudiced toward one type because he realizes as a breeder the overall quality of a good animal. It is relatively easy, even for a beginner, to judge a bad specimen or a really beautiful one, but the majority of dogs in the ring fall between these extremes. These are the most difficult to equate for it takes a great deal of experience to relate in importance the good and bad points. Here is where variety of opinion comes in and divergences from the Standard (in relation to the importance of various virtues and faults) become a matter of opinion.

GOING DOWNHILL

Another problem arises when a top-quality dog starts to "go down hill." It is easy for a judge to keep on placing the sensational winner on top, but even these dogs have good and bad days, and the judge with a keen eye and the courage of his convictions will see this and place another contender higher. All dogs get old, and the judge who starts putting the consistent winner down is either popular or unpopular depending on who is watching and how close his association is with the particular dog or its owner.

COMPETITIVE SPIRIT

The competitive spirit is strong in some persons, and the showing of dogs can satisfy this with a minimum of effort, especially when the dog is shown by a professional. A person of this type should acquire a male as a bitch rarely gets to the top, and even gaining a Championship for a bitch is more difficult because of the physical make-up of the female. There is not much sense in wanting to go Best in Show with all the expense and difficulties involved unless

DUAL CH. SHED OF ARDEN 1949 with his progeny at 1949 Labrador Specialty. By Ch. Raffles of Earlsmoor ex F.T. Ch. Decoy of Arden. Bred by the Hon. W. Averill Harriman owned and handled by Paul Bakewell III. Three times National Champion. He was the outstanding stud dog of his era with practically all field trial dogs and many bench champions going back to him today. This breeding produced three Dual Champions, Braes and Gorse of Arden as well as Shed, and four bench champions, Bass, Heather, Earlsmoor Moor and Marlin of Arden. In this photograph, Shed is on the right with Paul Bakewell.

you are relatively sure that your Labrador is of that quality and you are ready, in these days of hot competition, to keep him in top condition as well as to campaign him continually. When it is understood that the dogs entered in shows all over the country run into the thousands and only one Best is possible in each show, it can be understood that most of us had better be satisfied with something else. A breeder must show his dogs to the point of demonstrating their quality but should otherwise rather set his sights on producing successively better animals. He should make an effort to gain championship status for his dogs or run them in trials but leave to others the seeking of satisfaction through campaigning them further.

The British system of arriving at a Championship for a dog is different from ours and much more difficult in that dogs over there that are already Champions compete in the same class as dogs that are not. Therefore the Labrador trying to become a Champion must defeat Champions along the way; and, with relatively few shows where it is possible to gain a CC (challenge certificate) not many champions are made up each year. In place of our point system, a dog in England must gain three CCs under three different judges to be a Champion.

A SPORT, PLEASE!

It is well always to keep in mind that the showing of dogs in competition is rated as a sport; and, whether we like it or not, the decisions of the judge are final. We could learn something from our dogs in the way they handle themselves. Some are glad to get out of the ring and others want to go right back in again, but they do not bite the judge because of not being given a ribbon, as some exhibitors seem nearly ready to do.

SPECIALTY SHOWS

Our most important show is that put on once a year by the Labrador Club. In the beginning these were informal affairs held without being involved with an all-breed show, but things have changed primarily for the reason that members of the Labrador Club in general have little interest in shows and prefer to concentrate on field trials.

The purpose of a Specialty show is to bring out as many outstanding examples of the breed as possible to be looked over by a knowledgeable judge who will pick out for Best of Breed a truly superior type. All persons interested in Labradors, both old-timers and beginners, should go to these Specialty shows and it should be here that decisions are made for the future of the breed. Extra classes are allowed by the AKC for the purpose of showing what stud dogs and brood bitches produce, and these classes bring in the puppies with their parents. There are also classes for braces (two dogs) and teams (four dogs) owned by one person. These brace and team classes are important as they show strains within the breed that are being developed with uniformity as the objective.

PROGENY CLASS

The most important class at a Specialty show should be the progeny class, which unfortunately is never well-attended. In this

DUAL CH. ALPINE CHEROKEE ROCKET 1955 By Dual Ch. Cherokee Buck ex Nelgard's Madam Queen. This dog was the fourth Dual Champion in a straight line back to Dual Ch. Shed of Arden. His pedigree shows important American breeding on both sides. (Pedigree 31.)

class, only the progeny are supposed to be judged and could demonstrate the worth of particular bitches, especially wherein the same stud dog was used on various bitches with the resulting puppies showing the differences between bitches. The valuable assets of sires and dams would be made visible if enough progeny could be seen. Dogs are short-lived and bitches are capable of producing only a limited number of puppies during their all-too-brief productive years. Often their worth is not realized until after they are dead. Here is a chance to make a pedigree become important with only the need for progeny being present to prove the breeding impact of a dog or bitch. This evaluation could take the place of counting wins at the shows.

A Specialty should not be just another show but a special kind of a show, emphasizing in particular the art of breeding. However nothing is done by the Labrador Club to encourage owners to enter their dogs. Also since Best of Breed is judged before these classes, an anticlimax occurs and spectators move away from ringside. Special inducements could be given toward inviting and promoting entries in such classes. Special pens could be set up in some section of the field for puppies, with attendants watching over them night and day. Signs on the pens should indicate the sires, dams, and persons coming from a distance might bring more puppies under such circumstances. A special judge, who understands puppies of various ages, should be appointed, or perhaps it would not be important to have any judge. I realize that all this would mean extra work for somebody but it should be a more important function for the Club and the fancy than collecting silverware and ribbons.

FIELD TRIAL CLASS

Field trial classes are attended poorly, for one reason because the show is often held on the day of an important field trial. Another reason is that field trial dogs are not usually in what is called show condition. They should compete against each other only in special classes provided for them. However, any owner wishing to enter his dog in a regular class could do so with pride. The field trial class should be strictly limited to honest field trial dogs and not just show dogs which happened into a trial. I do not blame owners of field dogs for disliking to have their dogs compete against seasoned show dogs any more than I, the owner of a show dog (which may be an excellent hunting dog), want to compete against the super-trained field trial dog. Field trial dogs and brood bitches should not have their general condition count against them; they should be judged on other qualities.

HUNTING AND FIELD TRIALS

Since a Labrador is primarily a sporting dog, this fact should not be lost sight of by breeders who might only be interested in raising Labradors that look like Labradors regardless of how they act.

Field Trial training is a very complicated and specialized subject and as there are many excellent books on the subject, I omit discussion here. However, since the Labrador Club requires that any member having a dog that has completed its AKC Championship may not use that title until it has passed a working test, I will write about that because it is important. Unfortunately the Club has in the past made it very difficult for the average person to manage the testing, which in itself is very easy, and most Labradors could pass it with practically no training. The dog need not be steady but can be held on a line until sent by the judge. It must retrieve to hand a pheasant and enter water twice to retrieve dead or shackled ducks and must not be gun-shy, which is perhaps the hardest thing for an amateur to teach his dog. Any dog first exposed to gunfire while near the gun may become forever gun-shy. A dog's hearing is very much more acute than that of a human being, and introduction to any loud sharp sound such as a gunshot should be done with extreme caution. Introduction to sounds of percussion should begin when a puppy is quite small by making noises such as banging on a metal feed dish or even starting with hand clapping while the puppy is eating. Any accustoming to loud sound should be done while the puppy is concentrating on other things, such as food, or while excited at entering the water to retrieve a duck. The gun should be kept a long distance away at first and gradually moved nearer until the dog seems to pay no attention to it except to connect the sound with something interesting. It might be well to have an experienced person help in introducing your dog to gunshots as it is not as simple a proceeding as many would believe and can cause irreversible gun-shyness if done in the wrong way.

Most show-type Labradors will make excellent hunting dogs if handled by a person who understands training. A Labrador owner who sends his dog to a professional for training as a hunter and never handles it until the season opens, blames poor training on his lack of success when in reality it is his own fault in not learning the proper signals in the control of his dog. The dog is willing and understands the problem but is unable to understand what his owner is trying to tell him and the result is utter confusion, and loss of temper on the part of the owner.

Mutual trust and understanding are required between hunter and dog before a satisfactory retrieving companion is developed. The

CH. RUPERT BROOKHAVENS ANGELL CD By Zelstone Mr. Ben ex Rupert Daphne. Bred, owned and handled by Dorothy Howe.

intelligent Labrador, brought up as a house pet with the love and understanding of the person who is to take him hunting, requires a minimum of training in order to accomplish the job. Much of this training can be done in the house and a few minutes a day is enough. Such things as blind retrieves and hand signals can become a game in the house with the dog learning to trust his nose as one of the important by-products. Introduction to feathers can be accomplished by tying feathers on a dummy or using a pigeon or chicken wing with the feathers intact. Remember that a Labrador should hand you the object retrieved and not drop it on the ground as is allowed with other breeds. This is also one of the requirements for a working certificate for a show dog. One important thing should not be overlooked and that is allowing persons to throw just anything for a dog and not requiring the dog to bring it back and give it to them. Let toys be toys, but certain definite other things should be reserved for training. If a dog has a tendency to go off with the object you are training with out-of-doors, it is a good idea to reduce the available working space so that evading you is minimized. In such circumstances, moving away from the dog may induce following and the training object may be retrieved as the dog passes. His game of keep-away is thus converted to delivering the object for reward of the praise bestowed upon surrender of the object.

For outside work, training involves getting your dog to go far out, which is not possible in the house. Introducing him to gunfire must also be done outdoors. There is on the market a dummy thrower that is very useful, but test it without your dog the first time as the dummy goes a long way.

For persons wishing to use a whistle for signals, the best one is the Acme Thunderer. With this type of whistle, one can almost talk as it is possible to trill and make various other sounds. One blast is commonly used for a dog to sit wherever it is, and three blasts to summon the dog to come towards or all the way back to you. The single blast is used also to signal for the dog to pay attention when you plan to use hand signals.

Introducing a puppy to water should be done carefully. It is a good idea in warm weather to have a pan of water in the pen so the dog will·walk through it and get used to the feel of water. Introduction to deep water wherein the puppy's feet are off the ground for the first time can be terrifying and the puppy should be treated like a child with his head held up and being given lots of words of encouragement. It is well to take it in a brook first and if possible with its dam or some other older dog along, or to go in yourself for reassurance. If introduced to deep water properly, a Labrador will love the water and be difficult to keep out of it.

There should be no problem in transferring of the idea of hand signals in the house to the out-of-doors, but it should be understood that dogs cannot distinguish angles and it is confusing to them to bring your arm back and forth when signaling to them. Keep your arm out straight from your side and move your hand, but

252

do not bring the arm back. The only other direction a dog understands besides *right* and *left* is *back*, indicated with an overhead signal. When taking your dog for a walk, get him used to being called back; and, if there is any chance of his getting out of control and taking off after a rabbit or deer, do not let him get too far distant as the farther away a dog goes the less control you have over him.

A specialized type of training is involved in preparation for field trials. Competing is rather on the order of a show dog going after Group and Best in Show wins. Relatively few dogs make the grade and the competition is exceedingly stiff. With plenty of time and a special ability in handling a dog, it is possible for an amateur to entertain the idea of making up a Field Trial Champion, but relatively few dogs acquire the title unless much of the training is done by a professional.

One indication of the enthusiastic beginner is his conviction that his dog will some day be a Dual Champion (both bench and field trial), not realizing that in the history of Labradors in this

AYMES MICHAEL COLLIER (3 months) By Ch. Shamrock Acres Ebony Lancer × Ch. Shamrock Acres Cotton Candy.

National Geographic Magazine photo shows young Labrador puppy retrieving duck.

country fewer than thirty dogs have become Dual Champions, and even fewer have obtained the title in England.

For the person who has the ability and loves to work with his dog as a relaxation from a busy life, training can be very satisfactory, especially when done with friends and their dogs. In fact, no matter how much training is done alone, some of it must be done with other dogs or your dog will not be steady and will "break" in the excitement of seeing birds shot down that another dog retrieves while he is supposed to sit quietly by your side. The field trial Clubs have sanction matches as do the show groups. These can be fun for all concerned and satisfy that certain competitive spirit of some persons without the highly specialized organization of a field trial. Sometimes as many as 150 dogs show up at a sanction match with relatively few going on to the regular trials. No amount of wishful thinking about your dog's ability to compete against another dog in any situation will prove to be true in most cases since there must be complete cooperation between dog and man as well as continuous training for every known and anticipated situation. The competition in most trials has many unnatural tests devised by the judges in order to reduce the number of dogs running in the trial. There is nothing more thrilling than watching a well-trained, co-operative dog and a loving master working together in the field, yet it is maddening to see a man lose his temper with his dog when the blame for what happened should be upon him rather than upon the dog. It is not surprising that many hunters with a

CH. ROOKWOOD SILVER DEW 1961 AV By Roncott Shandy ex Ch. Rookwood Honeysuckle. Bred and owned by Mrs. Marion Saffell.

Labrador trained to bring in every bird shot down and to act in every way as a perfect retriever refuse to believe such a dog will not win a field trial. The hunter's pride in his dog's accomplishments and a misunderstanding of what is required of a field dog create bitter tensions when owners of differently-trained dogs start arguing the merits of their animals.

Unfortunately the separation between attributes of show and field trial dogs and the views of their owners is wide and becoming wider with more and more persons entering each type of competition. Field trial people are bored with shows, and show people do not have the time or inclination (and usually not the cash needed) for field trial competition. Show dogs must obtain their title at a young age, and during this age span a field trial dog is in training for his future attempts at winning his title. If it happens that the field trial dog receives his title at a young age and the owner and trainer condescend to let this dog start a show career, a dual title may be possible to attain. However, if the show title is not acquired quickly, the dog is withdrawn from competition and most field trial people care little about having their working dog become a bench Champion. Some field trial people will not have dogs in their kennels that are not a true type Labrador. Credit is due Grace Lambert for starting the trend back to having good-looking field trial dogs, and Mr. John Olin also has many in his kennel that might become bench Champions as well as field trial Champions.

Among the show group, there seems to be inclination to insist on other qualities besides beauty among show Labradors. Perhaps someday the Labrador Club will extend a helping hand and start bringing the two groups together as the situation was when the Labrador Club was founded.

PROFESSIONAL HANDLERS

As competition becomes more keen in any sport, more time and effort must be spent in training and what started out as a friendly relaxed affair becomes highly specialized and intense. All persons do not have the urge or ability or even the time to handle their own dogs in competition. Some persons are satisfied with the pride of owning a winner, whereas others get the most satisfaction from handling their dogs in competition. Professionals enter the field

CH. WHYGIN SKIA & CH. WHYGIN JOHN DUCK 1954 By Ch. Whygin Poppitt × Ch. Rupert Desdemona. Bred by Helen Ginnel. Skia owned by Nancy Tuttle, John owned by Helen Ginnel.

as their chosen way of making a living, and many persons owning superior dogs believe professionals are more capable than themselves in presenting their dogs to best advantage. This view prevails particularly in field trial competition with the constant intensive training a necessity if one has much hope of ever winning top awards. The life of a dog is relatively very short; much has to be crowded into a few years, and not many amateurs are willing or able to give the necessary amount of time to make everything else secondary to their dog.

Professionals who decide to try making a living through dogs must have a number of them that are constantly being shown, with a definite proportion of these winning if they are to stay in business. The problem comes down to the ability of a professional to win over an amateur either with a superior dog or one shown to better advantage. The professional must also demonstrate to the owner of a particular dog that everything possible is being done to set the stage for his dog's winning.

There is really not much excuse for an interested amateur not being able to learn how to show his own dog. What is not understood is that practice with the dog must be done at home and not at the show.

257

There certainly should be an understanding between the owner and the professional as to the ultimate goal desired for the particular dog. If the owner would like to try to win Groups and go on to try for Best in Show, the professional should be fully convinced of the superior quality of that particular dog and explain very carefully the problems involved. On the other hand, if the owner of the Labrador desires a Championship for his dog and will be happy if that is acquired, he should explain this to the professional. It is up to the professional to talk over the expense involved and possible rewards to be obtained in going on circuits or to shows at great distances. For a stud dog, it is important for him to be seen; even if he does not win all the time, owners of bitches may appreciate his outstanding qualities and pedigree and decide to use him in their breeding programs.

When giving a dog to a professional for extensive showing, it should be understood that the animal must live in a small cage a great deal of the time, especially when traveling. Field trial dogs will get plenty of exercise, but a show dog will probably not have enough.

Show dogs can be given to a professional at the show for handling but should be in good condition as things can be too hectic for fussing with a Labrador on short notice. A field trial dog must live at the training quarters for months and sometimes years if you plan a big future for him. This dog will probably never know that he belongs to you unless you plan to handle him at trials yourself and work with him as you train together.

Owners giving a dog to a professional must understand that professional handling alone does not guarantee gathering points at every show and that other dogs are certainly going to win some of the time. Without wins by amateur handlers and their dogs, there would be no competition and no dog shows. Care should be taken to encourage amateurs, and professionals should do everything possible to help them learn the game. There is sometimes criticism that dogs with professionals do all the winning. Remarks detrimental to judges and dogs often come from the amateur with either an inferior dog or one out of condition. It should be kept in mind that the professional generally will not take an inferior specimen and that every dog he takes into the ring must be in top condition and be well-trained for showing. If the amateur wishes to take a bitch

CH. SPENROCK SANS SOUCI 1968 By Ch. Sandylands Midus ex Ch. Spenrock Banner. Bred by Spenrock Kennels, owned by John C. Valentine.

to a show too soon after raising a litter and she is not yet back in show condition, it is his privilege, but most judges will not give a second look at such a bitch and a professional will seldom consent to enter the ring with such a dog. The bred-by-exhibitor class was added for the purpose of encouraging breeders to show their stock without facing the competition of professional handlers (dogs must be handled by the breeder or specified relatives). Unfortunately, the classes are not well attended, probably for the reason that point

259

winners generally are chosen from the open class, and few judges give enough attention to bred-by-exhibitor classes.

When hiring a professional for your dog, it should be understood that it is expensive, and your dog may be away from home for long stretches of time. There should be an understanding about whether or not the dog is to be returned to the owner when he is shedding or in other ways be out of condition. The amateur should understand that the professional is generally more capable of keeping the dog in top condition or bringing him back into condition than the average owner. Success breeds success, and the professional who never or rarely makes up a Champion either has poor judgment in obtaining the right stock to work with or does not handle his charges well, either in the ring or in his kennel.

The professional handler is here to stay and is definitely needed in the dog game. However, I hope that the trend towards more and more Labradors being handled by them in the ring will stop and that amateurs will enter their dogs in other classes besides Open and enjoy competing for blue ribbons instead of always for points. There seems to be a tendency toward rushing for the top without working one's way up.

JUDGES

With the tremendous increase in the number of dog shows and of exhibitors at each show, many judges will be learning what is involved in grading various dogs they see before them. It takes actual judging, distinguished from giving a ringside opinion, to gain experience and become qualified to pass judgments that mean much. In the ring, a judge has a tremendous responsibility in shaping the future of the breed and the knowledgeable judge realizes this and takes his assignment very seriously. It is fortunate that personal opinion is allowed as to what constitutes a thing of beauty and that the Labrador Standard of Perfection gives freedom of choice among various points. It is human nature to have opinions that disagree with those of others and often both may be right. It is a rare judge who will find everyone agreeing with him and it is no job for a person who cannot take unjust criticism. Neither is it a job for anyone with strong prejudices for or against certain types of dogs, since a judge must evaluate what he sees before him without prejudice.

Unfortunately, as in all fields, there are never enough of the best to go around and judges are no exception. New judges, like new exhibitors, have to learn the game. The American Kennel Club does its best to approve for judging only those whom they can trust to do a competent job on the various breeds. Exhibitors should be more appreciative of the struggle some judges have in trying to

THE RAED JEANNIE of Pandocha (chocolate) 1968 By Ch. Indian Valley Raed Wulf ex Annette's Miss Mischief. Bred and owned by Annette Koplovsky.

CANADIAN AND AMERICAN DUAL CH. HAPPY PLAYBOY Canadian By Ch. Castlemore Shamus ex Susie. Owned by Grace Lambert in USA. Qualified several years for The National.

do what is right. Nobody likes to be a loser in the ring, and it should be remembered that this is true of the judge as well. He may honestly believe in the dog he puts to the top but gets criticized as influenced by the handler or by other factors. It is his responsibility to enter the ring with an open mind and with no preconceived idea of what dog he plans to put up.

It is important that amateur and professional handlers have every chance to show their dogs to best advantage, and the judge should prevent as far as possible any particular individual trying to attract undue attention to his dog.

Perhaps there is a beginner present who bought a puppy from a breeder who assured him the puppy was of show type. When this puppy reached the age of six months he was entered in a show, then days were devoted to brushing and training the puppy. At last the great day comes and they arrive at the show convinced that no dog could possibly be better than this one. The beginner is terribly deflated if a judge passes a fleeting glance at his dog and sends him to the end of the line or perhaps out of the ring without a word of encouragement. The way everyone at the show treats a beginner has great influence on whether or not that particular dog and handler ever go to another show, and without beginners there would be no dog shows. Since we must continually have new exhibitors in order to keep shows going, judges and seasoned handlers should be particularly tolerant of these newcomers.

Ringside judges should also be careful what they talk about when beginners are present. There is nothing more discouraging than to hear people at the ringside say in no uncertain terms how crazy they think the judge is and how he put the worst possible specimen at the top. It should be understood that people at the ringside do not know the whole answer to what is being judged and might once in a while give the judge the benefit of the doubt.

Many times judges are called on to face delicate decisions such as a breeder stacking the entries in an effort to make up a champion which otherwise would not become one. Usually it is quite obvious which dog the breeder wants to have win and judges resent this kind of situation and will often put as winner another though poorer type than the one desired by the handler. It is a judge's privilege to withhold first place, which I believe should be done more often, but this is rarely done. The conflict here is whether a judge grades the dogs he sees before him or does he refuse first place if there is no first class dog in the group.

Another case where a judge is put on the spot is when a dog that he has bred is entered under him at a show. Here is the tendency to put his own breeding to the top as this is usually the type he likes. If, however, he does not do this, some people will think he is down-grading his own stock. Knowledgeable people will realize the truth that here is an ethical judge and put it down to bad taste that the dog in question was entered in the first place.

Much the same situation holds when influence peddling seems

apparent in cases involving a judge and close friends. In other cases a judge may be looking for future assignments and may be tempted to put up a dog coming from a particular area. Anyway it is very easy for disgruntled exhibitors to find reasons to back up their belief that a blue ribbon rather than a red one should have been theirs.

It is well to remember that as long as your dog wins, the judge is considered wonderful and it is in just as poor taste to be a poor winner as a poor loser. For a judge to have chosen for Best of Breed a dog that eventually goes on to become Best in Show he too must be careful about showing how smart he is and what good judgment he used, that was confirmed by the Group and Best in Show judges. It is just as important to be thoughtful and kindly toward man and beast at a show as it is anywhere else.

The beginner himself all too often has an attitude that prejudices all those he comes in contact with at a dog show. There is the type who becomes angry and tells the world what he thinks of a judge who does not know a good specimen when he sees it. There is a tendency for a novice to believe that a judge should see a good dog regardless of how it is presented. In principle this is all right, but how can anyone evaluate a dog being dragged around the ring with its head down or stood up with its back humped up in the middle and its tail between its legs.

The first-time exhibitor with the attitude of listening and seeking information through intelligent questions will not stay a beginner long and will be welcome in any group where people are talking about dogs. However, he must be careful not to abuse the privilege of being allowed to listen and should not repeat gossip about dogs or persons which is so bandied about within a group of close friends.

In this country, a judge is not expected to give reasons for his placings, and handlers are supposed to accept what he does without asking why. This rather puts the judge on a pedestal, and only the beginner dares go back into the ring and ask for an explanation. Whether or not this custom causes the excessive amount of ringside criticism one hears is open to debate, but the beginner should be careful to confine himself to listening and not quoting.

Those of us who show bitches must understand that we must start them young, and judges should realize that a bitch is usually

AMERICAN, CANADIAN, BERMUDA CHAMPION SPENROCK BAN-NER 1964 By Ch. Lockerbie Sandylands Tarquin ex Ch. Sandylands Spungold of Penyfan. Bred by Dorothy Francke, owned by Janet Churchill. Labrador of the Year 1967. (Phillips system.) (Pedigree 35.)

retained for breeding. A bitch has her six-month heat periods and is bred once a year, resulting, of course, in several months at home before she is in show condition again. She generally looks better after one litter but not after she has had several. In other words, it is much more difficult to "make up" a bitch and she must be shown often when in condition. Judges should learn to recognize a good brood bitch, and forgive minor faults and lack of condition in favor of understanding what is important and remember that the whole future of the breed depends on good bitches.

I think that the patience judges show under all kinds of circum-stances is remarkable. Although I have seen many a handler become furious, I have never seen a judge anything but a lady or gentleman. They are a good breed and we exhibitors should appreciate what they do or we might find ourselves trying to do their job.

DUAL CH. BANCHORY BOLO 1929 owned by Mrs. Robert Clark Jr. painted by Ward Binks.

22. WINNER LISTINGS

AMERICAN DUAL CHAMPIONS

BENGAL OF ARDEN—Good Hope Angus × Burma of Arden

BRACKENS SWEEP—Glenhead Sweep × Bracken of Timbertown

BRAES OF ARDEN—Ch. Raffles of Earlsmoor × F.T.Ch. Decoy of Arden

CHEROKEE BUCK—Dual Ch. Grangemead Precocious × Grangemead Sharon

GORSE OF ARDEN—Ch. Raffles of Earlsmoor × F.T.Ch. Decoy of Arden

GRANGEMEAD PRECOCIOUS—Dual Ch. Shed of Arden × Huron Lady

HELLO JOE OF ROCHELTREE—Snikeb's Ding Ding Ding × Billy's Black Babe

LITTLE PIERRE OF DEER CREEK—Eng. Am. Ch. Hiwood Mike × F.T.Ch. Tar of Arden

MATCHMAKER FOR DEER CREEK—Dual Ch. Little Pierre of Deer Creek × Tops of Bigstone

MICHAEL OF GLENMERE—Ace of Whitmore × Vixen of Glenmere

SHED OF ARDEN—Ch. Raffles of Earlsmoor × F.T.Ch. Decoy of Arden

TREVEILYR SWIFT (import)—Penlon Don × Treveilyr Starlight

YODEL OF MOREXPENSE—F.T.Ch. Freehaven Jay × Ch. Echo of Arden

ALPINE CHEROKEE ROCKET—Dual Ch. Grangemead Precocious × Nelgards Madam Queen

DELA-WINN'S TAR OF CRAIGNOOK—Dela-Winn's Mike × Dela-Winn's Gilda

NILO POSSIBILITY—F.T.Ch. Staindrop Murton Marksman × Pawlesta Tinki Poo

PROBLEM BOY DUKE OF WAKE—Ponto's Ponto of Wake × Kavanaugh's Ripple

BEAU BRUMMEL OF WHYDALE—F.T.Ch. Rip's Bingo × Shady Lady IV

BOLEY'S TAR BABY—King Chukker of Robinsdale × Mem of Greeymar

KINGSWERE BLACK EBONY—F.T.Ch. The Spider of Kingswere × Stylish Patsy of Deer Creek

BURNHAM BUFF (yellow bitch)—Ch. Deer Creek Toddy Time II × Tuffy of Bar Mur Farm

HAPPY PLAYBOY (also Canadian Dual Ch.)—Can. & Am. Ch. Castlemore Shamus × Susie

RIDGEWOOD PLAYBOY—La Sage's Smoky × Nelgard's Counterpoint

PETITE ROUGE—Robbet's Black Hope × Cuzz's Corky

SHAMROCK ACRES SIMMER DOWN—Brodhead's Bar Booze × Ch. Whygin Gentle Julia of Avec

CALYPSO CLIPPER—F.T.Ch. Yankee Clipper of Reo Raj × Bigstone Robber

BRAMHOPE BOATING 1960 AW By Bramhope Blackbird ex Bramhope Banana. Bred by Mary Scott, owned in Australia by Mrs. Helen Sapio. She had an important influence in Australia.

ALL-TIME HIGH SCORING FIELD TRIAL DOG

F.T.Ch. SPIRIT LAKE DUKE—Smudge of Prairie Creek Farm × Random Lake Black Ghost

BRITISH DUAL CHAMPIONS

BANCHORY BOLO AA—Scandal of Glynn × Caerhowell Nettle

BANCHORY SUNSPECK AA—Ch. Ilderton Ben × Ch. Manor House Belle

TITUS OF WHITMORE AA—Twist of Whitmore × Teazle of Whitmore

BRAMSHAW BOB MM—Ch. Ingleston Ben × Bramshaw Brimble

LOCHAR NESSIE RR (bitch)—Lochar Peter × Lochar Biddy

BANCHORY PAINTER PP—Peter the Painter × Glenhead Bess

STAINDROP SAIGHDEAR AD (yellow)—Glenhead Jimmy × Our Lil

KNAITH BANJO AE (yellow)—Poppleton Golden Russet × Knaith Brilliantine

ROCKSTEAD FOOTSPARK AD—Ludford Razor × Jaala

FLUTE OF FLODDEN EE—Dual Ch. Titus of Whitmore × Wemyss Rachael

CASTLEMORE CORONET—Ch. Whatstandwell Coronet × Ch. Hilldown Sylver

CASTLEMORE BLACK GEM (bitch)—Ch. Strokestown Duke of Blaircourt × Ch. Hilldown Sylver

Outstanding dogs of all breeds are listed in the Kennel Club Stud Book, published annually by the English Kennel Club, with each volume (starting in 1897 with A) code lettered to designate year of cataloging. (Actual publication occurs during the next year.) As each dog is originally listed therein, it is assigned a registration number to which is added the letter-code designating the volume then current. In subsequent listings of any dog, the letter-numeral identification is noted, but information contained in the original entry is not repeated and one must refer to the volume indicated by the letters for such data.

Code letters used herein and the registration years indicated are H 1904, J 1905, L 1907, M 1908, N 1909, P 1910, R 1912, S 1913, T 1914, and U 1915; a double letter code was begun in 1921 and is as follows:

		KK	1930	VV	1940	AG	1950	AS	1960	BD	1970
AA	1921	LL	1931	WW	1941	AH	1951	AT	1961	BE	1971
BB	1922	MM	1932	XX	1942	AJ	1952	AU	1962		
CC	1923	NN	1933	YY	1943	AK	1953	AV	1963		
DD	1924	PP	1934	ZZ	1944	AL	1954	AW	1964		
EE	1925	QQ	1935	AB	1945	AM	1955	AX	1965		
FF	1926	RR	1936	AC	1946	AN	1956	AY	1966		
GG	1927	SS	1937	AD	1947	AP	1957	AZ	1967		
HH	1928	TT	1938	AE	1948	AQ	1958	BA	1968		
JJ	1929	UU	1939	AF	1949	AR	1959	BC	1969		

ENG. AM. CH. BALLYDUFF SEAMAN BA 1966. By Ch. Ballyduff Holly-branch of Keithray AV ex Cookridge Negra. Bred by Mrs. R. Harrison. Owned by Mrs. B. M. Docking. Owned in the USA by Mr. Martin.

LABRADOR CLUB SPECIALTY SHOW WINNERS

(no record of first 20 shows)

WARDWYN WHISKERS—Ch. Earlsmoor Moor × Ch. Buddah of Arden

GOOD HOPE ABERDEEN—F.T.Ch. Hiwood Mike × Dhulochnan Dance of Timber Town (black bitch)

Ch. HUGGER MUGGER—Ch. Bancstone Bob of Wingan × Marsh

Ch. WARDWYN WELCOME—Ch. Earlsmoor Moor × Ch. Buddah of Arden (black bitch)

Ch. STOWAWAY AT DEER CREEK—Dual Ch. Shed of Arden × Ch. Buddah of Arden

Ch. CHIDLEY SPOOK—Ch. Hugger Mugger × Wendy Jinx (black bitch)

Ch. CHIDLEY SPOOK (black bitch)—See above

CHIMNEY SWEEP II—Dual Ch. Bracken's Sweep × Wardwyn Warbler

TOOTS OF DUNECHT (import)—Branchory Soot × Rose of Dunecht

MISS DELA-WINN (black bitch)—F.T.Ch. Gun of Arden × Blackhawk Queen Susan

Ch. CHIDLEY SPOOK—See above

Ch. ASHUR DEACON—Ch. Hugger Mugger × Ch. Rupert Desdemona

Port Fortune Smoke Screen—South Dartmouth Black Night × Hobbimoors Bullfinch

Udalia's Trace (black bitch)—Udalia's Target × Ledgeland's Susie

Chidley Genii (black bitch)—Ch. Hugger Mugger × Ch. Chidley Spook

Gunner of Land Fall—Lucky × Thorn of Catawba

Chidley Goldfinch (yellow bitch)—Ch. Hugger Mugger × Chidley Honey Bun

Whygin Skia of Southdown (black bitch)—Ch. Whygin Poppitt × Ch. Rupert Desdemona

Ch. Lockerbie Blackfella—Ballyduff Treesholme Terryboy × Ch. Ballyduff Candy

Golden Chance of Franklin (yellow bitch)—Ch. Troublemaker of Franklin × Pretty Iris

Ore Hill Sunday Punch—Ch. Wardwyn's Hi-Tail Mike × Wardwyn Shooting Star

Ch. Golden Chance of Franklin—See above

Land Fall's Vulcan—Ch. Gunner of Landfall × Strokestown Twinkle

Ch. Ore Hill's Sunday Punch—See above

Ch. Golden Chance of Franklin—See above

CH. SANDYLANDS TARA AV 1961 By Australian Ch. Sandylands Tan ex Sandylands Shadow. Bred by Mrs. G. Broadley, owned in USA by J. Lewis III.

CH. GOLDSBORO TWEED 1963 By Ch. Harris Tweed of Ide ex Ch. Kimvalley Deborah. Bred by A. Pollin, owned by Mrs. Robert Clark Jr.

Ch. DARK STAR OF FRANKLIN—Ch. Labcroft Mister Chips × Ch. Pitch of Franklin

Ch. GOLDEN CHANCE OF FRANKLIN—See above

Ch. WHYGIN CAMPAIGN PROMISE (black bitch)—Ch. Wildfield Mickey Finn × Ch. Whygin the Bedford Brat

Ch. LEWISFIELD GUNSLINGER—Ch. Jolor's Talisman × Ch. Sandylands Tara

Ch. SPENROCK BANNER—Ch. Lockerbie Sandylands Tarquin × Ch. Sandylands Spun Gold

Ch. LOCKERBIE GOLDENTONE JENSEN (yellow import)—Diant Jaysgreen Jasper × Moiban Trudy

SPENROCK SAN SOUCI—Ch. Sandylands Midas × Ch. Spenrock Banner

Ch. SPENROCK SAN SOUCI—See above

Ch. GOLDSBORO TWEED—Ch. Harris Tweed of Ide × Ch. Kimvalley Deborah

Ch. HILLSBORO WIZARD OF OZ—Ch. Shamrock Acres Light Brigade × Ch. Goldsboro Toto of Oz

Ch. SPRINGFIELD'S MISS WILLING—Ch. Harris Tweed of Ide × Ch. Kimvalley Cinderella

Ch. DIANT JUPITER (yellow import)—Ch. Landyke Lancer × Nokeener Novel Cracker

Ch. WHYGIN GOLD BULLION (yellow)—Ch. Kinley Comet × Whygin Popsickle

Ch. WHYGIN BLACK GAMIN (black bitch)—Ch. Whygin John Duck × Whygin Dark Magic

Ch. SAM OF BLAIRCOURT (import)—Hawk of Luscander × Olivia of Blaircourt

Ch. INKY OF DEERHAVEN (black bitch)—Chidley Winks

Ch. SAM OF BLAIRCOURT—See above

SANDYLANDS TARA (black bitch import)—Australian Ch. Sandylands Tan × Sandylands Shadow

Ch. SAM OF BLAIRCOURT—See above

GOLDSBORO STAR (black bitch)—Ch. Harris Tweed of Ide × Ch. Kimvalley Deborah

Ch. LEWISFIELD CHIMNEY SWEEP C.D.—Ch. Jo Lor's Talisman × Sandylands Tara

ALVASTAN DIANT WHIMSEY (yellow bitch import)—Dobrudden Tank Commander × Diant Julietta

Ch. LOCKERBIE KISMET (yellow)—Lockerbie Panda × Lockerbie Sandylands Tidy

Ch. RUPERT JURISPRUDENCE (yellow bitch)—Ch. Glenarvey Barrister × Rupert Grace

Ch. LEWISFIELD'S GUNSLINGER—Ch. Jolor's Talisman × Sandylands Tara

Ch. SPENROCK'S BANNER (black bitch)—Lockerbie Sandylands Tarquin × Ch. Sandylands Spungold

Ch. LOCKERBIE GOLDENSTONE JENSEN (yellow import)—Diant Jaysgreen Jasper × Moiban Trudy

SPENDROCK'S SAN SOUCI (yellow bitch)—Ch. Sandylands Midas × Ch. Spendrock's Banner

Ch. SPENDROCK'S SAN SOUCI—See above

Ch. GOLDSBORO TWEED—Ch. Harris Tweed of Ide × Ch. Kimvalley Deborah

NATIONAL CHAMPIONS (Field & Stream)

BLIND OF ARDEN (sister of F.T.Ch. Decoy of Arden)—Odds On × Peggy of Shipton (import)

BANCHORY NIGHT LIGHT—Blackworth Midnight × Dinah of Wongatee

NIGGER OF BARRINGTON—Fresco Smut × Kitty of Barrington

TAR OF ARDEN (bitch)—Hiwood Risk × Peggy of Shipton

272

NATIONAL CHAMPIONS

Dual Ch. SHED OF ARDEN (1942, 1943, 1946)—Ch. Raffles of Earlsmoor × F.T.Ch. Decoy of Arden

BLACK MAGIC OF AUDLON (bitch)—F.T.Ch. Hiwood Mike × F.T.Ch. Tar of Arden

Dual Ch. BRACKENS SWEEP—Glenhead Sweep × Bracken of Timer Town

BRIGNALS GRINGO—Freehaven Lucky × Victoria Crescent

MARVADEL BLACK GUM—Mint of Barrington × Marvadel Cinders

KING BUCK (1952, 1953)—Timothy of Arden × Alta Banchory

MAJOR VI—F.T.Ch. Shadows Ebony Bob × Wardwyn Windbound

SPIRIT LAKE DUKE (1957, 1959)—Smudge of Prairie Creek Farm × Random Lake Black Ghost

CORK OF OAKWOOD LANE (1955)—Coastal Charger of Deer Creek × Akona Liza Jane of Kingdale

MASSIE'S SASSIE BOOTS—Shadow II × Penny of Wingan

NILO POSSIBILITY—F.T.Ch. Black Prince of Sag Harbor × Kingswere Black Widow

DOLOBRAN'S SMOKE TAIL—F.T.Ch. Dolobran's Spook × Dolobran's Mighty Mite

DEL TONE COLVIN (1961, 1963)—Nat'l Ch. Cork of Oakwood Lane × Del Tone Bridget

BIGSTONE HOPE (bitch)—Nat'l Ch. Cork of Oakwood Lane × Bigstone Ricky

RIPCO'S V.C. MORGAN—Ripco's Peter Pan × Peggy of Lopez

WHYGIN CORK'S COOT—Nat'l Ch. Cork of Oakwood Lane × Whygin Dark Ace

BUTTE BLUE MOON—Beavercrest Storm Cloud × Mascushla of Rockmont

SUPER CHIEF—F.Ch. & AF.Ch. Paha Sapa Chief II × Ironwood Cherokee Chica

CRUFTS WINNERS

MUNDEN SENTRY H—Munden Sixty × Munden Scottie H
MUNDEN SINGLE H—Munden Sixty × Munden Scottie H
DAPHNE J—Rock × Gulnar J
SIR RICHARD J—Netherby Tar × Nell (Craw's)
DUNBOYNE J—Rock × Gulnar J
MUNDEN SINGLE—See above
MUNDEN SENTRY—See above
SYBIL J—Spratt × Munden Solitary H
BRAYTON SWIFT L—Sir Richard J × Betty
BRAYTON SWIFT—See above
SELINA M—Munden Sentry H × Snavernake Countess
Ch. BROOME PARK BOB M—Munden Sovereign H × Munden Sixpence
Ch. BELLE CHIENNE M—Timothy M × Zoe M
MUNDEN SOOTY P—Warwick Collier × Munden Scottie H
DUNGAVEL THOR P—Flapper L × Dungavel Juno M
ZILLAH N (bitch)—Brayton Swift L × Jilt
Ch. BRAYTON SWIFT L—See above
FOXLEY COUNTESS S—Sultan × Bendysh Bess
Ch. BRAYTON SWIFT—See above
Ch. MANOR HOUSE BELLE R—Timothy M × Joan N
TYPE OF WHITMORE T—Ch. Brayton Swift L × Arbury Countess
Ch. MANOR HOUSE BELLE—See above
Ch. TYPE OF WHITMORE T—See above
Ch. MANOR HOUSE BELLE R—See above
HORTON MAX U—Beechgrove Peter S (flatcoat) × Horton Flo
Ch. MANOR HOUSE BELLE R—See above
THELMA OF WHITMORE U—Crosshill Bruce T × Toddy T
Ch. WITHINGTON DORANDO T—F.T.Ch. Peter of Faskally P × Ch.
    Manor House Belle R
Ch. BANCHORY RANDO AA—Withington Bream × Withington Darkie
BANCHORY FIDGET BB—Tango U × Bess
F.T.Ch. BANCHORY BOLO AA—Scandall of Glynn × Caerhowell Nettle
BALCOMBE COUNTESS BB—Tramp × ?
TEAZLE OF WHITMORE AA—Ch. Ilderton Ben R × Phlox V
Ch. GRATELEY BEN BB—Ch. Ilderton Ben R × Dungavel Bell
Ch. WITHINGTON BEN AA—Banchory Don Y × Withington Dinah AA
WOLFERTON SHELAH DD—Withington Dan CC × Pallinsburn Quest CC
Ch. WITHINGTON BEN AA—See above
HAWKESBURY DAINTY EE (yellow)—Worlington Dick × Ruthless of
    Kettledean

NOKEENER NIGHTLIGHT 1962 By Cliveruth Black Night ex Nokeener Novelty. Bred and owned by Mrs. R. Williams.

Ch. BANCHORY DANILO EE—Dual Ch. Banchory Bolo AA × Munden Scarcity

HAILES PETER DD—Withington Ben AA × Hailes Lal BB

HAWKESBURY DAINTY EE—See above

Ch. BANCHORY DANILO EE—See above

JUNO HH—Castledown Lynch BB × Heathland Tess FF

SIMON CALLED PETER JJ—Dellshot Sable EE × Imperial Beauty

TANSEY OF WHITMORE FF—Tax of Whitmore CC × Thelma of Whitmore U

Ch. BENNINGBROUGH TANGLE DD—Dual Ch. Banchory Bolo AA × Thyme

THRONE OF WHITMORE KK—Dual Ch. Titus of Whitmore AA × Trifle of Whitmore

Ch. ALBY TWINK KK (yellow)—Golden Morn HH × Myrtle

REYEN LASS LL (yellow)—Storey × Helen

BRAMSHAW BOB MM—Ch. Ingleston Ben JJ × Bramshaw Brimble HH

JUDY OF PRESTWOOD MM—Bruce of Prestwood × Pietsmead Trix

Ch. BRAMSHAW BOB MM—See above

275

CH. BALLYDUFF WHATSTANDWELL ROWENA 1947 AG By Whatstandwell Ballyduff Robin ex Sandylands Juny. Bred by Mr. and Mrs. H. Taylor, owned by Dr. Acheson. CC Crufts.

GROSMONT JEWELL NN—Ch. Ingleston Ben JJ × Grosmont Judith JJ

INGLESTON NITH KK—Lochar Mac EE × Kinmount Juno CC

Ch. REYEN LASS LL (yellow)—See above

Ch. INGLESTON BEN JJ—Duke of Kirkmahoe FF × Ingleston Nancy FF

ABBESS OF HARPOTTS QQ—Monk of Winscales JJ × Judy of Woodlea KK

Ch. CHEVERELLS BEN OF BANCHORY RR—Ch. Ingleston Ben JJ × Xmas Nora MM

Ch. BANCHORY SHELAGH RR—Mitton Laddie × Bellendene

ORCHARDTON DONALD SS—Ch. Ingleston Ben JJ × Orchardton Dawn LL

Dual Ch. LOCHAR NESSIE RR—Lochar Peter × Lochar Biddy NN

GREATFORD BROOM VV—Burymanor Ben UU × Bisham Gypsy

HOLTON JOYFUL UU—Ch. Liddly Jonquil MM × Towyriver Bee MM

CRUDENBAY BLACK DIAMOND AD—Colwill Diamond UU × Crudenbay Lass SS

ANNETTE OF STAITHES AE—John of Sandylands YY × Black Emblem of Glengour

276

Dual Ch. STAINDROP SAIGHDEAR AD (yellow)—Glenhead Jimmy × Our Lil

Ch. BALLYDUFF WHATSTANDWELL ROWENA AG—Whatstandwell Ballyduff Robin AE × Sandylands Juny AC

Ch. BRITISH JUSTICE AG—Banchory Jack AD × Pont-Du-Fahs AD

SPURSTOW SCAWFELL SNIFF AG—Grouse of Spurstow·AD × Langnore Jane

Ch. BRITISH JUSTICE AG—See above

PRINCESS DEIRDRE AG (yellow)—Irish Ch. Jackie of Crossgar × Ballykine Kitty

HIGH ANGERTON SHOT AM—Triumph of Treesholme AH × Reek AF

Ch. BALLYDUFF WHATSTANDWELL ROWENA AG—See above

Ch. WHATSTANDWELL CORONET AM (yellow)—F.T.Ch. Whatstandwell Hiwood Brand AD × Honey of Whatstandwell AB

ROBERTA OF COOHOY AP—Whatstandwell Ballyduff Robin AE × Wanda of Coohoy AH

CEDAR WOODLAND AL (yellow)—Sandalwood AK × Susan of Haywood

Ch. LADY OF TRING AM (yellow)—Ballyduff Orangeman AF × Queenie of Battlesgreen

SILVER STANSHANG OF ZOAR AQ (yellow)—Ch. General of Garshangan AL × Shelagh of Zoar AQ

Ch. DIANT JULIET AP (yellow)—Ch. Diant Swandyke Cream Cracker AJ × Diant Reflection

Ch. RULER OF BLAIRCOURT AQ (Reserve Best in Show)—Forbes of Blaircourt AL × Olivia of Blaircourt AP

Ch. KINLEY CURLEW OF ULPHATHWAITE AP (yellow)—Kinley Comet AM × Oriole of Ulphathwaite AM

Ch. LANDYKE STOMER AR (yellow)—Nokeener Novelcracker AQ × Ch. Landyke Poppy AL

Ch. KINLEY CURLEW OF ULPHATHWAITE AP—See above

Ch. LANDYKE LANCER AR (yellow)—Nokeener Novelcracker AQ × Ch. Landyke Poppy AL

Ch. BALLAD OF BARRA AR (yellow)—Ch. Kinley Matador AL × Lady Copper AN

Ch. BALLYDUFF HOLLYBRANCH OF KEITHRAY AV—Ch. Sandylands Tweed of Blaircourt AS × Ch. Hollybank Beauty AT

Ch. SANDYLANDS TRUTH AU—Australian Ch. Sandylands Tan AT × Sandylands Shadow

DUNLIN OF ULPHATHWAITE AQ (yellow)—Kinley Comet AM × Oriole of Ulphathwaite AM

Ch. REANACRE MALLARDHURN THUNDER AV—Ch. Sandylands Tweed of Blaircourt AS × Mallardhurn Pat

CH. MACH ZERO CD By Crooks El Torro ex Lewisfield Contessa. Owned and handled by Mrs. A. L. Foote.

Ch. KINLEY COPPER AW (yellow)—Ch. Kinley Skipper AT × Kinley Tango

Ch. BIG BROTHER OF OLDFORGE AW—Ch. Sandylands Sam AT × Princess of Oldforge

Ch. KINLEY COPPER AW—See above

TANYA OF KEITHRAY AY (yellow)—Ch. Sandylands Tweed of Blaircourt AS × Ch. Hollybank Beauty AT

Ch. COOKRIDGE CORMORANT AX—Ch. Cookridge Jasper AW × Cookridge Olga

Ch. CORNLANDS MY FAIR LADY AZ (yellow)—Cornlands Kimvalley Crofter AZ × Cornlands Lady Be Good AU

CORNLANDS NOKEENER HIGH LIGHT AZ (yellow)—Cliveruth Harvester × Nokeener Night Light

KINGSBURY NOKEENER MOONSTAR (yellow puppy)—Nokeener Moon Rocket × Nokeener Night Light

Ch. POOLSTEAD POWDER PUFF AY (yellow)—Ch. Reanacre Mallardhurn Thunder AV × Braeduke Julia of Poolstead AU

COLINWOOD FERN—Ch. Sandylands Tandy × Redgame Liz's Daughter

KINKY OF KEITHRAY—Ch. Ballyduff Seaman BA × Ch. Hollybeaut of Keithray AX

PEDIGREES

① BUCCLEUCH SAILOR — 1892 — GREAT BRITAIN

BRED BY LORD GRIMSTON OWNED BY BUCCLEUCH KENNELS

BLACK DOG

Sire:

SCIPIO II (LORD GRIMSTON)

- SANCHO (LORD GRIMSTON)
  - NETHERBY KIELDER (SIR F. GRAHAM)
    - NETHERBY BOATSWAIN — FROM THE EARL OF HOME
    - NETHERBY NELL — FROM THE DUKE OF BUCCLEUCH
  - SUSAN (LORD GRIMSTON)
    - SAM (LORD GRIMSTON) — DACRE (LORD SALISBURY FROM LORD DACRE) / GYP (J.B. MYER)
    - JET (H. EATON) — NETHERBY BOATSWAIN / NETHERBY NELL
- SAPPHO (LORD GRIMSTON)
  - SANCHO (LORD GRIMSTON)
    - NETHERBY KIELDER (SIR F. GRAHAM) — SAM (LORD GRIMSTON) / JET (H. EATON)
    - SUSAN (LORD GRIMSTON) — NETHERBY BOATSWAIN / NETHERBY NELL
  - SIREN (LORD GRIMSTON)
    - NETHERBY KIELDER (SIR F. GRAHAM) — SAM (LORD GRIMSTON) / JET (H. EATON)
    - SUSAN (LORD GRIMSTON)

Dam:

GORHAMBURY SAPPHO II (LORD GRIMSTON)

- SANCHO (LORD GRIMSTON)
  - NETHERBY KIELDER (SIR F. GRAHAM)
    - NETHERBY BOATSWAIN — FROM THE EARL OF HOME
    - NETHERBY NELL — FROM THE DUKE OF BUCCLEUCH
  - SUSAN (LORD GRIMSTON)
    - SAM (LORD GRIMSTON) — DACRE (LORD SALISBURY FROM LORD DACRE) / GYP (J.B. MYER)
    - JET (H. EATON) — FROM THE EARL OF HOME
- SCANDAL (LORD GRIMSTON)
  - NETHERBY KIELDER (SIR F. GRAHAM)
    - NETHERBY BOATSWAIN — FROM THE DUKE OF BUCCLEUCH
    - NETHERBY NELL
  - SUSAN (LORD GRIMSTON)
    - SAM (LORD GRIMSTON) — DACRE (LORD SALISBURY FROM LORD DACRE) / GYP (J.B. MYER)
    - JET (H. EATON)

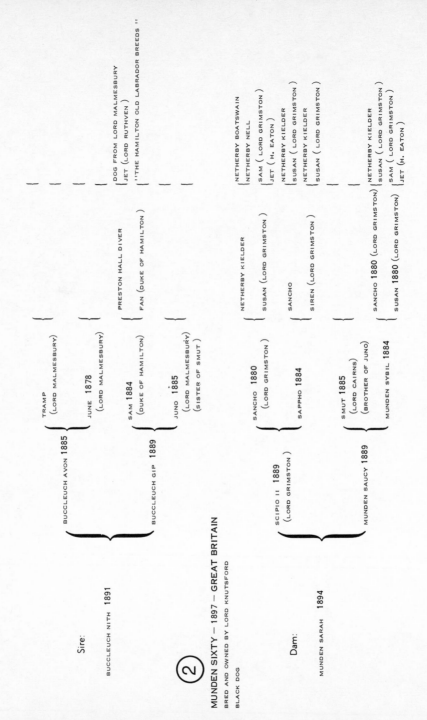

MUNDEN SIXTY – 1897 – GREAT BRITAIN

BRED AND OWNED BY LORD KNUTSFORD

③ BIRKHILL JULIET (DAM OF F.T.CH. PETER OF FASKALLY) ALSO STEWARDESS AND SOUVENIR — 1906 — GREAT BRITAIN

BRED AND OWNED BY CAPT. BALL
BLACK FEMALES

Sire: MUNDEN SOVEREIGN 1902 (HON. H. HOLLAND HIBBERT)

- SIR RICHARD 1899 (BRAYTON)
  - NETHERBY TAR 1894
    - SWEEP 1889 (LORD VERULUM)
      - SANCHO 1880 (LORD GRIMSTON)
      - SCANDAL 1880 (LORD GRIMSTON)
    - NETHERBY ESK 1892 (SIR R. GRAHAM)
      - BUCCLEUCH NED 1882
      - BUCCLEUCH TRICK 1888
  - NELL 1896 (CRAW)
    - BUCCLEUCH JOCK 1892
      - BUCCLEUCH NED 1882
      - BUCCLEUCH NELL 1889
    - JUNO 1891 (EARL OF HOME)
      - BUCCLEUCH AVON 1885
      - BUCCLEUCH TRICK 1888
- MUNDEN SINGLE 1899
  - MUNDEN SIXTY 1897
    - BUCCLEUCH NITH 1891
      - BUCCLEUCH AVON 1885
      - BUCCLEUCH GIP 1889
    - MUNDEN SARAH 1894
      - SCIPIO II (LORD GRIMSTON)
      - MUNDEN SAUCY 1889
  - MUNDEN SCOTTIE 1897
    - BUCCLEUCH DRAKE 1891
      - BUCCLEUCH AVON 1885
      - BUCCLEUCH GIP 1889
    - BUCCLEUCH BELLE 1892
      - BUCCLEUCH NED 1882
      - BUCCLEUCH TRICK 1888

Dam: SUSAN 1902 (CAPT. BALL)

- BUCCLEUCH BRUCE 1896
  - BUCCLEUCH SAILOR 1892
    - SCIPIO II (LORD GRIMSTON)
      - SANCHO 1880 (LORD GRIMSTON)
      - SAPPHO (LORD GRIMSTON)
    - SAPPHO II (LORD GRIMSTON)
      - SANCHO (LORD GRIMSTON)
      - SCANDAL (LORD GRIMSTON)
  - BUCCLEUCH BELLE 1892
    - BUCCLEUCH NED 1882
      - SWEEP 1877 (LORD MALMESBURY)
      - JUNO 1878 (LORD MALMESBURY)
    - BUCCLEUCH TRICK 1888
      - SAM 1884 (DUKE OF HAMILTON)
      - DINAH 1885 (LORD HOME)
- NINNIE 1898 (LIDDELL) (SISTER OF BETSY)
  - BEN 1894 (LIDDELL)
    - SAM 1890 (LIDDELL)
      - SCIPIO II (LORD GRIMSTON)
      - SAPPHO II (LORD GRIMSTON)
    - JUNO II 1891 (BARNETT)
      - SWEEP 1889 (MR. FENWICK)
      - JUNO I 1885 (MR. BARNETT)
  - SAL OR SAH 1891 (STRAKER) (MORE LIKE A LABRADOR)
    - DACRE "WAS A RATHER HEAVY SLOW, LONG COATED DOG!"
      - SIRE UNKNOWN
      - DAM IMPORTED BY AN AMERICAN
    - NELL 1881 (MR. STRAKER)

WATERDALE GAMESTER (SIRE OF PETER OF FASKALLY) — 1906 — GREAT BRITAIN

BRED BY K.R.FAULCONER

BLACK DOG

(4)

Sire:

SHERFIELD SPRATT 1900

- MUNDEN SIXTY (HON.A.H.HIBBERT)
  - BUCCLEUCH NITH
    - BUCCLEUCH AVON
      - TRAMP (LORD MALMESBURY)
      - JUNO 1878 (LORD MALMESBURY)
    - BUCCLEUCH GIP
      - SAM (DUKE OF HAMILTON)
      - BUCCLEUCH NELL (LORD MALMESBURY)
  - MUNDEN SARAH
    - SCIPIO II (LORD GRIMSTON)
      - SANCHO (LORD GRIMSTON)
      - SAPPHO II (LORD GRIMSTON)
    - MUNDEN SAUCY
      - SMUT (LORD CAIRN)
      - MUNDEN SYBIL
- MUNDEN SCOTTIE
  - BUCCLEUCH DRAKE
    - BUCCLEUCH AVON
      - TRAMP (LORD MALMESBURY)
      - JUNO (LORD MALMESBURY)
    - BUCCLEUCH GIP
      - SAM (DUKE OF HAMILTON)
      - BUCCLEUCH NELL (LORD MALMESBURY)
  - BUCCLEUCH BELLE
    - BUCCLEUCH NED
      - SWEEP (LORD MALMESBURY)
      - JUNO (LORD MALMESBURY)
    - BUCCLEUCH TRICK
      - SAM (DUKE OF HAMILTON)
      - DINAH (LORD HOME)

Dam:

WATERDALE TWINKLE 1904

- MUNDEN SENTRY
  - MUNDEN SIXTY
    - BUCCLEUCH NITH
      - BUCCLEUCH AVON
      - BUCCLEUCH GIP
    - MUNDEN SARAH
      - SCIPIO II (LORD GRIMSTON)
      - MUNDEN SAUCY
  - MUNDEN SCOTTIE
    - BUCCLEUCH DRAKE
      - BUCCLEUCH AVON
      - BUCCLEUCH GIP
    - BUCCLEUCH BELLE
      - BUCCLEUCH NED
      - BUCCLEUCH TRICK
- VENUS 1902 (R.WARD)
  - BRAMBLE (R. WARD)
    - BUCCLEUCH JOCK
      - BUCCLEUCH NELL
      - "SAID TO BE OF MIXED BREED"
    - ROSE (WARD)
      - "THOUGHT TO BE FROM LANGHOLM LODGE"
  - SOLO (F. SCHOOL BRED)
    - NETHERBY OTTER (SIR R.GRAHAM)
    - ROCK (MENZIES)

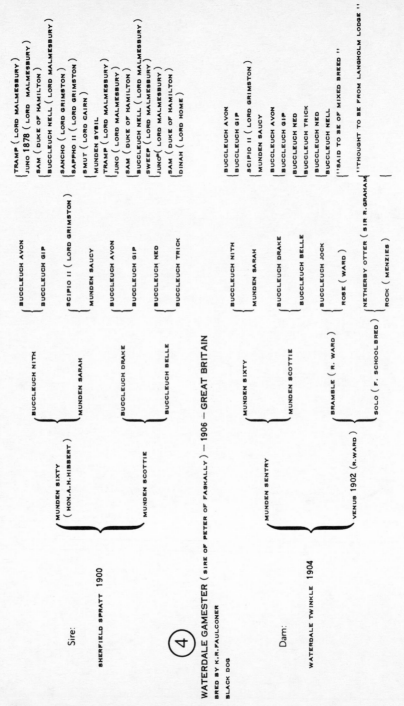

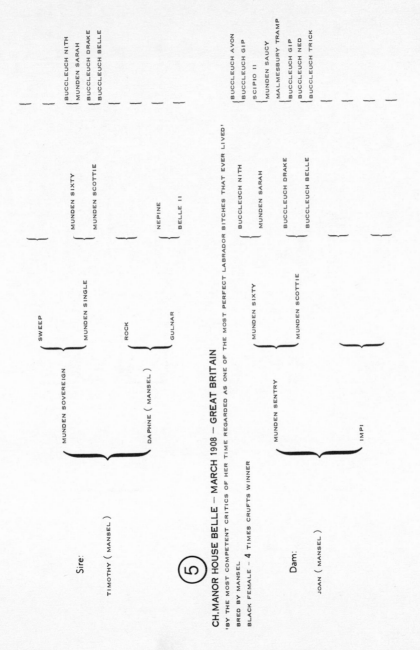

CH. MANOR HOUSE BELLE — MARCH 1908 — GREAT BRITAIN

'BY THE MOST COMPETENT CRITICS OF HER TIME REGARDED AS ONE OF THE MOST PERFECT LABRADOR BITCHES THAT EVER LIVED'

BRED BY MANSEL.

BLACK FEMALE — 4 TIMES CRUFTS WINNER

⑤

Sire:

TIMOTHY (MANSEL)

MUNDEN SOVEREIGN

SWEEP

MUNDEN SINGLE

MUNDEN SIXTY

MUNDEN SCOTTIE

DAPHNE (MANSEL)

ROCK

GULNAR

NEPINE

BELLE II

BUCCLEUCH NITH
MUNDEN SARAH
BUCCLEUCH DRAKE
BUCCLEUCH BELLE

Dam:

JOAN (MANSEL)

MUNDEN SENTRY

MUNDEN SIXTY

MUNDEN SCOTTIE

BUCCLEUCH NITH
MUNDEN SARAH
BUCCLEUCH DRAKE
BUCCLEUCH BELLE

IMPI

BUCCLEUCH AVON
BUCCLEUCH GIP
SCIPIO II
MUNDEN SAUCY
MALMESBURY TRAMP
BUCCLEUCH GIP
BUCCLEUCH NED
BUCCLEUCH TRICK

YELLOW JESTER — 1914 — GREAT BRITAIN

BRED BY J.H.HEAPS   OWNED BY N.G.ATKINSON CLARKE

YELLOW DOG

(6)

Sire: GENUINE 1913 (YELLOW)

- HARBORO PAT BLACK
  - RANGER (HIRSCH) BLACK
    - KING RICHARD — NO FURTHER RECORD
    - BESS — NO FURTHER RECORD
  - BENDYSH BESS
    - PRINCE — NO FURTHER RECORD
    - BLACK BESS — NO FURTHER RECORD
- BRAXTED ROSE (CLARKE) BLACK
  - KAAL (MAJ.PHILLIPS)
    - FLAPPER (MAJ.PORTAL)
      - STAG (BARNETT) 1898
      - BETSY (COL.BATES) 1898
    - KUTUSHKA (MAJ.PHILLIPS)
      - MUNDEN SIXTY
      - KATANGA (MAJ.PHILLIPS)
  - PUNDICTA (CROSS)
    - HICKORY
      - MUNDEN SOVEREIGN
      - MUNDEN SOLITARY
    - RATCHELL
      - WARICK COLLIER
      - THE DUCHESS

Dam: VETE 1918 (YELLOW)

- PRATT (CLARKE) YELLOW
  - BEN OF HYDE (RADCLYFFE) FIRST YELLOW LABRADOR
    - NEPTUNE (RADCLYFFE) BLACK
      - SWEEP II (GUEST)
      - NELL (RADCLYFFE) 1887
    - DUCHESS (TAPPER) BLACK
      - PROBABLY FROM CRANFORD OF MILTON ABBEY
      - LORD WIMBORNE'S BITCH
  - NELL (SWAN) BLACK
    - BUCCLEUCH NITH
      - BUCCLEUCH AVON 1885
      - BUCCLEUCH GIP 1890
    - SQUAW (BARNETT)
      - SAM (LIDDELL) 1890
      - JUNO II (BARNETT) 1891
- HURRY (CLARKE) YELLOW
  - ANGERTON RUST (STRAKER) YELLOW
    - ROVER (STRAKER)
      - RED DOG PROBABLY FROM LORD TWEEDMOUTH
      - BELL (HOGG) RED – PROBABLY SAME AS ABOVE
    - NANCY (STRANGHAN)
      - SPORTSMAN (RED)
      - NELL (SWAN) BLACK
  - FLEET 1908 (CLARKE) YELLOW
    - SANDY (CAPT.RICHMAN) YELLOW
      - TWEED (NO FURTHER RECORD)
      - CAPT.RICHMAN WAS ADJ. AT ALNWICK
    - SLOE (CLARKE) YELLOW
      - STAG (BARNETT)
      - SUSAN (BROWNE) SISTER OF NELL (SWAN)

DUAL CHAMPION KNAITH MONKBOY — 1919 — GREAT BRITAIN

BRED AND OWNED BY MRS. WORMALD

(7)

Sire: BRITZ (YELLOW) — YELLOW DOG

- MANNIE (YELLOW)
  - BEN OF HYDE (FIRST YELLOW LABRADOR)
    - NEPTUNE (RADCLYFFE) BLACK
      - SWEEP II (SIRE AND DAM IMPORTED)
      - NELL (RADCLYFFE) SIRE AND DAM IMPORTED
    - DUCHESS (TAPPER) BLACK
      - PROBABLY FROM CRANFORD OF MILTON ABBEY
      - LORD WIMBORNE'S BITCH
  - VELVET 1907 BLACK (MRS. WORMALD)
    - LIFT (MAJ. BROWNE)
      - FLAPPER (MAJ. PORTAL) 1902
      - SLOE (G. ATKINSON CLARKE)
    - NELL (MAJ. BROWNE)
      - BEN OF HYDE
      - PINK (SWAN)
- NELL (SWAN) BLACK
  - BUCCLEUCH NITH 1891
    - BUCCLEUCH AVON 1885
      - TRAMP (LORD MALMESBURY)
      - JUNE 1882 (LORD MALMESBURY)
    - BUCCLEUCH GIP 1889
      - SAM (DUKE OF HAMILTON) 1884
      - NELL 1886 (LORD MALMESBURY)
  - SQUAW 1893 (BARNETT)
    - SAM (LIDDELL) 1890
      - SCIPIO II
      - SAPPHO II
    - JUNE II (BARNETT) 1891
      - SWEEP 1889
      - JUNO (LORD MALMESBURY)

Dam: MEALIE (YELLOW)

- MANNIE (YELLOW)
  - BEN OF HYDE YELLOW
    - NEPTUNE (BLACK)
      - SWEEP "BRED FROM STOCK IMPORTED"
      - NELL (RADCLYFFE) SIRE AND DAM IMPORTED
    - DUCHESS (TAPPER)
      - PROBABLY FROM CRANFORD OF MILTON ABBEY
      - LORD WIMBORNE'S BITCH
  - VELVET (MRS. WORMALD) BLACK
    - LIFT (MAJ. BROWNE)
      - FLAPPER 1902
      - SLOE 1903
    - NELL (MAJ. BROWNE)
      - BEN OF HYDE
      - PINK (SWAN) FROM LORD TWEEDMOUTH'S DOG
- NAWTON BROWNIE P (REGISTERED AS DARK LIVER BLACK WITH BROWN MARKINGS - LABRADOR CLUB BOOK)
  - LANSDOWNE BENJAMIN
    - SATRAP (BLACK)
      - MUNDEN SENTRY
      - SYBIL J
    - DAPHNE (MANSEL) BLACK
      - ROCK
      - GULNAR J
  - ZADIE
    - SATRAP (MANSEL)
      - MUNDEN SENTRY
      - SYBIL (FAULCONER)
    - BELINDA (MANSEL)
      - MUNDEN SOVEREIGN
      - DAPHNE (MANSEL)

KIRKMAHOE DINA, BROCKLEHIRST NELL, KINMOUNT PAX — 1919 — GREAT BRITAIN

BRED BY J. DINWOODIE
BLACK BITCHES

⑧

Sire:
KINMOUNT DON

- BROCKLEHIRST BOB
  - ESK (PATTISON)
    - WARWICK COLLIER
      - NETHERBY TAR
      - NINNIE (LIDDELL) SISTER OF BETSY
    - NELL
      - NETHERBY KIELDER II
      - NEP (PATTISON)
  - BROCKLEHIRST FLORA
    - COPESHAW SAM
      - SULTAN (LORD VERULAM)
      - NETHERBY KATE
    - NETHERBY BESS
      - BUCCLEUCH ALLAN
      - DI (EARL CAIRN)
- STEWARDESS
  - MUNDEN SOVEREIGN
    - SIR RICHARD (BRAYTON)
      - NETHERBY TAR
      - NELL (CRAW)
    - MUNDEN SINGLE
      - MUNDEN SIXTY
      - MUNDEN SCOTTIE
  - SUSAN (CAPT. PARRY)
    - MUNDEN SENTRY
      - BUCCLEUCH SAILOR
      - BUCCLEUCH BELLE
    - NETHERBY KATE
      - BEN (LIDDELL)
      - SAL (STRAKER)

Dam:
MURRAYFIELD NORA

- CH. ILDERTON BEN
  - BOBBY (BOSWELL)
    - SMILER
      - NO RECORD
    - ATHOL LASS
      - NO RECORD
  - NELL (THOMPSON)
    - ROGER
      - NO RECORD
    - JET
      - NO RECORD
- MURRAYFIELD KATE
  - PETER OF WHITMORE II
    - F.T.CH. PETER OF FASKALLY
      - WATERDALE GAMESTER
      - BIRKHILL JULIET (SISTER OF STEWARDESS)
    - LOGAN LORNA
      - BUCCLEUCH MONK
      - LADY (DALGLEISH)
  - BROCKLEHIRST JET
    - ESK (PATTISON)
      - WARWICK COLLIER
      - NELL
    - BROCKLEHIRST FLORA
      - COPESHAW SAM
      - NETHERBY BESS

286

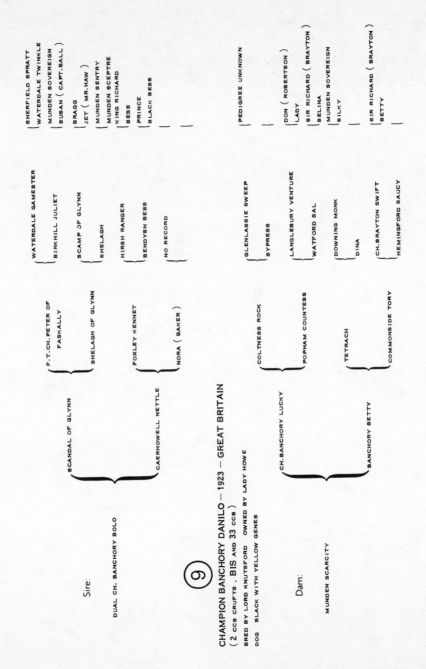

⑨ CHAMPION BANCHORY DANILO — 1923 — GREAT BRITAIN
(2 CCS CRUFTS , BIS AND 33 CCS)
BRED BY LORD KNUTSFORD   OWNED BY LADY HOWE
DOG   BLACK WITH YELLOW GENES

Sire:

DUAL CH. BANCHORY BOLO

- SCANDAL OF GLYNN
  - F.T.CH. PETER OF FASKALLY
    - WATERDALE GAMESTER
      - SHERFIELD SPRATT
      - WATERDALE TWINKLE
    - BIRKHILL JULIET
      - MUNDEN SOVEREIGN
      - SUSAN (CAPT. BALL)
  - SHELAGH OF GLYNN
    - SCAMP OF GLYNN
      - BRAGG
      - JET (MR. HAW)
    - SHELAGH
      - MUNDEN SENTRY
      - MUNDEN SCEPTRE
- CAERHOWELL NETTLE
  - FOXLEY KENNET
    - HIRSH RANGER
      - KING RICHARD
      - BESS
    - BENDYSH BESS
      - PRINCE
      - BLACK BESS
  - NORA (BAKER)
    - NO RECORD

Dam:

MUNDEN SCARCITY

- CH. BANCHORY LUCKY
  - COLTNESS ROCK
    - GLENLASSIE SWEEP
      - PEDIGREE UNKNOWN
    - SYPRESS
  - POPHAM COUNTESS
    - LANGLEBURY VENTURE
      - DON (ROBERTSON)
      - LADY
    - WATFORD SAL
      - SIR RICHARD (BRAYTON)
      - SELINA
- BANCHORY BETTY
  - TETRACH
    - DOWNING MONK
      - MUNDEN SOVEREIGN
      - SILKY
    - DINA
  - COMMONSIDE TORY
    - CH. BRAYTON SWIFT
      - SIR RICHARD (BRAYTON)
      - BETTY
    - HEMINGFORD SAUCY

CH. ALBY TWINK – 1927 – GREAT BRITAIN

FIRST YELLOW CHAMPION
BRED BY S.C. DYER
YELLOW DOG

(10)

Sire: GOLDEN MORN (YELLOW)

- CHUM OF BOGHURST
  - SHERRY OF KETTLEDEAN (RED)
    - SCARLET (LORD FEVERSHAM)
      - SAM (BROTHER OF MANNIE)
      - ROUGE (CAPT. SWAN)
    - PSYCHE
      - PRINCIPAL (BROTHER OF MEALLIE)
      - NAWTON PEG
  - HAWKESBURY JUDY
    - WORLINGTON DICK
      - NAWTON LION
      - NAWTON PANSY
    - RUTHLESS OF KETTLEDEAN
      - PRATT
      - NEREID (MRS. WORMALD)
- GOLDEN DAWN (YELLOW) (SISTER OF VELVET)
  - SCALTBACK VIMY
    - NAWTON LION
    - NAWTON PANSY
  - VESTA
    - PETER
      - DUKE
      - BESS
    - TRACE

Dam: MYRTLE

- KNAITH BOUCE
  - SAILOR (MAJ. RADCLYFFE)
    - SAM (MRS MOLYNEUX)
    - ROUGE (COL. SWAN)
      - BEN OF HYDE
      - VELVET (BLACK)
  - MEALIE
    - MANNIE
      - BEN OF HYDE
      - VELVET (BLACK)
    - NAWTON BROWNIE (DARK LIVER)
      - LANDSDOWNE BENJAMIN
      - ZADIE
- LORBOTTLE BELLE
  - KNAITH SAM
    - FOXDENTON NEPTUNE
      - BEN OF HYDE
      - NELL (SWAN)
    - KNAITH LADY
  - RESTLESS OF KETTLEDEAN (RED)
    - SCARLET (LORD FEVERSHAM)
      - SAM (BROTHER OF MANNIE)
      - ROUGE (COL. SWAN)
    - PSYCHE
      - PRINCIPAL (BROTHER OF MEALLIE)
      - NAWTON PEG

288

FIELD TRIAL CHAMPION BRAEROY RUDDY — 1932 — GREAT BRITAIN

BRED BY MRS. WILSON   OWNED BY MRS. MACPHERSON

FEMALE

Sire:

BRAEROY RAB

- HIELANT LADDIE
  - GLENCOE MAC
    - REMUS
    - PINS
  - CRESTONA
    - PETER
    - VICK
- F.T.CH. BRAEROY ROE
  - WESTERN RIEVER
    - CLYDE (LIKE A CHESAPEAKE)
    - DUNSKEY JEAN
      - DUKE (BUCCLEUCH BLOOD)
      - BUIE (BUCCLEUCH BLOOD)
  - ASHDALE PRIMROSE
    - GLENCOE MAC
      - REMUS
      - PINS
    - ASHDALE POPPY
      - REMUS
      - PRETTY

Dam:

BRAEROY RANDY
(CHOCOLATE GENES)

- WESTERN RIEVER
  - CLYDE (LIKE A CHESAPEAKE)
  - DUNSKEY JEAN
    - DUKE
      - BUCCLEUCH BLOOD
    - BUIE
      - BUCCLEUCH BLOOD
- TANGERINE
  - WOOLMERS SULTAN
    - KNAITH BOUNCE
      - SAILOR
      - MEALIE
    - WOOLMERS SUSAN
      - WOOLMERS SANDAL
      - PECHE MELBA
  - LADY

289

DUAL CHAMPION LOCHAR NESSIE — 1933 — GREAT BRITAIN

BRED AND OWNED BY J.DINWOODIE

BLACK BITCH

⑫

Sire:

LOCHAR PETER

- LOCHAR JOCK
  - INGLESTON NITH
    - LOCHAR MAC
      - GEOFFREY OF NORTHAW
      - LOCHAR KATE
    - KINMOUNT JUNO
      - BACHELOR
      - KINMOUNT PAX
  - INGLESTON NANCY
    - BANCHORY ROGER
      - DUAL CH.BANCHORY BOLO
      - PATIENCE OF FASKALLY
    - BROCKLEHIRST NELL
      - KINMOUNT DON
      - MURRAYFIELD NORA
- KIRKBEAN GYP
  - DUAL CH.FLUTE OF FLODDEN
    - DUAL CH.TITUS OF WHITMORE
      - TWIST OF WHITMORE
      - TEAZLE OF WHITMORE
    - WEMYSS RACHAEL
      - MUTO
      - DINA
  - CRAIGHOUSE GYP
    - SUMITT
    - GYP

Dam:

LOCHAR BIDDY

- CH.BROCKLEHIRST DONNER
  - DUAL CH.BANCHORY BOLO
    - SCANDAL OF GLYNN
      - F.T.CH.PETER OF FASKALLY
      - SHELAGH OF GLYNN
    - CAERHOWELL NETTLE
      - FOXLEY KENNETT
      - NORA (BAKER)
  - MURRAYFIELD BET
    - MURRAYFIELD DAN
      - PETER OF WHITMORE
      - BROCKLEHIRST JET
    - MURRAYFIELD KATE
      - CH.WITHINGTON DORANDO
      - WITHINGTON TESS
- LOCHAR NELL
  - WITHINGTON BANTER
    - WITHINGTON BREAM
      - WITHINGTON BEN
      - QUEENIE OF HALE BARNES
    - HOLFORD FREDA
      - SCANDAL OF GLYNN
      - CAERHOWELL NETTLE
  - BROCKLEHIRST DAISY
    - DUAL CH.BANCHORY BOLO
      - KINMOUNT DON
      - MURRAYFIELD NORA
    - BROCKLEHIRST NELL

F.T.CH. PAINTED LADY OF WILBURY AND PETTISTREE DAN AND MUNTHAM QUAINT (BITCH) — 1934 — GREAT BRITAIN

A KNICKING LITTER   ONE DOG TWO BITCHES (OTHERS)   ALL BLACK

BRED BY MAJOR DES PENCER-ROBERTSON

(13)

Sire:

DUAL CH. BANCHORY PAINTER
- PETER THE PAINTER
  - F.T.CH. LEDSHAM PETER
    - ST MARY'S DONSON
      - CH. ILDERTON BEN
      - DUNGAVEL DIDO
    - DALBEATTIE ROSE
      - TIM OF WHITMORE
      - FAIRGIRTH BELL
  - DINAH
- GLENHEAD BESS
  - F.T.CH. LEDSHAM PETER
    - ST MARY'S DONSON
      - CH. ILDERTON BEN
      - DUNGAVEL DIDO
    - DALBEATTIE ROSE
      - TIM OF WHITMORE
      - FAIRGIRTH BELL
  - L'ILLE BOUNCING GIRL
    - INGLESIDE DON
      - ISLA DON
      - ISLA BESS
    - HEATHERBELLE

Dam:

F.T.CH. QUEST OF WILBURY
- CH. INGLESTON BEN
  - DUKE OF KIRKMAHOE
    - CH. WITHINGTON BANTER
      - WITHINGTON BEAM
      - HOLFORD FREEDA
    - KIRKMAHOE DINA
      - KINMOUNT DON
      - MURRAYFIELD NORA
  - INGLESTON NANCY
    - BANCHORY ROGER
      - DUAL CH. BANCHORY BOLO
      - PATIENCE OF FASKALLY
    - BROCKLEHIRST NELL
      - KINMOUNT DON
      - MURRAYFIELD NORA
- F.T.CH. MUNTHAM RAVEN
  - BANCHORY CORBIE
    - DUAL CH. BANCHORY BOLO
      - SCANDAL OF GLYNN
      - CAERHOWELL NETTLE
    - KIRKMAHOE DINA
      - KINMOUNT DON
      - MURRAYFIELD NORA
  - BENINGBROUGH TANSEY
    - F.T.CH. TAG OF WHITMORE
      - F.T.CH. PATRON OF FASKALLY
      - TACTFUL OF WHITMORE
    - RAFFLES

291

CHAMPION POPPLETON GOLDEN FLIGHT — 1944 — GREAT BRITAIN

BRED BY E.PARKER   OWNED BY MRS.OUTHWAITE

Sire:

POPPLETON GOLDEN RUSSET
YELLOW DOG

- CH.POPPLETON GOLDEN MAJOR
  - CH.POPPLETON BLACK LANCER
    - HAYLERS DANILO
      - CH.BANCHORY DANILO
      - BORRISDEMAIN
    - HAWLMARK TWILIGHT
      - BLACKWORTH MIDNIGHT
      - WORTH FOLLY
  - GOLD GLEAM OF POPPLETON
    - POPPLETON GOLDEN MILLER
      - BILSDALE BARLEY
      - RANI OF BOSSVILLE
    - QUEENIE OF POPPLETON
      - GOLDEN MORN
      - PRIDE OF POPPLETON
- POPPLETON GOLDEN DAWN
  - ILTON ROGER
    - GATEBURTON STOREY
      - STALKER
      - MINTO
    - BILSDALE BUNTY
      - STANTHORNE SERENUS
      - REST
  - POPPLETON BLACK LILAC
    - GROSMONT JAN
      - CH.INGLESTON BEN
      - GROSMONT JUDITH
    - POPPLETON BLACK TULIP
      - HAYLERS DANILO
      - HAWLMARK TWILIGHT

Dam:

MODNEY CROCUS

- FOLKINGHAM SOLO
  - CH.BADGERY RICHARD
    - CH.BANCHORY DANILO
      - DUAL CH.BANCHORY BOLO
      - MUNDEN SCARCITY
    - COODENBEACH NELL
      - COODENBEACH DON
      - FAIRTHORNE DINAH
  - MORMOND BABS
    - CH.BANCHORY DANILO
      - DUAL CH.BANCHORY BOLO
      - MUNDEN SCARCITY
    - MORMOND MOLLY
      - BURO OF STRICKEN
      - STANTHORNE SUSAN
- BESTWOOD BELLE
  - REX
  - GINGER

CH. DIANT SWANDYKE CREAM CRACKER 1950 AJ By Ch. Poppleton Golden Flight AD ex Lassie of Freiston. Bred by W. Tillson, owned by Mrs. L. Wilson Jones. This dog and his sister, Ch. Landyke Poppy were great producers of yellow Labradors.

CH. POPPLETON LIEUTENANT 1949 AH By Poppleton Beech Flight ex Poppleton Golden Sherry. Bred and owned by Mrs. B. M. Outhwaite. Poppleton Kennels had great influence on the popularity of yellow Labradors. Ch. Kinley Comet is line bred to Ch. Poppleton Golden Flight.

DUAL CHAMPION STAINDROP SAIGHDEAR — 1947 — GREAT BRITAIN

BRED BY J.J.MURRAY DEWAR   OWNED BY EDGAR WINTER

YELLOW DOG

(15)

Sire:

GLENHEAD JIMMY

CH.KINPURNIE KAM

CH.ORCHARDTON DONALD

CH.INGLESTON BEN
{ DUKE OF KIRKMAHOE
INGLESTON NANCY

ORCHARDTON DAWN
{ CH.BROCKLEHIRST DONNER
HARDIES CHOICE

F.T.CH.KINPURNIE KATE

KINPURNIE JOE
{ NITH OF HALLEATHS
KINPURNIE GYPSEY

CATTER BETTY
{ SOOT OF KEAVIL
LADY BETTY OF STRUTHERS

KNAPPIES LASS

DUAL CH.BRAMSHAW BOB

CH.INGLESTON BEN
{ DUKE OF KIRKMAHOE
INGLESTON NANCY

BRAMSHAW BRIMBLE
{ F.T.CH.KIRKMAHOE ROVER
CH.BALBEARDIE

GLENHEAD BESS

F.T.CH.LEDSHAM PETER
{ ST.MARY'S DONSON
DALBEATTIE ROSE

L'ILLE BOUNCING GIRL
{ INGLESTON DON
HEATHER BELLE

Dam:

OUR LIL (YELLOW)

F.T.CH.GLENRAVEL
NIMROD

F.T.CH.TAG OF CLAVA

DUAL CH.TITUS OF WHITMORE
{ TWIST OF WHITMORE
TEAZLE OF WHITMORE

CH.DRINKSTONE GYP
{ WOLFERTON DAN
CH.PRIDE OF SOMERSBY

QUEEN OF THE MAY

BLACK HAWK
{ GREAT SCOTT
CRAIGETTA

LIDDLY KINGFISHER
{ CH.TAR OF HAMYAX
LIDDLY VANITY

GLENRAVEL GLYNTER

CH.TOWRIVER JAMES

BANCHORY BOLO'S TRUST
{ DUAL CH.BANCHORY BOLO
BEAULIEU NANCE

TOWRIVER BRAMBLE
{ DUAL CH.TITUS OF WHITMORE
TOWRIVER BEAD

WILD WHISPER

CH.BANCHORY DANILO
{ DUAL CH.BANCHORY BOLO
MUNDEN SCARCITY

CH.REYEN LASS
{ STOREY
HELEN

294

CHAMPION KINLEY COMET — 1953 — GREAT BRITAIN

(16)

BRED BY F.G.WRIGLEY   OWNED BY HAROLD FLORSHEIM IN USA

YELLOW DOG

Sire: CH.KINLEY MATADOR

- POPPLETON BEECH FLIGHT
  - CH.POPPLETON GOLDEN FLIGHT
    - POPPLETON GOLDEN RUSSET
      - CH.POPPLETON GOLDEN MAJOR
      - POPPLETON GOLDEN DAWN
    - MODNEY CROCUS
      - FOLKINGHAM SOLO
      - BESTWOOD BELLE
  - LIME BEECH
    - CH.DURLEY BEECH
      - WARRICK OF WINSCALES
      - BADGERY BRIDGET
    - LIDDLY LIMEJUICE
      - CH.LIDDLY GERANIUM
      - LIDDLY HONEY
- KINLEY SPARROW HAWK
  - CH.POPPLETON GOLDEN FLIGHT
    - POPPLETON GOLDEN RUSSET
      - CH.POPPLETON GOLDEN MAJOR
      - POPPLETON GOLDEN DAWN
    - MODNEY CROCUS
      - FOLKINGHAM SOLO
      - BESTWOOD BELLE
  - FLAXEN LADY
    - GOLD GLEAM OF GLOAMIN
      - ARCADIAN
      - GOLDEN DAWN OF GLENGOUR
    - FENSIDE MEG
      - NIDD JULIAN
      - AKETON JUDY

Dam: CH.KINLEY CHARM

- KINLEY TOSTIG TINTAGEL
  - DUAL CH.STAINDROP SAIGHDEAR
    - GLENHEAD JIMMY
      - CH.KINPURNIE KAM
      - KNAPPIES LASS
    - OUR LIL
      - F.T.CH.GLENRAVEL NIMROD
      - GLENRAVEL GLYNTER
  - TOSTIG SOLGA
    - DAMSTEAD SOLGO
      - STAINDROP WYNDEN
      - CLOVER OF KEEWATIN
    - TOSTIG EBONY
      - DANPRU OF TIBSHELF
      - WYBERTON WENDY
- KINLEY KESTREL
  - CH.POPPLETON GOLDEN FLIGHT
    - POPPLETON GOLDEN RUSSET
      - CH.POPPLETON GOLDEN MAJOR
      - POPPLETON GOLDEN DAWN
    - MODNEY CROCUS
      - FOLKINGHAM SOLO
      - BESTWOOD BELLE
  - FLAXEN LADY
    - GOLD GLEAM OF GLOAMIN
      - ARCADIAN
      - GOLDEN DAWN OF GLENGOUR
    - FENSIDE MEG
      - NIDD JULIAN
      - AKETON JUDY

DUAL CH.CASTLEMORE BLACK GEM (BITCH) IRISH CH.CASTLEMORE CLODAGH AND IRISH, AM.,CAN.CH.CASTLEMORE SHAMUS — 1953 — IRISH

BRED BY MRS.EUSTACE DUCKETT   CLODAGH OWNED BY MISS M.P.DOWLING   SHAMUS OWNED BY H.CROZIER IN CANADA

BLACK WITH YELLOW GENES

(17)

Sire:

IRISH CH.STROKESTOWN DUKE OF BLAIRCOURT

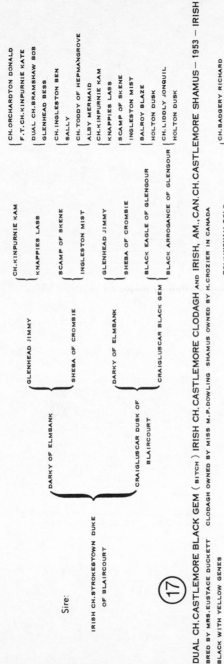

DARKY OF ELMBANK
- GLENHEAD JIMMY
  - CH.KINPURNIE KAM
    - CH.ORCHARDTON DONALD
    - F.T.CH.KINPURNIE KATE
  - KNAPPIES LASS
    - DUAL CH.BRAMSHAW BOB
    - GLENHEAD BESS
- SHEBA OF CROMBIE
  - SCAMP OF SKENE
    - CH.INGLESTON BEN
    - SALLY
  - INGLESTON MIST
    - CH.TODDY OF HEPMANGROVE
    - ALBY MERMAID

CRAIGLUSCAR DUSK OF BLAIRCOURT
- DARKY OF ELMBANK
  - GLENHEAD JIMMY
    - CH.KINPURNIE KAM
    - KNAPPIES LASS
  - SHEBA OF CROMBIE
    - SCAMP OF SKENE
    - INGLESTON MIST
- CRAIGLUSCAR BLACK GEM
  - BLACK EAGLE OF GLENGOUR
    - BALROY BLAZE
    - HOLTON DUSK
  - BLACK ARROGANCE OF GLENGOUR
    - CH.LIDDLY JONQUIL
    - HOLTON DUSK

Dam:

IRISH ENGLISH CH. HILLDOWN SYLVER (YELLOW)

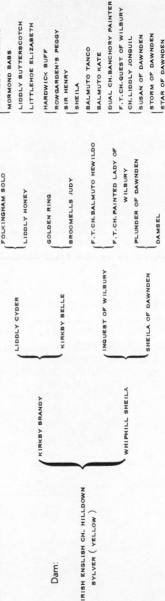

KIRKBY BRANDY
- LIDDLY CYDER
  - FOLKINGHAM SOLO
    - CH.BADGERY RICHARD
    - MORMOND BABS
  - LIDDLY HONEY
    - LIDDLY BUTTERSCOTCH
    - LITTLEHOE ELIZABETH
- KIRKBY BELLE
  - GOLDEN RING
    - HARDWICK BUFF
    - ROWGARDEN'S PEGGY
  - BROOMELLS JUDY
    - SIR HENRY
    - SHEILA

WHIPHILL SHEILA
- INQUEST OF WILBURY
  - F.T.CH.BALMUTO HEWILDO
    - BALMUTO TANCO
    - BALMUTO KATE
  - F.T.CH.PAINTED LADY OF WILBURY
    - DUAL CH.BANCHORY PAINTER
    - F.T.CH.QUEST OF WILBURY
- SHEILA OF DAWNDEN
  - PLUNDER OF DAWNDEN
    - CH.LIDDLY JONQUIL
    - SUSAN OF DAWNDEN
  - DAMSEL
    - STORM OF DAWNDEN
    - STAR OF DAWNDEN

CH. STROKESTOWN SULIA 1964 AH By Greatford Nero ex Phillipine Dipper. Bred by Mrs. Field-Marcham, owned by Major Pakenham-Mahon.

CANADIAN AND AMERICAN CH. LISNAMALLAD TARENTALLA 1953 By Ch. Strokestown Duke of Blaircourt AJ ex Irish and English Ch. Hilldown Sylver AH. Bred by Col. G. Craster, owned in Canada by Frank Jones. Best of opposite sex two years at Westminster.

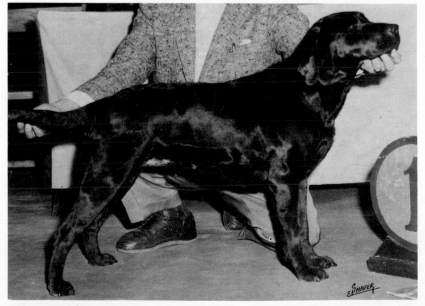

COOKRIDGE GAY PRINCESS — 1956 — GREAT BRITAIN

OWNED BY MRS. PAULING

FEMALE — BLACK WITH YELLOW AND CHOCOLATE GENES

(18)

Sire: CH.COOKRIDGE OTTER

- COOKRIDGE ROAMER
  - CH.BRAMHOPE BRUTUS
    - SANDYLANDS BEN
      - CH.DURLEY BEECH
      - CH.JUNE OF SANDYLANDS
    - TRIXIE OF KEEWATIN
      - CH.POPPLETON BLACK LANCER
      - LONESOME LASS
  - SUSAN OF HEATHEREDGE
    - LIEGE OF METESFORD
      - CH.LIDDLY JONQUIL
      - JULIETTE OF METESFORD
    - FRIEND'S CHOICE OF SANDYLANDS
      - BIG BEN
      - TRIXIE OF KEEWATIN
- CH.CAREENA OF HEATHEREDGE
  - CORNBLADE OF METESFORD
    - JOKER OF METESFORD
      - LIEGE OF METESFORD
      - JEAN OF SYDNOPE
    - IVORY OF GLOAMIN
      - MARQUIS OF GLOAMIN
      - DIGNITY OF GLOAMIN
  - SUSAN OF HEATHEREDGE
    - LIEGE OF METESFORD
      - CH.LIDDLY JONQUIL
      - JULIETTE OF METESFORD
    - FRIEND'S CHOICE OF SANDYLANDS
      - KEEWATIN BIG BEN
      - TRIXIE OF KEEWATIN

Dam: NEWLEY LASS

- CH.COOKRIDGE INTELLIGENCE
  - COOKRIDGE ROAMER
    - CH.BRAMHOPE BRUTUS
      - SANDYLANDS BEN
      - TRIXIE OF KEEWATIN
    - SUSAN OF HEATHEREDGE
      - LIEGE OF METESFORD
      - FRIEND'S CHOICE OF SANDYLANDS
  - COOKRIDGE PATIENCE
    - CH.DONNYBROOK THUNDER
      - BLACK EAGLE OF GLENGOUR
      - DONNYBROOK WENDY
    - LOCHAR DAINTY
- CORAL OF FIELDHEAD
  - CH.BLACKSMITH OF IDE
    - IRISH CH.JACKIE OF CROSSGAR
      - JACKIE OF TIBSHELF
      - RITA OF MAYMORE
    - CH.SANDYLANDS HARLEY PRINCESS
      - IRISH CH.PRINCE OF MOUNTPANTHER
      - BANKER BESS
  - GAD FLY
    - GOLDEN RING
      - HARDWICK BUFF
      - ROWGARDEN'S PEGGY
    - WIGGIE WUM
      - CRAFTSMAN
      - BROOMEL'S JUDY

BIN SENDVADA bred by Fru Brit-Marie Brulin. 13 CCs in Sweden.

COOKRIDGE JASPER 1961 AW By Ch. Sandylands Tweed of Blaircourt ex Cookridge Gay Princess. Bred and owned by Mrs. M. Y. Pauling. Litter brother of Ch. Cookridge Tango AW.

ENGLISH, CANADIAN, AMERICAN CHAMPION SAM OF BLAIRCOURT — 1957 — GREAT BRITAIN

BRED BY GRANT CAIRNS IMPORTED AND OWNED BY GRACE LAMBERT

BLACK DOG

(19)

Sire: HAWK OF LUSCANDER

- CH.HOLTON BARON
  - SANDYLANDS BOB
    - SANDYLANDS BEN
      - CH.DURLEY BEECH
      - CH.JUNE OF SANDYLANDS
    - CH.SANDYLANDS HARLEY PRINCESS
      - DALMAS JEWELL
      - CATTERBRIDGE MIMOSA
  - HOLTON WHIMBREL
    - JOCK OF MIDVILLE
      - RUFUS OF EDALE
      - LEVERTON QUIZ
    - HOLTON GLEANER
      - HOLTON EAGER
      - HOLTON ELEGANCE
- CRAIGLUSCAR CROCUS
  - DARKY OF ELMBANK
    - GLENHEAD JIMMY
      - CH.KINPURNIE KAM
      - KNAPPIES LASS
    - SHEBA OF CROMBIE
      - SCAMP OF SKENE
      - INGLESTON MIST
  - CRAIGLUSCAR BLACK GEM
    - BLACK EAGLE OF GLENGOUR
      - BALROY BLAZE
      - HOLTON DUSK
    - BLACK ARROGANCE OF GLENGOUR
      - CH.LIDDLY JONQUIL
      - HOLTON DUSK

Dam: OLIVIA OF BLAIRCOURT

- LAWRIE OF BLAIRCOURT
  - TREESHOLME TRIGGER
    - CH.DONNYBROOK THUNDER
      - BLACK EAGLE OF GLENGOUR
      - DONNYBROOK WENDY
    - TREESHOLME TWILIGHT
      - TREESHOLME TOPPER
      - SANDYLANDS BRIAR OF WEIRBRAKE
  - FIONA OF BLAIRCOURT
    - TREESHOLME THUNDER
      - TRIUMPH OF TREESHOLME
      - TREESHOLME TUNE
    - CRAIGLUSCAR DUSK OF BLAIRCOURT
      - DARKY OF ELMBANK
      - CRAIGLUSCAR BLACK GEM
- CRAIGLUSCAR DUSK OF BLAIRCOURT
  - DARKY OF ELMBANK
    - GLENHEAD JIMMY
      - KINPURNIE KAM
      - KNAPPIES LASS
    - SHEBA OF CROMBIE
      - SCAMP OF SKENE
      - INGLESTON MIST
  - CRAIGLUSCAR BLACK GEM
    - BLACK EAGLE OF GLENGOUR
      - BALROY BLAZE
      - HOLTON DUSK
    - BLACK ARROGANCE OF GLENGOUR
      - CH.LIDDLY JONQUIL
      - HOLTON DUSK

COOKRIDGE LIKIM 1967 BC By Ch. Cookridge Cormorant ex Cookridge Widgen. Bred and owned by Mrs. M. Y. Pauling.

RUPERT PAMELA OF TEDCO 1963 By Eng. Can. Am. Ch. Sam of Blaircourt ex Ch. Rupert Aurora Borealis. Bred by Dorothy Howe, owned by Chris Woelfel.

CHAMPION SANDYLANDS TWEED OF BLAIRCOURT — 1958 — GREAT BRITAIN

BRED BY MR. AND MRS. GRANT CAIRNS   OWNED BY MRS. GWEN BROADLEY

MALE — BLACK YELLOW AND CHOCOLATE GENES

（20）

Sire: CH.RULER OF BLAIRCOURT

- FORBES OF BLAIRCOURT
  - TREESHOLME THUNDER
    - TRIUMPH OF TREESHOLME
      - LOCHAR GOLD FLAKE
      - POPPLETON GOLDEN SHERRY
    - TREESHOLME TUNE
      - DONNYBROOK THUNDER
      - TREESHOLME TWILIGHT
  - CH.CRAIGLUSCAR DUSK OF BLAIRCOURT
    - DARKY OF ELMBANK
      - GLENHEAD JIMMY
      - SHEBA OF CROMBIE
    - CRAIGLUSCAR BLACK GEM
      - BLACK EAGLE OF GLENGOUR
      - BLACK ARROGANCE OF GLENGOUR
- OLIVIA OF BLAIRCOURT
  - LAWRIE OF BLAIRCOURT
    - TREESHOLME TRIGGER
      - CH.DONNYBROOK THUNDER
      - TREESHOLME TWILIGHT
    - FIONA OF BLAIRCOURT
      - TREESHOLME THUNDER
      - CRAIGLUSCAR DUSK OF BLAIRCOURT
  - CH.CRAIGLUSCAR DUSK OF BLAIRCOURT
    - DARKY OF ELMBANK
      - GLENHEAD JIMMY
      - SHEBA OF CROMBIE
    - CRAIGLUSCAR BLACK GEM
      - BLACK EAGLE OF GLENGOUR
      - BLACK ARROGANCE OF GLENGOUR

Dam: TESSA OF BLAIRCOURT

- CH.LAIRD OF LOCHABER
  - TREESHOLME TRIGGER
    - CH.DONNYBROOK THUNDER
      - BLACK EAGLE OF GLENGOUR
      - DONNYBROOK WENDY
    - TREESHOLME TWILIGHT
      - TREESHOLME TOPPER
      - SANDYLANDS BRIAR OF WEIRBRAKE
  - THRILL OF TREESHOLME
    - CH.GOLD RAND OF GLENGOUR
      - KNAITH BOBOY
      - GOLDEN DOT OF GLENGOUR
    - CH.TREAT OF TREESHOLME
      - LOCHAR GOLD FLAKE
      - POPPLETON GOLDEN SHERRY
- CH.IMP OF BLAIRCOURT
  - CH.CRAIGLUSCAR EMPEROR OF BLAIRCOURT
    - DARKY OF ELMBANK
      - GLENHEAD JIMMY
      - SHEBA OF CROMBIE
    - CRAIGLUSCAR BLACK GEM
      - BLACK EAGLE OF GLENGOUR
      - BLACK ARROGANCE OF GLENGOUR
  - SANDRA OF BLAIRCOURT
    - LOCHAR GOLD FLAKE
      - LOCHAR BLOSSOM
      - KNAITH BOOMERANG
    - TAUNA OF TREESHOLME
      - TOMBOY OF TREESHOLME

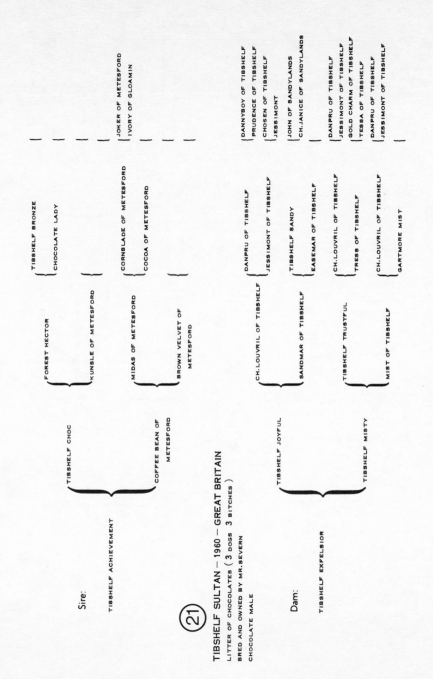

TIBSHELF SULTAN — 1960 — GREAT BRITAIN

㉑ LITTER OF CHOCOLATES (3 DOGS 3 BITCHES)

BRED AND OWNED BY MR.SEVERN

CHOCOLATE MALE

Sire:

TIBSHELF ACHIEVEMENT

   TIBSHELF CHOC
      FOREST HECTOR
         TIBSHELF BRONZE
         CHOCOLATE LADY
      KUNSLE OF METESFORD

   COFFEE BEAN OF METESFORD
      MIDAS OF METESFORD
         CORNBLADE OF METESFORD
         COCOA OF METESFORD
      BROWN VELVET OF METESFORD
         JOKER OF METESFORD
         IVORY OF GLOAMIN

Dam:

TIBSHELF EXFELSIOR

   TIBSHELF JOYFUL
      CH.LOUVRIL OF TIBSHELF
         DANPRU OF TIBSHELF
         JESSIMONT OF TIBSHELF
      SANDMAR OF TIBSHELF
         TIBSHELF SANDY
         EASEMAR OF TIBSHELF

   TIBSHELF MISTY
      TIBSHELF TRUSTFUL
         CH.LOUVRIL OF TIBSHELF
         TRESS OF TIBSHELF
      MIST OF TIBSHELF
         CH.LOUVRIL OF TIBSHELF
         GARTMORE MIST

DANNYBOY OF TIBSHELF
PRUDENCE OF TIBSHELF
CHOSEN OF TIBSHELF
JESSIMONT
JOHN OF SANDYLANDS
CH.JANICE OF SANDYLANDS
DANPRU OF TIBSHELF
JESSIMONT OF TIBSHELF
GOLD CHARM OF TIBSHELF
TESSA OF TIBSHELF
DANPRU OF TIBSHELF
JESSIMONT OF TIBSHELF

INTERNATIONAL NORWEGIAN, SWEDISH CHAMPION and SWEDISH F.T.CH. KAMRATE CAREENA — 1964 — SWEDEN

BRED BY INGE AND ING MARIE ESON THOOR, MJOLBY   OWNED BY FRAU BRIT-MARIE BRULIN

(22)

Sire: FINNISH AND NORWEGIAN CH. DIANT DOBRUDDEN BREYDEN (IMPORT)

- CH. SANDYLANDS TWEED OF BLAIRCOURT
  - CH. RULER OF BLAIRCOURT
    - FORBES OF BLAIRCOURT
      - TREESHOLME THUNDER
      - CH. CRAIGLUSCAR DUSK OF BLAIRCOURT
    - OLIVIA OF BLAIRCOURT
      - LAWRIE OF BLAIRCOURT
      - CH. CRAIGLUSCAR DUSK OF BLAIRCOURT
  - TESSA OF BLAIRCOURT
    - CH. LAIRD OF LOCHABER
      - TREESHOLME TRIGGER
      - THRILL OF TREESHOLME
    - CH. IMP OF BLAIRCOURT
      - CH. CRAIGLUSCAR EMPEROR OF BLAIRCOURT
      - SANDRA OF BLAIRCOURT
- CH. DOBRUDDEN DEBONNET
  - CH. COOKRIDGE INTELLIGENCE
    - COOKRIDGE ROAMER
      - BRAMHOPE BRUTUS
      - SUSAN OF HEATHEREDGE
    - COOKRIDGE PATIENCE
      - CH. DONNYBROOK THUNDER
      - LOCHAR DAINTY
  - DOBRUDDEN DERRYCAW EASTER BONNET
    - DUAL CH. STAINDROP SAIGHDEAR
      - GLENHEAD JIMMY
      - OUR LIL
    - CASTLEMORE BELVELLY BELLA
      - CH. PRINCE OF MOUNTPANTHER
      - FARNHAM PEACH

Dam: INT. SWEDISH CH. COOKRIDGE COLA (CHOCOLATE) IMPORT — CHOCOLATE FEMALE

- COOKRIDGE OSCAR
  - BICKERTON SALMON PRINCE
    - CORNBLADE OF METESFORD
      - JOKER OF METESFORD
      - IVORY OF GLOAMIN
    - BLONDIE OF GLOAMIN
      - RAIDER OF GLOAMIN
      - TREESHOLME TARETTE
  - COOKRIDGE GAY PRINCESS
    - CH. COOKRIDGE OTTER
      - COOKRIDGE ROAMER
      - CH. CAREENA OF HEATHEREDGE
    - NEWLEY LASS
      - CH. COOKRIDGE INTELLIGENCE
      - CORAL OF FIELDHEAD
- CH. COOKRIDGE OLGA
  - CH. COOKRIDGE OTTER
    - COOKRIDGE ROAMER
      - CH. BRAMHOPE BRUTUS
      - SUSAN OF HEATHEREDGE
    - CH. CAREENA OF HEATHEREDGE
      - CORNBLADE OF METESFORD
      - SUSAN OF HEATHEREDGE
  - TIBSHELF COCO
    - FOREST HECTOR
    - KUNZLE OF METESFORD

ENGLISH, AMERICAN CHAMPION SANDYLANDS MIDAS — 1965 — GREAT BRITAIN

BRED BY MRS. GWEN BROADLEY   IMPORTED BY MRS. GRACE LAMBERT USA

YELLOW DOG

(23)

Sire: CH.REANACRE MALLARDHURN THUNDER

- CH. SANDYLANDS TWEED OF BLAIRCOURT
  - CH.RULER OF BLAIRCOURT
    - FORBES OF BLAIRCOURT
      - TREESHOLME THUNDER
      - CRAIGLUSCAR DUSK OF BLAIRCOURT
    - OLIVIA OF BLAIRCOURT
      - LAWRIE OF BLAIRCOURT
      - CRAIGLUSCAR DUSK OF BLAIRCOURT
  - TESSA OF BLAIRCOURT
    - CH.LAIRD OF LOCHABER
      - TREESHOLME TRIGGER
      - THRILL OF TREESHOLME
    - CH. IMP OF BLAIRCOURT
      - CH.CRAIGLUSCAR EMPEROR OF BLAIRCOURT
      - SANDRA OF BLAIRCOURT
- MALLARDHURN PAT
  - CH.POPPLETON LIEUTENANT
    - CH.POPPLETON BEECH FLIGHT
      - CH.POPPLETON GOLDEN FLIGHT
      - LIME BEECH
    - POPPLETON GOLDEN SUNRAY
      - CH.POPPLETON GOLDEN MAJOR
      - POPPLETON GOLDEN DAWN
  - GUNSMITH SUESETTE
    - GUNSMITH SILVER FLIGHT
      - CH.POPPLETON GOLDEN FLIGHT
      - LASSIE OF FREISTON
    - GUNSMITH SUGAR
      - RUFUS OF EDALE
      - LEVERTON QUIZ

Dam: CH. SANDYLANDS TRUTH

- AUST.CH. SANDYLANDS TAN
  - CH.SANDYLANDS TWEED OF BLAIRCOURT
    - CH.RULER OF BLAIRCOURT
      - FORBES OF BLAIRCOURT
      - OLIVIA OF BLAIRCOURT
    - TESSA OF BLAIRCOURT
      - CH.LAIRD OF LOCHABER
      - CH.IMP OF BLAIRCOURT
  - SANDYLANDS ANNABEL
    - CH.CISSBURY ADVENTURE
      - CALCETTO CARLO
      - CALCETTO BRILLIANT
    - CH.SANDYLANDS JUNO
      - CH.BRITISH JUSTICE
      - CH.SANDYLANDS BELLE OF HELENSPRING
- SANDYLANDS SHADOW
  - ENG.CAN.AM.CH.SAM OF BLAIRCOURT
    - HAWK OF LUSCANDER
      - CH.HOLTON BARON
      - CRAIGLUSCAR CROCUS
    - OLIVIA OF BLAIRCOURT
      - LAWRIE OF BLAIRCOURT
      - CRAIGLUSCAR DUSK OF BLAIRCOURT
  - DIANT PRIDE
    - CH.POPPLETON LIEUTENANT
      - CH. POPPLETON BEECH FLIGHT
      - POPPLETON GOLDEN SUNRAY
    - CH.DIANT JULIET
      - CH.DIANT SWANDYKE CREAM CRACKER
      - DIANT REFLECTION

CH. NOKEENER MOONROCKET at two years of age. By Ch. Candlemas Rookwood Silver Moonlight. Bred and owned by Mrs. R. Williams.

CORNLANDS NOKEENER HIGHLIGHT 1965 AZ by Cliveruth Harvester BA ex Nokeener Night Light. Bred by Mrs. R. Williams, owned by Mrs. D. P. Rae. CC Crufts.

CH. BALLYDUFF HOLLYBRANCH OF KEITHRAY 1962 AV By Ch. Sandylands Tweed of Blaircourt AS ex Ch. Hollybank Beauty AT. Bred by Mrs. M. Wilkinson, owned by Dr. T. S. Acheson. Another of that famous Keithray litter. CC Crufts.

CH. HOLLYBANK BEAUTY AT 1958 By Bickerton Salmon Prince ex Cookridge Gay Princess. Bred by Mrs. M. Pauling. Owned by Mrs. M. Wilkinson.

CH. HOLLYBANK BEAUTY

CHAMPION NOKEENER PINCHBECK SEAFARER — 1967 — GREAT BRITAIN

BRED BY E.DALTON   OWNED BY DOROTHY HOWE   USA

BLACK DOG

Sire:

CH.BALLYDUFF SEAMAN

- CH.BALLYDUFF HOLLYBRANCH OF KEITHRAY
  - CH.SANDYLANDS TWEED OF BLAIRCOURT
    - CH.RULER OF BLAIRCOURT
      - FORBES OF BLAIRCOURT
      - OLIVIA OF BLAIRCOURT
    - TESSA OF BLAIRCOURT
      - CH.LAIRD OF LOCHABER
      - CH.IMP OF BLAIRCOURT
  - CH.HOLLYBANK BEAUTY
    - BICKERTON SALMON PRINCE
      - CORNBLADE OF METESFORD
      - BLONDIE OF GLOAMIN
    - COOKRIDGE GAY PRINCESS
      - CH.COOKRIDGE OTTER
      - NEWLEY LASS
- COOKRIDGE NEGRA
  - COOKRIDGE JASPER
    - CH.SANDYLANDS TWEED OF BLAIRCOURT
      - CH.RULER OF BLAIRCOURT
      - TESSA OF BLAIRCOURT
    - COOKRIDGE GAY PRINCESS
      - CH.COOKRIDGE OTTER
      - NEWLEY LASS
  - COOKRIDGE NINA
    - CH.COOKRIDGE OTTER
      - COOKRIDGE ROAMER
      - CH.CAREENA OF HEATHEREDGE
    - CELLE OF IMPHAL
      - BICKERTON SALMON PRINCE
      - BUTTONGRANGE PENNY

(24)

Dam:

NOKEENER CINCHONA

- CORNLANDS CEDAR
  - CH.SANDYLANDS TWEED OF BLAIRCOURT
    - CH.RULER OF BLAIRCOURT
      - FORBES OF BLAIRCOURT
      - OLIVIA OF BLAIRCOURT
    - TESSA OF BLAIRCOURT
      - CH.LAIRD OF LOCHABER
      - CH.IMP OF BLAIRCOURT
  - CORNLANDS LADY BE GOOD
    - CORNLANDS PETER SO GAY
      - CH.DIANT SWANDYKE CREAM CRACKER
      - FLUSH OF CORNLANDS
    - FORESTDELL LADY REJOICE
      - CH.CORNLANDS WESTELM FLIGHT
      - LADY REGIVY
- NOKEENER NOVEL BLACK
  - CLIVERUTH BLACK NIGHT
    - CH.SANDYLANDS TWEED OF BLAIRCOURT
      - CH.RULER OF BLAIRCOURT
      - TESSA OF BLAIRCOURT
    - CLIVERUTH SHERRY OF BEECHWOOD
      - CH.CEDAR WOODLAND
      - TIO PEPE
  - NOKEENER NOVELTY
    - CH.LANDYKE LANCER
      - NOKEENER NOVEL CRACKER
      - CH.LANDYKE POPPY
    - DIANT CHLOE
      - CH.DIANT SWANDYKE CREAM CRACKER
      - DIANT TORRENTIAL

COOKRIDGE GAY PRINCESS 1956. By Ch. Cookridge Otter AM ex Newley Lass. Owned by Mrs. M. Y. Pauling. A great producing bitch of both show and working Labradors. A black that carries both yellow and chocolate genes.

CH. CORNLANDS MY FAIR LADY 1965 AZ By Cornlands Kimvalley Crofter AZ ex Cornlands Lady Be Good AU. Bred and owned by Mrs. D. P. Rae.

ENGLISH, AMERICAN CHAMPION POOLSTEAD PILGRIM — 1968 — GREAT BRITAIN

BRED BY MR AND MRS R HEPWORTH   OWNED BY MRS ROBERT CLARK JR IN USA

YELLOW DOG

(25)

Sire: CH.SANDYLANDS TANDY

AUSTRALIAN CH. SANDYLANDS TAN
- CH.SANDYLANDS TWEED OF BLAIRCOURT
  - CH.RULER OF BLAIRCOURT
    - FORBES OF BLAIRCOURT
    - OLIVIA OF BLAIRCOURT
  - TESSA OF BLAIRCOURT
    - LAIRD OF LOCHABER
    - CH.IMP OF BLAIRCOURT
- SANDYLANDS ANNABEL
  - CH.CISSBURY ADVENTURE
    - CALCETTO CARLO
    - CALCETTO BRILLIANT
  - SANDYLANDS JUNO
    - CH.BRITISH JUSTICE
    - CH.SANDYLANDS BELLE OF HELENSPRING

SANDYLANDS SHADOW
- ENG.CAN.AM.CH.SAM OF BLAIRCOURT
  - HAWK OF LUSCANDER
    - CH.HOLTON BARON
    - CRAIGLUSCAR CROCUS
  - OLIVIA OF BLAIRCOURT
    - LAWRIE OF BLAIRCOURT
    - CRAIGLUSCAR DUSK OF BLAIRCOURT
- DIANT PRIDE
  - CH.POPPLETON LIEUTENANT
    - POPPLETON BEECH FLIGHT
    - POPPLETON GOLDEN SUNRAY
  - CH.DIANT JULIET
    - CH.DIANT SWANDYKE CREAM CRACKER
    - DIANT REFLECTION

Dam: CH.POOLSTEAD POWDER PUFF

CH.REANACRE MALLARDHURN THUNDER
- CH.SANDYLANDS TWEED OF BLAIRCOURT
  - CH.RULER OF BLAIRCOURT
    - FORBES OF BLAIRCOURT
    - OLIVIA OF BLAIRCOURT
  - TESSA OF BLAIRCOURT
    - CH.LAIRD OF LOCHABER
    - CH.IMP OF BLAIRCOURT
- MALLARDHURN PAT
  - CH.POPPLETON LIEUTENANT
    - POPPLETON BEECH FLIGHT
    - POPPLETON GOLDEN SUNRAY
  - GUNSMITH SUESETTE
    - GUNSMITH SILVER FLIGHT
    - GUNSMITH SUGAR

BRAEDUKE JULIA OF POOLSTEAD
- CH.LANDYKE STORMER
  - NOKEENER NOVEL CRACKER
    - DERWIN CRACKERJACK
    - DIANT CHLOE
  - CH.LANDYKE POPPY
    - CH.POPPLETON GOLDEN FLIGHT
    - LASSIE OF FREISTON
- DIANT JOY OF BRAEDUKE
  - CH.POPPLETON LIEUTENANT
    - POPPLETON BEECH FLIGHT
    - POPPLETON GOLDEN SUNRAY
  - CH.DIANT JULIET
    - CH.DIANT SWANDYKE CREAM CRACKER
    - DIANT REFLECTION

CH. TROUBLEMAKER OF FRANKLIN 1955 By Ch. Labcroft Mr. Chips ex Ch. Pitch of Franklin. Bred, owned and handled by Mrs. B. Ziessow.

DUAL CH. CHEROKEE ROCKET 1955 By Dual Ch. Alpine Cherokee Buck ex Nelgard's Madam Queen. Owned by Charles C. Cook. One of the long line of Dual Champions.

F.T. Ch. SUNGO 1954 By Buck of Rodall ex Brookstone Dixie (sister of Dauntless of Deer Creek) owned by Mr. and Mrs. Guy Cherry.

Sire:

HIWOOD RISK (IMPORT)

F.T.CH.HIWOOD D'ARCY
- CH. BANCHORY DANILO
  - DUAL CH. BANCHORY BOLO
    - SCANDAL OF GLYNN
    - CAERHOWELL NETTLE
  - MUNDEN SCARCITY
    - CH. BANCHORY LUCKY
    - BANCHORY BETTY
- SATINA
  - DUAL CH. TITUS OF WHITMORE
    - TWIST OF WHITMORE
    - TEAZLE OF WHITMORE
  - KINGSWALDEN SADIE

HIWOOD BETTY
- CH.INGLESTON BEN
  - DUKE OF KIRKMAHOE
    - CH. WITHINGTON BANTER
    - KIRKMAHOE DINAH
  - INGLESTON NANCY
    - BANCHORY ROGER
    - BROCKLEHIRST NELL
- F.T.CH. HIWOOD CHANCE
  - F.T.CH.BENINGBROUGH TANCO
    - BANCHORY CORBIE
    - BENINGBROUGH TANSEY
  - ROCKSTEAD SWIFT
    - RAG TAG
    - LORENTOR NELLIE

(26)

FIELD TRIAL CHAMPION TAR OF ARDEN — 1937 — USA

BRED BY W.AVERILL HARRIMAN   OWNED BY PAUL BAKEWELL III

FEMALE   BLACK WITH YELLOW GENES

Dam:

PEGGY OF SHIPTON (IMPORTED IN WHELP)

RONALD OF CANDAHAR
- RAG TAG
  - F.T.CH. TAG OF WHITMORE
    - F.T.CH.,PATRON OF FASKALLY
    - TACTFUL OF WHITMORE
  - SQUIB OF BELVOIR
    - TETRACK
    - COMMONSIDE TORY
- LORENTOR NELLIE
  - LORENTOR DAN
    - KNAP
    - KILBA
  - PIGFACE EARNSHAW
    - ZOG
    - DAFFODEL

GEHTA OF SIGEFORDA
- BANCHORY BLUFF
  - DUAL CH. BANCHORY BOLO
    - SCANDAL OF GLYNN
    - CAERHOWELL NETTLE
  - BROCKLEHIRST NELL
    - KINMOUNT DON
    - MURRAYFIELD NORA
- BALBEARDIE
  - MUTO
    - GLENMUIR NERO
    - FRAULEIN
  - BALMUTO PINKIE
    - WEMYSS NERO
    - CAMILLA MAGGIE

313

CEDARHILL WHYGIN — 1947 — USA

OWNED BY HELEN GINNEL

FEMALE   BLACK WITH YELLOW GENES

(27)

Sire:

TAR ROCK PLUTO

- MICKIE
  - PUCK
    - MICK
    - LASSIE II
  - HILL HOUSE LASSIE (IMPORT)
    - CARL OF BOGHURST
    - BEEDING LILAC (IMPORT)
- TAR ROCK JET
  - DECCO OF GLENMERE (IMPORT)
    - SAB OF TULLIALIAN
    - NEIGHLA
  - NITHI'S DOUBLE (IMPORT)
    - F.T.CH. NITH OF HALLEATHS
    - KINPURNIE GIFSEY

- CAUMSET DON OF KENJOCKETY
- KATEREN OF KENJOCKETY
- DIVER OF LIPHOOK (IMPORT)
- RIDGELAND BLACK DIAMOND (IMPORT)
- CORONA OF BOGHURST
- HAYLERS LINDA
- WESTERN REIVER
- AMBER JOY
- SAM OF INVERTROSSAKS (IMPORT)
- DILBEY
- KHETO
- CHAGFORD VEENA
- DUAL CH. BANCHORY BOLO
- BROCKLEHIRST NELL
- FINTRY SAM
- FAN

Dam:

CEDAR HILL'S KATE

- WYCOMBE CHIPS
  - CH. MICHAEL OF WYNWARD
    - CH.EARLSMOOR MOOR
    - BRIGHT OF BLAKE
  - BELLE OF WYCOMBE
    - CH. WEST COAST JERRY (IMPORT)
    - JOAN
- BOULINKA TINKERTOT
  - BENDER
    - CH. BANCSTONE BEN
    - CINDERS
  - TINKER
    - EBONY
    - GRUSHENKA

- CH.RAFFLES OF EARLSMOOR (IMPORT)
- F.T.CH. DECOY OF ARDEN
- F.T.CH.BANCHORY VARNISH (IMPORT)
- CHEVERELS DINA (IMPORT)
- GROSMONT JAN
- WILD WHISPER
- TOWYRIVER JAMES (IMPORT)
- LOCHANHEAD JET
- DUAL CH. BRAMSHAW BOB
- CH.DRINKSTONE PEG (IMPORTED IN WHELP)
- DIVER OF LIPHOOK (IMPORT)
- RIDGELAND BLACK DIAMOND (IMPORT)
- ZULU
- ZULINKA
- CAUMSET BANKER
- JUDY OF CAUMSET

CHAMPION CHIDLEY ALMOND CRISP – 1947 – USA

FIRST AMERICAN BRED YELLOW CHAMPION

BRED BY JOAN READ OWNED BY MRS. REDMOND

FEMALE

(28)

Sire:

LOKI OF CLARENDON

- PICKLE OF CHALE
  - FEARLESS BOB (BRITISH)
    - KNAITH BOGEY
      - KNAITH BOUNCE
      - HELEN
    - HER LADYSHIP
      - FEARLESS RUFUS
      - LADY PONGO
  - MORRISTOWN JUDY (BRITISH)
    - ROY OF JUPITER
      - HAWKESBURY JUPITER
      - HAWKESBURY JEANNIE
    - GLORY OF THE BANYERS
      - WARLOCK OF THE HURST
      - CHARMING MORN
- LADY ANN OF CLARENDON
  - CH.KOLANEKA MAZADA
    - ALBERT'S ARGUS
      - WARRENVILLE SHANDY
      - DAKOTA TOOTS
    - BRAEROY MAIZE (IMPORT)
      - BRAEROY TONY
      - BRAEROY RANDY
  - LADY LOU OF POUND HOLLOW
    - BANCHORY SNOWDRIFT
      - WITHINGTON HEMP
      - ARKLAND
    - BELLE OF POUND HOLLOW (IMPORT)
      - KENJOCKETY TUCSON
      - DIAMOND LIL

Dam:

CH.CHIDLEY MARSHMALLOW

- CHIPS
  - PETER OF COOKHILL (IMPORT)
    - CH. ALBY TWINK (FIRST YELLOW CHAMPION)
      - GOLDEN MORN
      - MYRTLE
    - OLD PARK MOLLIE
      - DUAL CH. TITUS OF WHITMORE
      - BELL
  - LEDGELANDS BRIDGET
    - ST. MARY'S DUKE (IMPORT)
      - MONK OF WINSCALES
      - SWIFT DUSKIE
    - CH. BANTRY TESS
      - BANTRY BROKER
      - BARONESS
- DAWN II
  - CH. BANCSTONE BOB OF WINGAN
    - DUAL CH. BRAMSHAW BOB
      - CH. INGLESTON BEN
      - BRAMSHAW BRIMBLE
    - CH.DRINKSTONE PEG (IMPORTED IN WHELP)
      - TOI OF WHITMORE
      - CH. PRIDE OF SOMERSBY
  - MARSH
    - CH. EARLSMOOR MOOR
      - CH. RAFFLES OF EARLSMOOR (IMPORT)
      - F.T.CH.DECOY OF ARDEN
    - WINGAN'S MAID O'THE MIST
      - CH.LIDDLY BULFINCH (IMPORT)
      - CH.DRINKSTONE SPAN (IMPORT)

CH. RUPERT DESDEMONA 1947. By Dauntless of Deer Creek ex Lena. Bred by D. Howe, owned and handled by Mrs. Johnson Smith.

RUPERT DOMINO AND RUPERT DAMIRI 1947 By Dauntless of Deer Creek ex Lena. Bred by D. Howe, owned by Mr. and Mrs. Henry Loomis.

CHAMPIONS RUPERT DAHOMEY, RUPERT DAPHNE, RUPERT DESDEMONA, and RUPERT DUSKY — 1947 — USA

BRED BY DOROTHY B. HOWE
1 DOG 3 BITCHES – ALL BLACK

(29)

Sire:
DAUNTLESS OF DEER CREEK

- DUAL CH.SHED OF ARDEN
  - CH.RAFFLES OF EARLSMOOR (IMPORT)
    - THATCH OF WHITMORE
      - DUAL CH.TITUS OF WHITMORE
      - TEE OF WHITMORE
    - TASK OF WHITMORE
      - TOI OF WHITMORE
      - TEAZLE OF WHITMORE
  - F.T.CH.DECOY OF ARDEN
    - ODDS ON (IMPORT)
      - THE FAVORITE
      - JEST
    - PEGGY OF SHIPTON (IMPORT)
      - RONALD OF CANDAHAR
      - GEHTA OF SIGEFORDA
- BROOKSTONE BURMA
  - F.T.CH.GLENAIRLIE ROVER
    - DALBEATTIE TANGO
      - DALBEATTIE DON
      - NELL
    - LADY MATILDA (BRITISH)
      - F.T.CH.KIRKMAHOE ROVER
      - CH.BALBEARDIE
  - BROOKSTONE TINKERBELLE
    - NIGEL MALUK
      - TWENTY GRAND
      - MISS CANADA
    - BROOKSTONE JODY
      - BLOOIE OF RIPLEY
      - BROOKSTONE SPECK

Dam:
LENA

- F.T.CH.TIMBERTOWN CLANSMAN
  - PONS JR. OF WINGAN
    - CH.DRINKSTONE PONS (IMPORT)
      - CH.BANCHORY DANILO
      - CH.DRINKSTONE PEG
    - ORCHARDTON DORIS (IMPORT)
      - CH.INGLESTON BEN
      - ORCHARDTON DAWN
  - BLACK AND BLUE RAIN
    - BLACK AND BLUE JET
      - BEECHGROVE DICK
      - BEECHGROVE GYPSY
    - WARBRIDE (IMPORT)
      - DIVER OF LIPHOOK
      - RIDGELAND BLACK DIAMOND
- WINGAN'S PRIMROSE
  - CH.DRINKSTONE PONS (IMPORT)
    - CH.BANCHORY DANILO
      - DUAL CH.BANCHORY BOLO
      - MUNDEN SCARCITY
    - CH.DRINKSTONE PEG
      - TOI OF WHITMORE
      - PRIDE OF SOMERSBY
  - KITTY OF HILLWOOD
    - PETER OF COOKHILL (IMPORT)
      - CH.ALBY TWINK
      - OLD PARK MOLLIE
    - MERRY (IMPORT)
      - USURPER OF HENDRE
      - BRICKWOOD BEAUTY

CHAMPION DARK STAR OF FRANKLIN — 1953 — USA

BRED AND OWNED BY MR. AND MRS. ZIESSOW

BLACK MALE

(30)

Sire:

CH. LABCROFT MR CHIPS

- LABCROFT GAME BOY
  - DUAL CH. SHED OF ARDEN
    - CH. RAFFLES OF EARLSMOOR (IMPORT)
      - THATCH OF WHITMORE
      - TASK OF WHITMORE
    - F.T.CH. DECOY OF ARDEN
      - ODDS ON (IMPORT)
      - PEGGY OF SHIPTON (IMPORT)
  - MUELLER'S JUDY
    - F.T.CH. GUN OF ARDEN
      - TOFF OF HAMYAX (IMPORT)
      - F.T.CH. DECOY OF ARDEN
    - DUCHESS HICKORY HURST
      - BANNRIG BANNER (BRITISH)
      - JUDY OF TARNBANK
- LABCROFT NORTH WIND
  - F.T.CH. CHIEF OF OLDBRIDGE (IMPORT)
    - F.T.CH. OLDBRIDGE BOB
      - PONTO BONES (BRITISH)
      - OLDBRIDGE FANCY
    - GLENRAVEL TRYST (BRITISH)
      - F.T.CH. GLENRAVEL JOCK
      - TRYST OF TEIGN
  - BLACK MEG OF AVANDALE
    - CAN. DUAL CH. L'ILLE LARRY (BRITISH)
      - PETER MUNROE
      - L'ILLE FANNY ATKINS
    - MEG OF GREEYMAR
      - F.T.CH. TIMBERTOWN CLANSMAN
      - GYP OF GREEYMAR

Dam:

CH. PITCH OF FRANKLIN

- PICKPOCKET FOR DEER CREEK
  - DUAL CH. SHED OF ARDEN
    - CH. RAFFLES OF EARLSMOOR (IMPORT)
      - THATCH OF WHITMORE
      - TASK OF WHITMORE
    - F.T.CH. DECOY OF ARDEN
      - ODDS ON (IMPORT)
      - PEGGY OF SHIPTON (IMPORT)
  - PEGGY OF PHEASANT LAWN
    - BANCHORY TRUMP (IMPORT)
      - BLENHEIM SCAMP
      - LADY DAPHNE
    - LAQUER
      - F.T.CH. BANCHORY VARNISH (IMPORT)
      - CHEVERELLS DINA (IMPORT)
- WARDWYN WARBLER
  - CH. EARLSMOOR MOOR
    - CH. RAFFLES OF EARLSMOOR (IMPORT)
      - THATCH OF WHITMORE
      - TASK OF WHITMORE
    - F.T.CH. DECOY OF ARDEN
      - ODDS ON (IMPORT)
      - PEGGY OF SHIPTON (IMPORT)
  - CH. BUDDAH OF ARDEN
    - FIFE OF KENNOWAY
      - JERICHO PAUL (BRITISH)
      - JUDY OF KENNOWAY
    - PITCH OF ARDEN
      - HIWOOD RISK (IMPORT)
      - PEGGY OF SHIPTON (IMPORT)

DUAL CHAMPION ALPINE CHEROKEE ROCKET — 1955 — USA

OWNED BY CHARLES C. COOK

BLACK DOG

(31)

Sire:

DUAL CH.CHEROKEE BUCK
IN THIS LITTER ALSO -
DUAL CH.CHEROKEE MEDICINE MAN AND
F.T.CH.FREEHAVEN MUSCLES

- DUAL CH.GRANGEMEAD PRECOCIOUS
  - DUAL CH.SHED OF ARDEN
    - CH.RAFFLES OF EARLSMOOR (IMPORT)
      - THATCH OF WHITMORE
      - TASK OF WHITMORE
    - F.T.CH.DECOY OF ARDEN
      - ODDS ON (IMPORT)
      - PEGGY OF SHIPTON (IMPORT)
  - HURON LADY
    - CH.BANCHORY TRUMP (IMPORT)
      - BLENHEIM SCAMP
      - LADY DAPHNE
    - CH.BANCSTONE LORNA OF WINGAN
      - DUAL CH.BRAMSHAW BOB
      - CH.DRINKSTONE PEG (IMPORT) (IN WHELP)
- GRANGEMEAD SHARON
  - F.T.CH.HIWOOD MIKE (IMPORT)
    - PETTISTREE DAN
      - DUAL CH.BANCHORY PAINTER
      - F.T.CH.QUEST OF WILBURY
    - PETTISTREE POPPET
      - CEDARS MICHAEL
      - CRANSFORD FLAPPER
  - GRANGEMEAD ANGEL
    - F.T.CH.FREEHAVEN JAY
      - F.T.CH.GLENAIRLIE ROVER
      - SPOT OF BARRINGTON
    - LANGBOURNE DARKIE
      - CARIBOO OF LANBOURNE
      - LANGBOURNE BLACK BESS

Dam:

NELGARD'S MADAM QUEEN

- DUAL CH.BRACKEN'S SWEEP
  - GLENHEAD SWEEP (IMPORT)
    - BANCHORY BENMHORE
      - INGLESTON NITH
      - GAY'S VERA
    - GLENHEAD BIDDY
      - TERRANCE OF LINTRATHEN
      - GLENHEAD BESS
  - BRACKEN OF TIMBER TOWN
    - F.T.CH.TIMBERTOWN CLANSMAN
      - PONS JR. OF WINGAN
      - BLACK AND BLUE RAIN
    - CONNIE
      - F.T.CH.BANCHORY NIGHT LIGHT (IMPORT)
      - CH.BANCSTONE PEGGY OF WINGAN
- F.T.CH.LADIES DAY AT DEER CREEK
  - DUAL CH.LITTLE PIERRE OF DEER CREEK
    - F.T.CH.HIWOOD MIKE (IMPORT)
      - PETTISTREE DAN
      - PETTISTREE POPPET
    - F.T.CH.TAR OF ARDEN
      - HIWOOD RISK (IMPORT)
      - PEGGY OF SHIPTON (IMPORT)
  - TOPS OF BIGSTONE
    - F.T.CH.BANCHORY NIGHT LIGHT (IMPORT)
      - BLACKWORTH MIDNIGHT
      - DINAH OF WONGALEE
    - CH.SCARBOROUGH SHENKA
      - EBONY
      - GRUSHENKA

CHAMPION WHYGIN CAMPAIGN PROMISE — 1959 — USA

BRED BY HELEN GINNEL   OWNED BY SHAMROCK ACRES KENNELS

BLACK FEMALE

(32)

Sire: CH.WILDFIELD MICKEY FINN

- CH.HUGGER MUGGER
  - CH.BANCSTONE BOB OF WINGAN
    - DUAL CH.BRAMSHAW BOB
      - CH.INGLESTON BEN
      - BRAMSHAW BRIMBLE
    - CH.DRINKSTONE PEG (IMPORTED IN WHELP)
      - TOI OF WHITMORE
      - CH.PRIDE OF SOMERSBY
  - MARSH
    - CH.EARLSMOOR MOOR
      - CH.RAFFLES OF EARLSMOOR (IMPORT)
      - F.T.CH.DECOY OF ARDEN
    - WINGAN'S MAID O'THE MIST
      - CH.LIDDLY BULFINCH (IMPORT)
      - CH.DRINKSTONE SPAN (IMPORT)
- CH.WOODCROFT DAISY
  - WARDWYN THUNDERCLAP
    - DUAL CH.SHED OF ARDEN
      - CH.RAFFLES OF EARLSMOOR
      - F.T.CH.DECOY OF ARDEN
    - CH.BUDDAH OF ARDEN
      - FIFE OF KENNOWAY
      - PITCH OF ARDEN
  - GOOD HOPE ABERDEEN
    - F.T.CH.HIWOOD MIKE (IMPORT)
      - PETTISTREE DAN
      - PETTISTREE POPPET
    - DHULOCHNAN DANCE OF TIMBERTOWN
      - ARDOCH SANDY
      - DONSIDE GWEN

Dam: CH.WHYGIN THE BEDFORD BRAT

- CH.WHYGIN JOHN DUCK
  - CH.WHYGIN POPPIT
    - CH.RUPERT DAHOMEY
      - DAUNTLESS OF DEER CREEK
      - LENA
    - CEDARHILL WHYGIN
      - TAR ROCK PLUTO
      - CEDARHILL KATE
  - CH.RUPERT DESDEMONA
    - DAUNTLESS OF DEER CREEK
      - DUAL CH.SHED OF ARDEN
      - BROOKSTONE BURMA
    - LENA
      - F.T.CH.TIMBERTOWN CLANSMAN
      - WINGAN'S PRIMROSE
- WHYGIN DARK MAGIC
  - CH.RUPERT DAHOMEY
    - DAUNTLESS OF DEER CREEK
      - DUAL CH.SHED OF ARDEN
      - BROOKSTONE BURMA
    - LENA
      - F.T.CH.TIMBERTOWN CLANSMAN
      - WINGAN'S PRIMROSE
  - CEDARHILL WHYGIN
    - TAR ROCK PLUTO
      - NICKIE
      - TAR ROCK JET
    - CEDARHILL KATE
      - WYCOMBE CLIPPER
      - BOULINKA TINKERTOT

AMATEUR F.T.CH. and NATIONAL CHAMPION 1967,1968 SUPER CHIEF — 1962 — USA

OWNED BY AUGUST BELMONT

BLACK DOG

(33)

Sire:

F.T.CH. AND AM.F.T.CH. PAHA SAPA CHIEF II

- F.T.CH.FREEHAVEN MUSCLES
  - DUAL CH.GRANGEMEAD PRECOCIOUS
    - DUAL CH.SHED OF ARDEN
      - CH.RAFFLES OF EARLSMOOR (IMPORT)
      - F.T.CH.DECOY OF ARDEN
    - HURON LADY
      - CH.BANCHORY TRUMP OF WINGAN (IMPORT)
      - CH.BANCSTONE LORNA
  - GRANGEMEAD SHARON
    - F.T.CH.HIWOOD MIKE (IMPORT)
      - PETTISTREE DAN
      - PETTISTREE POPPET
    - GRANGEMEAD ANGEL
      - F.T.CH.FREEHAVEN JAY
      - LANGBOURNE DARKIE
- TREASURE STATE BE-WISE
  - F.T.CH.THE SPIDER OF KINGSWERE
    - GOOD HOPE SMOKE
      - F.T.CH.HIWOOD MIKE
      - DRULOCHNAN DANCE OF TIMBERTOWN
    - JEAN OF SANDYLANDS (IMPORT)
      - CH.JERRYSLAD OF SANDYLANDS
      - JETTA OF SANDYLANDS
  - F.T.CH.DEER CREEK BE-WISE
    - NAT'L CH.MARVADEL BLACK GUM
      - MINT OF BARRINGTON
      - MARVADEL TOPSY
    - SYMPHONY AT DEER CREEK
      - DUAL CH.SHED OF ARDEN
      - F.T.CH.TAR OF ARDEN

Dam:

IRONWOOD CHEROKEE CHICA

- DUAL CH.CHEROKEE BUCK
  - DUAL CH.GRANGEMEAD PRECOCIOUS
    - DUAL CH.SHED OF ARDEN
      - CH.RAFFLES OF EARLSMOOR (IMPORT)
      - F.T.CH.DECOY OF ARDEN
    - HURON LADY
      - CH.BANCHORY TRUMP OF WINGAN
      - CH.BANCSTONE LORNA
  - GRANGEMEAD SHARON
    - F.T.CH.HIWOOD MIKE (IMPORT)
      - PETTISTREE DAN
      - PETTISTREE POPPET
    - GRANGEMEAD ANGEL
      - F.T.CH.FREEHAVEN JAY
      - LANGBOURNE DARKIE
- GLEN WATER FANTOM
  - NAT'L CH.CORK OF OAKWOOD LANE
    - COASTAL CHARGER OF DEER CREEK
      - F.T.CH.HIWOOD MIKE (IMPORT)
      - F.T.CH.TAR OF ARDEN
    - AKONA LIZA JANE OF KINGDALE
      - DUAL CH.BRACKEN'S SWEEP
      - KINGDALE'S BELLE
  - LITTLE PEGGY BLACK GUM
    - NAT'L CH.MARVADEL BLACK GUM
      - MINT OF BARRINGTON
      - MARVADEL TOPSY
    - COMAY CLASSEY CHASSEY
      - DUAL CH.LITTLE PIERRE OF DEER CREEK
      - WARDWYN WARBLER

CHAMPION SHAMROCK ACRES LIGHT BRIGADE — 1964 — USA

BRED BY SALLY MCCARTHY   OWNED WITH MRS. JAMES R. GETZ

(34)

Sire:
YELLOW DOG

CH. SHAMROCK ACRES CASEY JONES

- CH. WHYGIN GOLD BULLION
  - CH. KINLEY COMET (IMPORT)
    - CH. KINLEY MATADOR
      - POPPLETON BEECH FLIGHT
      - KINLEY SPARROW HAWK
    - CH. KINLEY CHARM
      - KINLEY TOSTIG TINTAGEL
      - KINLEY KESTREL
  - WHYGIN POPSICLE
    - CH. WHYGIN POPPIT
      - CH. RUPERT DAHOMEY
      - CEDARHILL WHYGIN
    - CEDARHILL WHYGIN
      - TAR ROCK PLUTO
      - CEDARHILL KATE
- CH. GENTLE JULIA OF AVEC
  - CH. WHYGIN GOLD BULLION
    - CH. KINLEY COMET (IMPORT)
      - CH. KINLEY MATADOR
      - CH. KINLEY CHARM
    - WHYGIN POPSICLE
      - CH. WHYGIN POPPIT
      - CEDARHILL WHYGIN
  - WHYGIN BLACK GAMBIT OF AVEC
    - CH. SMOKEY OF THE DAHL'S HOUSE
      - F.T. CH. GUN OF ARDEN
      - BARTI'S ECHO'S CHLOE
    - CH. WHYGIN BLACK GAMIN OF AVEC
      - CH. WHYGIN JOHN DUCK
      - WHYGIN DARK MAGIC

Dam:

WHYGIN BUSY BELINDA

- CH. WHYGIN POPPIT
  - CH. RUPERT DAHOMEY
    - DAUNTLESS OF DEER CREEK
      - DUAL CH. SHED OF ARDEN
      - BROOKSTONE BURMA
    - LENA
      - F.T. CH. TIMBER TOWN CLANSMAN
      - WONGAN'S PRIMROSE
  - CEDARHILL WHYGIN
    - TAR ROCK PLUTO
      - NICKIE
      - TAR ROCK JET
    - CEDARHILL KATE
      - WYCOMBE CHIPS
      - BOULINKA TINKERTOT
- BENGALI SARI (FROM AUSTRALIA)
  - CH. MICHAEL OF KANDAHAR
    - GOLD CLOUD OF WARRIGAL
      - WINLAYTON MICHAEL
      - GUNDAMAIN GOLD SKY
    - WINLAYTON GOLDEN SYRUP
      - WINLAYTON SULTAN
      - CH. LIDDLY QUEEN CAKE
  - CH. BENGALI PRINCESS
    - BENGALI TOREADOR
      - KAHIMA AJAX
      - KAHIMA BET
    - CH. SWALSDALE VIVERENE
      - CH. TRIEVADOR RODERICK
      - CH. BANCHTON FREDA

322

CHAMPION SPENROCK BANNER — 1964 — USA

㉟

BRED BY DOROTHY FRANCKE   OWNED BY JANET CHURCHILL

FEMALE – BLACK WITH YELLOW GENES

Sire:

CH.LOCKERBIE SANDYLANDS TARQUIN (IMPORT)

- CH.SANDYLANDS TWEED OF BLAIRCOURT
  - CH.RULER OF BLAIRCOURT
    - FORBES OF BLAIRCOURT
      - TREESHOLME THUNDER
      - CRAIGLUSCAR DUSK OF BLAIRCOURT
    - OLIVIA OF BLAIRCOURT
      - LAWRIE OF BLAIRCOURT
      - CRAIGLUSCAR DUSK OF BLAIRCOURT
  - TESSA OF BLAIRCOURT
    - CH.LAIRD OF LOCHABER
      - TREESHOLME TRIGGER
      - THRILL OF TREESHOLME
    - CH.IMP OF BLAIRCOURT
      - CH.CRAIGLUSCAR EMPEROR OF BLAIRCOURT
      - SANDRA OF BLAIRCOURT
- SANDYLANDS SHADOW
  - ENG.AM.CAN.CH.SAM OF BLAIRCOURT
    - HAWK OF LUSCANDER
      - CH.HOLTON BARON
      - CRAIGLUSCAR CROCUS
    - OLIVIA OF BLAIRCOURT
      - LAWRIE OF BLAIRCOURT
      - CRAIGLUSCAR DUSK OF BLAIRCOURT
  - DIANT PRIDE
    - CH.POPPLETON LIEUTENANT
      - POPPLETON BEECH FLIGHT
      - POPPLETON GOLDEN SUNRAY
    - CH.DIANT JULIET
      - CH.DIANT SWANDYKE CREAM CRACKER
      - DIANT REFLECTION

Dam:

CH.SANDYLANDS SPUNGOLD (IMPORT)

- CH.SANDYLANDS SAM
  - ENG.AM.CAN.CH.SAM OF BLAIRCOURT
    - HAWK OF LUSCANDER
      - CH.HOLTON BARON
      - CRAIGLUSCAR CROCUS
    - OLIVIA OF BLAIRCOURT
      - LAWRIE OF BLAIRCOURT
      - CRAIGLUSCAR DUSK OF BLAIRCOURT
  - DIANT PRIDE
    - CH.POPPLETON LIEUTENANT
      - POPPLETON BEECH FLIGHT
      - POPPLETON GOLDEN SUNRAY
    - CH.DIANT JULIET
      - CH.DIANT SWANDYKE CREAM CRACKER
      - DIANT REFLECTION
- PENTOWAN SANDYLANDS TIPTOES
  - CH.SANDYLANDS TWEED OF BLAIRCOURT
    - CH.RULER OF BLAIRCOURT
      - FORBES OF BLAIRCOURT
      - OLIVIA OF BLAIRCOURT
    - TESSA OF BLAIRCOURT
      - CH.LAIRD OF LOCHABER
      - CH.IMP OF BLAIRCOURT
  - SANDYLANDS CHARM
    - CH.WHATSTANDWELL CORONET
      - F.T.CH.WHATSTANDWELL HIWOOD BRAND
      - CH.HONEY OF WHATSTANDWELL
    - CH.SANDYLANDS BELLE OF HELENSPRING
      - SANDYLANDS BEN
      - CH.SANDYLANDS HARLEY PRINCESS

CH.SPRINGFIELD MISS WILLING and CH.SPRINGFIELD CHESHIRE CHEESE — 1966 — USA

BRED BY MRS. ROBERT V. CLARK JR.

Sire:

CH. HARRIS TWEED OF IDE
IMPORT

- CH. SANDYLANDS TWEED OF BLAIRCOURT
  - CH.RULER OF BLAIRCOURT
    - FORBES OF BLAIRCOURT
      - TREESHOLME THUNDER
      - CH. CRAIGLUSCAR DUSK OF BLAIRCOURT
    - OLIVIA OF BLAIRCOURT
      - CH.POPPLETON LIEUTENANT
      - CH.DIANT JULIET
  - TESSA OF BLAIRCOURT
    - CH. LAIRD OF LOCHABER
      - TREESHOLME TRIGGER
      - THRILL OF TREESHOLME
    - CH. IMP OF BLAIRCOURT
      - CH.CRAIGLUSCAR EMPEROR OF BLAIRCOURT
      - SANDRA OF BLAIRCOURT
- CINDY SUE OF IDE
  - BLACK SHEIK OF IDE
    - BLACK KNIGHT OF IDE
      - CH.JACKIE OF CROSSGAR
      - CH.SANDYLANDS HARLEY PRINCESS
    - CH.BLACK BESS OF IDE
      - CH.BLACKSMITH OF IDE
      - CH.BARROWBY FERN OF IDE
  - BLACK SARAH OF IDE
    - BLACK KNIGHT OF IDE
      - CH.JACKIE OF CROSSGAR
      - CH.SANDYLANDS HARLEY PRINCESS
    - CH.BLACK BESS OF IDE
      - CH.BLACKSMITH OF IDE
      - CH.BARROWBY FERN OF IDE

36

YELLOW BITCHES

Dam:

CH. KIMVALLEY CINDERELLA
IMPORT

- CH. SANDYLANDS TANDY
  - AUSTRALIAN CH. SANDYLANDS TAN
    - CH.SANDYLANDS TWEED OF BLAIRCOURT
      - CH.RULER OF BLAIRCOURT
      - TESSA OF BLAIRCOURT
    - SANDYLANDS ANNABEL
      - CH. CISSBURY ADVENTURE
      - CH. SANDYLANDS JUNO
  - SANDYLANDS SHADOW
    - CH.SAM OF BLAIRCOURT
      - HAWK OF LUSCANDER
      - OLIVIA OF BLAIRCOURT
    - DIANT PRIDE
      - CH. DIANT JULIET
      - DUAL CH.STAINDROP SAIGHDEAR
- KIMVALLEY GUILDOWN CASSANDRA
  - CH.WHATSTANDWELL CORONET
    - F. T. CH.WHATSTANDWELL HIWOOD BRAND
      - DAWN OF WHATSTANDWELL
      - HONEY BADGER
    - CH.HONEY OF WHATSTANDWELL
      - BRACKEN OF WHATSTANDWELL
      - CH.POPPLETON GOLDEN FLIGHT
  - GUILDOWN ECRU
    - CH.DIANT SWANDYKE CREAM CRACKER
      - LASSIE OF FREISTON
      - MAX OF DEN
    - GUILDOWN MARGHERITA
      - GUILDOWN GAY

324

GLOSSARY

BLOOM: Glossiness of coat.

BRISKET: Front of chest between forelegs.

CHALLENGE CERTIFICATE: awarded in England to a dog or bitch gaining first prize in an open class at a Championship show.

CHAMPIONSHIP: American—A Labrador must win fifteen points, of which there must be two major wins (3 points or more at one show) under two different judges.

English—A Labrador must win three challenge certificates at different shows under different judges and also have a working certificate. Without the working certificate a winning Labrador is called a Show Champion (Sh.Ch.).

COUPLINGS: That part of the body between the shoulders and hips. (Short-coupled is a desirable quality in a Labrador.)

DEW CLAWS: Rudimentary toes that are sometimes removed in puppyhood.

DUDLEY-NOSED: Pink-nosed, a fault mentioned in the Standard but allowed in winter.

FIELD TRIAL CHAMPIONSHIP: A retriever must win 1. a National Championship Stake or 2. a total of 10 points which may be acquired as follows: In each Open All Age or Limited All Age Stake there must be at least 12 starters. The winner of first place shall be credited with 5 points, second place 3 points, third place 1 point, and fourth place $\frac{1}{2}$ point; but before acquiring a championship a dog must win first place and acquire 5 points in at least one Open All Age or Limited All Age Stake open to all breeds of Retriever and not more than 5 points of the required 10 shall be acquired in trials not open to all breeds of Retriever.

HARE-FOOT: A long, narrow foot.

HOCKS: The joints above the pasterns of the hind legs.

OUT AT THE ELBOW: Having the joints of the front legs turning away from the body.

OVERSHOT: Having the upper jaw projecting over the lower.

PAD: The cushioned part of the foot.

PASTERN: That part of the leg below the knee (rear legs).

SNIPEY: Too long and narrow in the muzzle.

STIFLE: The upper joint (rear legs), corresponding to the human knee.

STOP: A depression between the eyes.

TUCKED-UP: Small-waisted; too shallow in front of hips.

WEEDY: Too lightly formed, especially in the region of the ribs.

INDEX

popularity, 37
pregnancy, 73, 158–162
progressive retinal atrophy, 86, 88–90
puppy matches, 235

R

rabies shots, 63, 66
Reanacre Mallardhurn Thunder, 198
Roberta of Coohoy, 32
Rookwood Gold Crest, 136
Rookwood Honeygold, 136
Rookwood Petergold, 136
Rookwood Silver Dew, 255
Ruler of Blaircourt, 21
runts, 149, 177
Rupert Brookhavens Angell, 251
Rupert Cedar of Birchwood, 53
Rupert Comet, 80
Rupert Counsellor, 46, 151
Rupert Dahomey, 195, 317
Rupert Damiri, 316
Rupert Daphne, 106, 317
Rupert Desdemona, 183, 316, 317
Rupert Domino, 316
Rupert Dusky, 183, 317
Rupert Jurisprudence, 117, 155
Rupert Kennels, 106
Rupert Marleigh Bingham, 111
Rupert Olivia, 176
Rupert Pamela of Tedco, 153, 301
Rupert Sam Howe, 24
Rupert Searchon, 164–167
Rupert Seashell, 181

S

Sam of Blaircourt, 205, 300
Sandylands Kennels, 136
Sandylands Midas, 305
Sandylands Spungold of Penyfan, 133
Sandylands Tara, 270
Sandylands Truth, 133
Sandylands Tweed of Blaircourt, 21, 38, 142, 208, 302
Scandal of Glynn, 17
Scawfell Seekon, 69
Shamrock Acres Kennels, 33

Shamrock Acres Light Brigade, 33, 207, 322
Shed of Arden, 246
show stance, 150–151, 227, 236–237
Spenrock Banner, 265, 323
Spenrock Sans Souci, 259
Springfield Cheshire Cheese, 324
Springfield Miss Willing, 213, 324
Staindrop Saighdear, 108, 294
standard, 146, 156, 209–215, 224, 244, 260
sterility, 54, 104
Strokestown Duke of Blaircourt, 18
Strokestown Sulia, 297
Strokestown Traveller, 202
stud agreement, 116
Sungo, 312
Super Chief, 321
supplementary food, 167–168, 177
swimming, 61

T

tapeworms, 80–81
Tar of Arden, 27, 40, 205, 207, 313
tattooing, 173
temperament, 20, 30, 35, 41–42, 47, 57, 155
temperature, 162
The Raed Jeannie of Pandocha, 261
Tibshelf Coffee, 135
Tibshelf Kennels, 142
Tibshelf Ochre, 140
Tibshelf Sultan, 206, 303
Titus of Whitmore, 20
traveling to the stud, 119
Troublemaker of Franklin, 311
tuck up, 214
Tudor Lincolnshire Poacher, 236
type, 11, 16, 35, 36, 123–127, 208

V

vitamin supplements, 67, 68

W

Wardwyn Kennels, 29
Waterdale Gamester, 282

RECOMMENDED READING LIST

Action, The Dog In, 1950, USA, McDowell Lyon.

Behavior, New Knowledge of Dog, 1964, USA, Clarence Pfaffenberger (The best of its kind).

Breaking & Training Gun Dogs, GB, C. Mackay Sanderson, editor of the 1949 British Labrador Club Stud Book.

Breaking, Observations on Dog, (ancient), William Floyd.

(Breaking) *About Dog Breaking*, 1873, GB, Dinks, Mayhew and Hutchinson.

    Dog Breaking, 1885, GB, (8th Edition), Gen. W. N. Hutchinson.

    Observations on Breaking Retrievers, 1879, GB, F. R. Bevan (an arresting old-timer).

Breed Your Dog, 1960, USA, Leon F. Whitney, DVM.

Breeding & Genetics of the Dog, 1959, USA, Anne FitzGerald Paramoure.

Breeding, The Anatomy of Dog, 1962, GB & USA, R. H. Smythe, M.R.C.V.S.

(Breeding) *How to Breed Dogs*, 1948, USA, Leon F. Whitney, DVM.

    The Dog Breeder's Manual, 1951 & 1954, GB, Eric Fitch Daglish.

    The New Art of Breeding Better Dogs, 1965, USA, Kyle Onstott (revised 1962 by Philip Onstott).

    The Theory and Practice of Breeding to Type, GB, C. J. Davies (an important book and a must for the serious breeder).

(Color) *The Inheritance of Coat Color in Dogs*, 1967, USA (2nd Edition) Clarence C. Little.

Conformation of the Dog, The, 1957, GB, R. H. Smythe, M.R.C.V.S.

Dog, Cassell's New Book of the, (old), GB, Robert Leighton (Labrador section by F. E. Schofield).

Dog, Family, 1963, USA, Richard A. Wolters (illustrated; excellent on training).

Dog, The, 1972, GB, Several editions by "Idstone" (The Rev. T. Pearce).

Dog, The, 1859, GB, Several editions by "Stonehenge" (J. H. Walsh, editor of *The Field*) (Edition of 1886 has a chapter on retrievers).

Dog Book, AKC Complete, (Standards of various breeds).

Dogs, 1888, GB, Hugh Dalziel (chapter on various retrievers and other hunting dogs).

Dogs: Naturalist Library, 1839 and 1840, GB, Lt. Col. Charles Hamilton Smith.

Dogs, Their History and Development, 1927, GB, Edward C. Ash (probably the most quoted book on dogs; much research into early developments).

Dogs & Hounds, 1932, GB, Croxton A Smith, editor (Labrador coverage by Lorna, Countess Howe).

Dogs, About Our, GB, Croxton A. Smith (introduction by Lorna, Countess Howe).

Dogs, Modern, 1902, GB, Rowden B. Lee (a few pages on Labradors).

Education The Scientific Education of Dogs for the Gun, GB, Holland Hibbert (many interesting training ideas)

Encyclopaedia, Hutchinson's Dog, (old), GB, (illustrated).

Encyclopaedia, The Retriever Owner's, 1968, GB, Gwen Broadley.

Encyclopedia, The Modern Dog, 1949, USA, Henry P. Davis.

Feeding Our Dogs, 1949, USA, Leon F. Whitney, DVM.

Flat Coated Retriever, A Review of the, 1969, GB, Dr. Nancy Laughton (an excellent summary of important books [many out of print] on retrievers).

Foxhounds of the 20th Century, 1914, GB, Cuthbert Bradley.

Genetics, The Dog Breeders Introduction to, 1966, GB, Dr. Eleanor Frankling.

Genetics of the Dog, The, GB, 1st edition 1952, Marca Burns; 2nd edition 1967, Marca Burns and Margaret N. Fraser (differing points of view on Labradors between editions).

Gun Dogs, Modern, 1936, USA, Lawrence B. Smith.

Hip Dysplasia *Canine Hip Dysplasia & How to Control it,* 1966, USA, Wayne H. Riser, DVM, and Harry Miller.

Hunting Dogs, How to Train, 1945, USA, William F. Brown.

Inbreeding, Practical, 1955, GB, W. Watmough.

Inheritance in Dogs, 1950, USA, Ojvind Winge, Ph.D. (translated from the Danish by Catherine Roberts, Ph.D.) (an important old standby).

Labrador, Our Friend the, USA, Rowland Johns.

Labrador, The Complete, 1964, USA, Helen Warwick.

Labrador, The Pet, 1954, USA, Frances Griscom.

Labrador Dog, The, Its Home and History, 1936, GB, (A very important book; out of print); Part I, Lt. Col. Lord Geroge Scott; Part II, Sir John Middleton.

Labrador Retriever Club, The Stud Book and Record of Field Trials, 1949, GB, Compiled by C. Mackay Sanderson, introduction by Lorna, Countess Howe. Complete pedigrees, records, and history to 1949 (out of print).

Labrador Retriever Training, 1950, USA, Ralston Purina Company in collaboration with Paul Bakewell III.

Labrador Retriever, How to Raise and Train a, 1964, USA, Stan Henschel

Labrador Retriever, The, 1931–1966, USA, edited by Thomas Merritt (complete information on shows and trials and breeding of US Labradors, also titles).

Labrador Retriever, The, 1933, GB, Leslie Sprake (an important book on the formation of the breed).

Labrador Retriever, The, 1936, USA, David D. Elliot.

Labrador Retriever in Australia, The, Labrador Retriever Club of Victoria.

Labrador Retriever, The Popular, 1957, 1959, 1961, 1964, GB, Lorna, Countess Howe.

Labradors, 1960, GB, F. Warner Hill (foreword by Lorna, Countess Howe).

Mendelism, 1927, GB, Reginald Grundall Punnett, F.R.S. (Not easy reading, but necessary for the serious breeder).

Mind of the Dog, The, 1958, GB, R. H. Smythe, M.R.C.V.S.

Nutrition of the Dog, 1946, USA, Clive M. McCay (no longer entirely timely).

Obedience, The Complete Book of, 1963, USA, Blanche Saunders.

Personality of the Dog, 1964, USA, Brant Aymar and Edward Sagarin.

Pointer and his Predecessors, The, 1906, William Arkwright (the Spanish Pointer, possibly in Labrador ancestry).

Puppy and Dog Care, 1956, USA, Harry Miller (easy reading, commonsense book).

Puppy and Dog Book, Complete, 1966, USA, Norman H. Johnson, DVM.

Puppy, How to Raise and Train a, 1958, USA, Arthur Liebers.

Puppy *Complete Book of Puppy Training and Care,* 1963, USA, Maxwell Riddle (excellent for the beginner).

Retriever Gun Dogs, 1945, USA, William F. Brown.

Retriever, You and Your, 1963, USA, Ralf W. Coykendall, Jr. (early field trials).

Retrievers, 1879, GB, The Hon. Gerald Lascelles (an amusing and interesting pamphlet on training).

Retrievers, Charles Morgan on, 1969, USA, edited by Ann Fowler and D. L. Walters (many useful hints on training and handling).

Retrievers, Golden, 1962, GB, Joan Gill (a history of the breed).

Retrievers, Hunting with, 1956, USA, Joe Stetson.

Setter, The Gordon, 1939, GB, Major Corn Schilbred.

Setter, The, 1872, GB, Edward Laverach (possibly some Setter cross in Labrador ancestry).

Social Behavior *Genetics and the Social Behavior of the Dog*, 1965, USA, John Paul Scott and John L. Fuller (difficult reading, but of interest to those desiring to know why dogs act in certain ways).

Stud Book of the Duke of Buccleuch's Labrador Retrievers, 1931, GB (this still existing kennel produced some of the most important foundation Labradors).

Training *Dog Training by Amateurs*, 1946, GB, R. Sharpe.

Training *Dog Training or Training Vs Breaking*, 1885, GB, S. T. Hammond.

Training, Gun Dogs and their, 1935, USA, Atwood Clark.

Training Gun Dogs to Retrieve, 1952, 1960, USA, David D. Elliot (a must for those needing help on timid dogs).

Training Hunting Dogs, USA, (Stackpole publication, photos of James Cowie training Labradors).

Training the Hunting Retriever, 1959, USA, Thomas R. Cofield.

Training Your Retriever, 1949 and 1963, USA, James Lamb Free (the so-called bible of retriever training, by the breeders of Freehaven Labradors. In my estimation, a bit rough on the dogs).

Trial, Retriever Handbook, 1961, USA, Eloise Heller (history of trials, AKC rules and regulations, complete information for those interested in trials).

Truth About Dogs, The, 1959, USA, Dr. Leon F. Whitney.

Visualization of Dog Standards, 1968, USA, Alice Wagner and Ab Sidewater, (illustrated, comprehensive).

Water Dog, 1964, USA, Richard A. 'Wolters (excellent on training, many illustrations).

Whelping *The Mating and Whelping of Dogs*, 1954, GB, Capt. R. Portman Graham (greatly detailed and very good on all sorts of problems).

Year Books of the Midland County Labrador Club, GB (excellent illustrations and listings of stud dogs and their breeding).

SUPPLEMENTAL
RECOMMENDED READING

BREED YOUR DOG, by Dr. Leon Whitney, 64 pp., $1.00. Instructive photos in color and black and white, covering breeding through puppyhood.

DOG OWNER'S ENCYCLOPEDIA OF VETERINARY MEDICINE, by Allan H. Hart, B.V.Sc., 186 pp., $9.95. A treatise on canine diseases, their causes, symptoms and treatments.

DOLLARS IN DOGS, by Leon F. Whitney, D.V.M., 255 pp., $6.95. Twenty-six chapters on vocations in the dog world.

FIRST AID FOR YOUR DOG, by Dr. Herbert Richards, 64 pp., $1.00. Illustrations in color and black and white.

GROOM YOUR DOG, by Leon F. Whitney, D.V.M., 64 pp., $1.00. Illustrations in color and black and white on various grooming techniques.

HOW TO FEED YOUR DOG, by Dr. Leon F. Whitney, 64 pp., $1.00. Diets and feeding routines for puppies and dogs, with illustrations.

HOW TO HOUSEBREAK AND TRAIN YOUR DOG, by Arthur Liebers, 80 pp., $1.00. Six educational chapters illustrated in color and black and white.

HOW TO RAISE AND TRAIN A PEDIGREED OR MIXED BREED PUPPY, by Arthur Liebers, 64 pp., $1.00. Nine chapters on choosing your puppy and breeding it. Illustrated in color and black and white.

HOW TO SHOW YOUR DOG, by Virginia Tuck Nichols, 252 pp., $4.95. For the novice who wants to show his dog.

HUNTING WITH FLUSHING DOGS, by Joe Stetson, 64 pp., $1.00. Illustrated text on training spaniels to flush and retrieve game. One of a series of TFH Publications, including *Hunting with Pointing Dogs, Hunting with Retrievers,* and *Hunting with Scent Hounds,* all $1.00 each.

All books published by TFH Publications, 211 West Sylvania Ave., Neptune City, NJ 07753, and available at pet shops everywhere. Titles not quickly obtainable locally can be ordered from the publisher; in such cases, please add 50c per copy to cover postage and handling.